Bhajan Supplement 2020

Omkara Divya Porule

Mata Amritanandamayi Center
San Ramon, California, USA

Bhajan Supplement 2020 – Omkara Divya Porule

Published By:
Mata Amritanandamayi Center
P.O. Box 613
San Ramon, CA 94583-0613, USA

In India:
www.amritapuri.org
inform@amritapuri.org

In Europe:
www.amma-europe.org

In US:
www.amma.org

About Pronunciation

The following key is for the guidance of those who are unfamiliar with the transliteration codes used in this book:

A	-as	a	in America
AI	-as	ai	in aisle
AU	-as	ow	in how
E	-as	e	in they
I	-as	ea	in heat
O	-as	o	in or
U	-as	u	in suit
KH	-as	kh	in Eckhart
G	-as	g	in give
GH	-as	gh	in loghouse
PH	-as	ph	in shepherd
BH	-as	bh	in clubhouse
TH	-as	th	in lighthouse
DH	-as	dh	in redhead
CH	-as	ch-h	in staunch-heart
JH	-as	dge	in hedgehog
Ñ	-as	ny	in canyon
Ṣ	-as	sh	in shine
Ś	-as	c	in efficient
Ṅ	-as	ng	in sing (nasal sound)
V	-as	v	in valley
ZH	-as	rh	in rhythm
R	-as	r	in ride

Vowels with a line on top are pronounced like the vowels listed above but held twice as long.
The letters with dots under them (ṭ, ṭh, ḍ, ḍh, ṇ) are palatal sounds. They are pronounced with the tip of the tongue against the hard palate.

Table of Contents of 3 the Volumes

1. abhayaṅkarī ammē (Malayalam) 2-19
2. abhinnatva torisi (Kannada) 1-19
3. aindezhuttu mandirattin (Tamil) 1-19
4. aisā dil (Hindi) 2-22
5. ājīvanāntam (Tamil version) 1-21
6. akaleyāṇenkilum (Malayāḷam) 1-22
7. akataḷiril aṭimalar (Malayalam) 2-20
8. akatāril azhalinde nizhal (Malayalam) 1-23
9. akhila brahmāṇḍaṅgaḷ (Malayalam) 1-24
10. akumu no youna (Japanese) 2-23
11. alalē lēnidē (Telugu) 1-25
12. āli paṭarum (Malayalam) 2-21
13. ālō kuṭhūna mī (Marathi) 1-27
14. ālōlam-ālōlam (Malayalam) 1-28
15. ambā gauri (Hindi) 2-24
16. ambā jananī (Sanskrit) 2-25
17. ambā kāḷī (Sanskrit) 2-25
18. ambā kṛpā varṣām (Sanskrit) 2-26
19. ammā ammā ammā (Tamil) 2-27
20. ammā dēvi jagadīśvari (Sanskrit) 2-27
21. Amma devi ma (French) 2-28
22. Amma Du bist mein (German) 2-29
23. Amma, hoy me siento lejos (Spanish) 2-30
24. Amma mother of my heart (English) 2-31
25. Amma my heart (English) 2-32
26. amma nin mugdhamām (Malayalam) 2-32
27. amma ninna prēma (Kannada) 1-29

28. Amma okaasam (Japanese) 2-33
29. Amma otzmat (Hebrew) 2-34
30. Amma tu danses (French) 2-35
31. amma unnai ariyāmal (Tamil) 2-36
32. ammā unnanbu (Tamil) 2-37
33. Amma wa itsumo (Japanese) 2-39
34. Amma, you are everything (English) 2-38
35. ammē abhayapradē (Malayalam) 2-39
36. ammē ammē amṛtēśvarī (Malayalam) 2-40
37. ammē ammē ennu (Malayalam) 2-42
38. ammē ammē nitya (Malayalam) 2-43
39. ammē dēvi amṛtēśvarī (Malayalam) 2-44
40. ammē dēvī snēha-svarūpiṇi (Malayalam) 2-45
41. ammē hṛdayēśvari (Malayalam) 2-47
42. ammē hṛdayēśvarī (Malayalam) 2-46
43. ammē karuṇāmayi (Malayalam) 2-48
44. ammē nin māyā (Malayalam) 2-49
45. ammē nin rūpam (Malayalam) 2-50
46. ammē parāśaktī (Malayalam) 2-51
47. ānandam-uḷḷil (Malayalam) 1-30
48. aṅgaḷake hāribandu (Kannada) 1-32
49. añjani putra (Malayalam) 2-52
50. ānondō ānondō (Bengali) 1-33
51. Antakaa Ammalle (Finnish) 2-53
52. antarātmāvil (Malayalam) 1-34
53. arikil-uṇḍenn-amma (Malayalam) 1-35
54. arinda nabarukkō (Tamil) 1-36
55. ārōmal pūmpaitalē (Malayalam) 1-37

56. ārtta-bandhuvāya dēvi (Malayalam) 1-38
57. aruṇōdayattiṅkal (Malayalam) 1-39
58. avanavanār-enn (Malayalam) 2-54
59. āvō muraḷīdhar (Hindi) 1-40
60. Awlaadi, awlaadi (Arabic) 2-55
61. āyēṅgē mērē kānhā āj (Hindi) 1-41
62. āyiram kātuḷḷa kāḷi (Malayalam) 2-56
63. āyōrē āyōrē kānhā (Hindi) 1-42
64. bahū divasāñcī (Marāṭhi) 1-43
65. bandu chē (Gujarati) 1-45
66. bārō bārō bālagōpāla (Kannada) 2-57
67. bhagavan ham par (Hindi) 2-58
68. bhagavān kahāṅ (Hindi) 1-46
69. bhajeham gaṇēśam (Sanskrit) 2-59
70. bhajlē rām rām rām (Hindi) 1-47
71. bhakti dē mā (Hindi) 1-49
72. bhayamannadi (Telugu) 2-61
73. bhītiyilāyen manam (Malayalam) 2-62
74. birahō āgune (Bengali) 1-50
75. bōlo śyām rādhē rādhē (Hindi) 1-51
76. Celebramos la vida (Spanish) 2-63
77. cēsēdi nīvamma (Telugu) 1-52
78. chod de mānase (Odiya version) 1-53
79. cilambōli kēṭṭuvō (Malayalam) 2-64
80. cinmay sundar (Marathi) 1-54
81. citaykkarikil (Malayalam) 1-55
82. Cógeme la mano (Spanish) 2-65
83. Cuando la madre tierra (Spanish) 2-66

84. ḍamaruka-nātha (Sanskrit) 2-67
85. dē darśan mā (Odiya version) 1-57
86. Desire leads to anger (English) 1-57
87. Devi awaken your children (English) 2-68
88. dēvi mahāśaktī (Malayalam) 2-68
89. dēvi mātē durgē (Malayalam) 2-69
90. dil kō banā dō (Hindi) 1-58
91. dīnabandhō (Sanskrit) 2-70
92. Don't let me waste this life (English) 1-59
93. Du er mit smukke hjem (Danish) 2-71
94. ē amma! (Telugu) 1-60
95. ē duniyā hai (Punjabi) 1-61
96. ēk dīp jalāyē ham (Hindi) 1-62
97. ēk ēk jap sē (Hindi) 2-71
98. ēk vacani ēk bāṇi (Marathi) 1-64
99. eḷimayānavaḷ (Tamil) 2-72
100. Em habria ahava (Hebrew) 2-73
101. Engulfed in this dark world (English) 2-74
102. en manaceppil (Malayalam) 2-75
103. enne nayikkuvān (Malayalam) 2-76
104. ennu kēḷkkum (Malayalam) 2-77
105. entinō vēṇḍi (Malayalam) 2-78
106. entinu śokam (Telugu version) 1-65
107. entu colvān-uddhavare (Malayalam) 2-79
108. Eons of lifetimes (English) 1-66
109. Epsahna stin nihta (Greek) 2-80
110. gaṇēśa namaḥ ōm (Odiya version) 1-66
111. gaṇēśa siddhi dātā (Hindi) 1-67

112. giri vana puri (Kannada) 1-68
113. gōkulanāthā gōpakumārā (Tamil) 1-69
114. gōpālak bāsurī (Hindi) 1-70
115. Gotts himmel (German) 2-82
116. gōvarddhanam uyartti (Malayalam) 2-84
117. Hakuna matata (Swahili) 2-85
118. Hana mo tori mo (Japanese) 2-86
119. hara hara śiva śiva (Malayalam) 2-87
120. hōli āyī dēkhō (Hindi) 2-89
121. hōli āyi khuśiyāṅ (Hindi) 1-71
122. Hør Gud, hvor (Danish) 2-90
123. hṛdayam dravicc-ozhukum (Malayalam) 1-73
124. hṛdayattin aṭittaṭṭil (Malayalam) 2-91
125. hṛdinivāsi (Kannada) 1-74
126. Illumina el mey camí (Catalan) 2-92
127. Ilumina ilumina (Spanish) 2-93
128. indranīladyutim (Sanskrit) 2-94
129. indu habba (Baḍuga) 1-75
130. indukalā-dhara (Sanskrit) 1-76
131. In every heart (English) 2-95
132. ini oru janmam (Tamil version) 1-77
133. innentē vannilla (Malayalam) 1-78
134. iṇṭilōkki (Telugu) 1-80
135. Io sono una bolla (Italian) 2-95
136. iruḷil ninnuṭal (Malayalam) 1-81
137. iruḷ māri teḷiyānāyi (Malayalam) 1-82
138. I see in this dark night (English) 2-96
139. jab se pāvan (Hindi) 2-97

140.	jagadambā prēmānē (Marathi)	1-83
141.	jagadīśvarī mā (Malayalam)	2-98
142.	jagatanātha (Odiya)	1-84
143.	jag spandan (Hindi)	2-102
144.	Jai jai mukunda (Spanish)	2-103
145.	jaya jaya śankara (Kannada)	1-85
146.	jaya rama rama ram (French)	2-99
147.	jay jay dēvi (Sanskrit)	2-100
148.	jay rām sītāpatē (Sanskrit)	2-100
149.	Je suis un rayon (French)	2-101
150.	jīvitam-ennoru tuṭarkatha (Malayalam)	1-86
151.	jīvita ommē (Kannada)	1-87
152.	jñāna-dīpam (Malayalam)	1-88
153.	jōt jalālē rām (Hindi)	1-90
154.	kaisā nāc nacāyā (Hindi)	1-92
155.	kāj karō (Hindi)	1-93
156.	kali devi jaganmata (Sanskrit)	2-104
157.	Kāḷī dēvī, mother to me (English)	1-94
158.	kāḷi kāḷi kāḷi kālasvarūpiṇi (Telugu)	1-95
159.	kāḷi kāḷi kapālini (Sanskrit)	2-105
160.	kāḷī karāḷī mahāśakti (Sanskrit)	2-106
161.	Kali mata zai (Chinese)	2-107
162.	kamanīya-rūpan (Malayalam)	1-96
163.	kaṇā kaṇā (Marathi)	1-98
164.	kāṇān-uzharunna (Malayalam)	2-107
165.	Kang a yo i wei (Chinese)	2-109
166.	kanivoṭakaṭṭuka (Malayalam)	2-109
167.	kaṇṇane kāṇān (Malayalam)	2-111

168.	kaṇṇan-en cārattu (Malayalam)	1-100
169.	kaṇṇā nin vēṇu (Malayalam)	1-99
170.	kaṇṇā nī ōṭi vāyō (Malayalam)	2-112
171.	kaṇṇirkkaṭalin karayil (Malayalam)	1-101
172.	kaṇṇunnīru tumbi (Badaga)	2-113
173.	karaḷ niraññu (Malayalam)	1-102
174.	karayāt-endōmana (Malayalam)	2-114
175.	karimukil varṇṇā (Malayalam)	2-115
176.	kar-lē dhyān tu bandē (Hindi)	1-103
177.	kārmukil varṇṇande līlakaḷ (Malayalam)	1-105
178.	kārtikēya subrahmaṇya (Telugu)	1-106
179.	karuṇārdra mānasē (Malayalam)	2-117
180.	karuṇayinda (Kannada)	1-107
181.	kāruṇyarūpiṇi ammē nin (Malayalam)	2-118
182.	kāttaruḷvāy dēvi (Tamil)	2-119
183.	kātyāyani dēvi (Hindi)	2-121
184.	Kmo navad hatoe (Hebrew)	2-122
185.	Kokoroyo nanio (Japanese)	2-122
186.	Kom hjem mit barn (Danish)	2-124
187.	Kom tillsammans (Swedish)	2-125
188.	koṇḍāṭṭamām (Tamil)	2-126
189.	krishna krishna jay jay (Chinese)	2-128
190.	kṛṣṇaghanā rē (Marathi)	1-109
191.	kṛṣṇā kṛṣṇā dēvakī nandana (Sanskrit)	2-127
192.	kṛṣṇā, nī ennil (Malayalam)	2-129
193.	kuṭilam-ākum (Malayalam)	1-110
194.	laḷitāmbikē ammē (Malayalam)	2-130
195.	Lämmössä tuulen (Finnish)	2-131

196.	Liebe Amma (German)	2-132
197.	Liefde voor God (Dutch)	2-132
198.	Llum de la llum (Catalan)	2-133
199.	Love is you, love is me (English)	2-134
200.	Lurreko mantu leuna (Basque)	2-135
201.	lūtayil ninnu (Malayalam)	1-111
202.	Maadare man (Persian)	2-136
203.	māḍī tārī (Gujarati)	1-112
204.	Mā inspire l'amour (French)	2-137
205.	maiyyājī huṇ mērā (Punjabi)	1-114
206.	Mā kālī devī (French)	2-138
207.	mākhan cōr (Hindi)	1-115
208.	manasā... cēyavē (Telugu)	1-116
209.	manasē ō manasē (Kannada)	2-140
210.	manasigē kaccikoḷuva āse (Kannada)	1-117
211.	manassil menayunna (Malayalam)	2-141
212.	mānava janmavu (Kannada)	1-118
213.	manavē kāraṇa (Kannada)	2-142
214.	manidā manidā (Tamil)	1-120
215.	maṇi-māṇiku (Hindi)	1-119
216.	maṇṇaiyaḷakka (Tamil)	1-121
217.	manōdarppaṇattil (Malayalam)	1-122
218.	man tō bandhi (Hindi)	1-124
219.	manvā rē tu (Hindi)	1-125
220.	mā ō mā mārī (Gujarati)	1-126
221.	maraṇattin-oru cuvaṭu (Malayalam)	1-127
222.	mārgamulu enni (Telugu)	1-129
223.	mā śakti hai (Punjabi)	2-143

224.	māyai adu niṙaindirukkum (Tamil)	2-144
225.	māye tanna (Kannada)	1-130
226.	mērī dēvīmā (Punjabi)	1-131
227.	Mir, lyubov' (Russian)	2-145
228.	mōr paṅkh (Hindi)	1-132
229.	Mother divine (English)	2-146
230.	Mother ocean (English)	2-147
231.	Moye serce byotsya (Russian)	2-148
232.	mṛtyuñjaya hara (Sanskrit)	2-151
233.	mukiloḷi niram (Malayalam)	1-134
234.	muḷam taṇḍil (Malayalam)	2-152
235.	muruga muruga (Malayalam)	2-153
236.	muttu muttu māriyamma (Tamil)	1-136
237.	nācē kānuḍō nācē (Gujarati)	1-137
238.	nā kaṇṭiki velugu (Telugu)	2-154
239.	Nakhtalifu (Arabic-Egyptian)	2-154
240.	nalvazhikāṭṭiṭu jayalakṣmi (Tamil)	2-156
241.	ñān aṙiyunnu (Malayalam)	2-157
242.	nandalālā yadu nandalālā (Hindi)	1-138
243.	narajanmōgu (Tulu)	1-139
244.	navvu navvu (Telugu)	1-141
245.	nēh mujhē dō (Hindi)	1-142
246.	nel tarum (Tamil)	1-143
247.	nīlāñjana mizhi (Kannada version)	1-145
248.	nīlō nīlō nīlōnē (Telugu)	1-146
249.	nin malarvāṭiyil (Malayalam)	2-158
250.	ninna naguvu (Kannada)	1-147
251.	ninna nirmala (Kannada)	1-148

252.	ninnapāda sēvēmāḍalū (Kannada)	2-159
253.	nin pādapadmattil aṇayān (Malayalam)	2-160
254.	ninu kīrtimpa (Telugu)	1-149
255.	nīr bharā (Hindi)	2-161
256.	niścala koḷada (Kannada)	1-150
257.	niṣphala-svapnattil (Malayalam)	2-162
258.	nit din tarsē (Hindi)	1-151
259.	nityānandattil (Malayalam)	2-163
260.	nī viral toṭṭāl (Malayalam)	1-144
261.	Noor a veen (Irish)	2-164
262.	nṛttamāḍu (Malayalam)	1-152
263.	O Amma, please come (English)	2-165
264.	Oh mind of mine (English)	2-166
265.	Oi Äiti (Finnish)	2-167
266.	ō man mālik (Hindi)	1-154
267.	ō mā ō mā (Hindi)	2-168
268.	ō mā sab lōkōṅ (Hindi)	2-168
269.	ōmkāra divya porūḷe 47 (Malayalam)	ODP-19
270.	ōmkāra divya porūḷe 48 (Malayalam)	ODP-33
271.	ōmkāra divya porūḷe 49 (Malayalam)	ODP-48
272.	ōmkāra divya porūḷe 50 (Malayalam)	ODP-63
273.	ōmkāra divya porūḷe 51 (Malayalam)	ODP-78
274.	ōmkāra divya porūḷe 52 (Malayalam)	ODP-94
275.	ōmkāra divya porūḷe 53 (Malayalam)	ODP-110
276.	ōmkāra divya porūḷe 54 (Malayalam)	ODP-126
277.	ōmkāra divya porūḷe 55 (Malayalam)	ODP-143
278.	ōmkāra divya porūḷe 56 (Malayalam)	ODP-160
279.	ōmkāra divya porūḷe 57 (Malayalam)	ODP-177

280. ōmkāra divya porūḷe 58 (Malayalam) ODP-195
281. ōmkāra divya porūḷe 59 (Malayalam) ODP-213
282. ōmkāra divya porūḷe 60 (Malayalam) ODP-231
283. ōmkāra divya porūḷe 61 (Malayalam) ODP-249
284. ōmkāra divya porūḷe 62 (Malayalam) ODP-267
285. ōmkāra divya porūḷe 63 (Malayalam) ODP-286
286. ōmkāra divya porūḷe 64 (Malayalam) ODP-305
287. ōmkāra divya porūḷe 65 (Malayalam) ODP-325
288. ōmkāra divya porūḷe 66 (Malayalam) ODP-345
289. ōmkāra svaramezhum (Malayalam) 1-155
290. ōm namō bhagavatē rudrāya (Sanskrit) 2-169
291. O Mother, when will I live your dream (English) 1-156
292. O my dear Kali (English) 2-170
293. onnum uriyāṭān (Malayalam) 2-171
294. On the banks of the river (English) 1-157
295. oru mazhakkālavum (Malayalam) 2-172
296. oru naḷil ñān en (Kannada version) 1-158
297. oru nerippōṭ-eriyunnu (Malayalam) 2-173
298. oru nōṭṭam-ēkāttat-entē (Malayalam) 1-158
299. oru piñcupaitalām (Malayalam) 2-175
300. oru vitumbal mātram (Malayalam) 1-159
301. Ote bondie (Kreole) 2-176
302. pāhimām pāhimām (Sanskrit) 2-176
303. pāhimām paramēśvarī (Malayalam) 1-160
304. pañcākṣara mandirattai (Tamil) 2-178
305. pannagaśāyi pārthasārathi (Kannada) 1-161
306. pantaḷa rājā ayyappā (Malayalam) 2-179
307. parandu virindu (Tamil) 2-180

308.	Pikimusta taivas (Finnish)	2-181
309.	pittā endrazhaittālum (Tamil)	1-162
310.	prabhu bin (Hindi)	2-183
311.	prabhuji tērā darśan (Hindi)	1-164
312.	prēmadondu (Kannada)	2-184
313.	prēma-gaṅgē ammē (Malayalam)	1-166
314.	prēmattin tūlika (Malayalam)	2-185
315.	prēm sē gāō (Hindi)	1-165
316.	puṭṭa puṭṭa kṛṣṇā (Kannada)	1-167
317.	rāma rāma jaya (Sanskrit)	2-186
318.	rām hamārē śyām hamārē (Hindi)	1-168
319.	rām hī rām (Hindi)	1-169
320.	rām rām rām (Sanskrit)	2-187
321.	raṅg jā tu maiyyā (Punjabi)	1-170
322.	ravikula-tilaka (Sanskrit)	1-172
323.	Reflect on life (English)	1-173
324.	ruṭhā hai kyōṅ mērē lāl (Hindi)	1-174
325.	sācō tērō nām (Hindi)	1-175
326.	sadāśivā mahēśvarā (Malayalam)	1-176
327.	sādi tōjāle (Tulu)	1-177
328.	śakti tū sab jīv (Hindi)	1-178
329.	samasta līḷārē (Odiya)	1-179
330.	śambho śaṅkara (Tamil)	2-188
331.	Seigneur Krishna (French)	2-189
332.	Sento le onde (Italian)	2-190
333.	śēr tē savār āyī (Punjabi)	1-181
334.	Shénshèng Mǔqīn (Chinese)	2-191
335.	Show me your real form (English)	2-192

336.	śibjē bhōlā (Bengali)	1-182
337.	siṭrinbam nāḍum (Tamil)	1-183
338.	Sitting in the dark (English)	2-193
339.	śiva mahādēva (Sanskrit)	2-193
340.	śiva śiva śiva śiva uraittiḍuvāyē (Tamil)	1-184
341.	śivōham śivōham (Hindi)	1-185
342.	Somos todos um (Portuguese)	2-194
343.	śrī rāma rāma raghurāma (Sanskrit)	2-195
344.	śrīśailavāsini (Sanskrit)	2-196
345.	sukhattilum (Malayalam)	2-197
346.	sumadhura sundara (Sanskrit)	1-186
347.	sun mēri mayyā (Hindi)	1-188
348.	sun sun mā (Hindi)	2-198
349.	Szukam cie w nocy (Polish)	2-199
350.	tabōnām (Bengali)	1-189
351.	taka dhimi taka jaṇu (Malayalam)	2-200
352.	tallī vallī kalpavallī (Telugu)	1-190
353.	tām tittām tey tey (Malayalam)	2-201
354.	tañjamena vandōm (Tamil)	1-191
355.	tannana tannana (English)	2-203
356.	tāyē unai (Tamil)	2-203
357.	teccippū piccippū (Malayalam)	1-192
358.	tēḍi tēḍi (Tamil)	1-194
359.	tellaccīra kaṭṭināvē (Telugu)	2-204
360.	tērā darśan karnē (Punjabi)	1-195
361.	tērē vicc maiyā (Punjabi)	1-196
362.	Thank you for this life (English)	2-206
363.	The pendulum of life (English)	1-197

364.	The world reels (English)	1-198
365.	tīn guṇōṅ kī (Hindi)	1-199
366.	toṭṭuṇartti (Tamil)	1-200
367.	tuḷaśīmāḷā gaḷā (Marathi)	1-201
368.	tuḷasīmālayāy (Malayalam)	2-206
369.	tūyi kālō (Bengali)	1-203
370.	tyāga diyā tūnē (Hindi)	1-204
371.	ulagam oru pūntōṭṭam (Tamil)	1-205
372.	ulakattin ādhāra (Tamil version)	1-206
373.	umaye uḷḷil (Malayalam)	2-207
374.	vāgiś nāgēś (Hindi)	1-207
375.	vāṇi sarasvati (Malayalam)	2-208
376.	vānōrum (Tamil)	1-208
377.	vattātta snēhattin (Malayalam)	1-209
378.	vāzhkeyenum paḍaku (Tamil)	1-210
379.	vēlavanē śakti (Tamil)	2-209
380.	vēlmurugā vēlmurugā (Tamil)	1-212
381.	veṇṇai uṇṇum (Tamil)	2-210
382.	viḍarātta tāmara (Kannada version)	1-214
383.	vinati hamare tune (Odiya version)	1-213
384.	Vind de vrede (Dutch)	2-211
385.	viṭhala viṭhala viṭhala viṭhala (Konkani)	1-214
386.	viṭhal hari viṭhal nām gajari (Marathi)	1-216
387.	vittumundā (Telugu)	1-217
388.	Vlepo thavmata (Greek)	2-212
389.	Warum suchen wir (German)	2-214
390.	yadukulam (Malayalam)	1-218

ōmkāra divya porūḷe 47 (Malayalam)

Disclaimer: The translations of certain verses are not literal; they aim to bring out the essential meaning from the Malayalam verses in a way that is easily understandable.

ōmkāra divya porūḷe varū
ōmanamakkaḷē vēgam
ōmanayāyvaḷarnnāmayaṅgaḷ nīkki
ōmkāravastuvāy tīrū

Come quickly darling children, you who are the divine essence of Om. Remove all sorrows, grow dear and adorable, and merge with the Absolute.

1
saumyatayōṭe carikkū – makkaḷ
sāmūhya-dharmam smarikkū
samphulla-mānasam sandēham-aṫṫātma
samvēdanattinn-iṇakkū

Children, move forward with a calm and quiet mind. Remember your *dharma* towards others. Let your blossoming and perfected mind know its Oneness with the *atman*.

2
bhūta-jālaṅgaḷil ellām – divya
snēham vazhiññ-ozhukaṭṭe
ānanda-pūrṇṇamāy ātmāvil ēkatā-
bhāvam niṙaññ-ozhukaṭṭe

May divine love overflow to all beings. May the bliss of Oneness overflow from the Self.

3
prārtthanā-nirbharam ākkām – vyakti
jīvitam sadbhāva-niṣṭham
ādyam manaḥ-sthiti pinne paristhiti
māṫṫām – maṙiccalla vēṇḍū

May our life be full of prayer and goodness. Let us transform our inner attitude first, and only then our external situation.

4
kālam talakīzh-maṙiññāl – vālu
nāyaye āṭṭān tuṭaṅgum
vṛkṣa-ttalappil vaḷam-vaykkuvōr vṛthā
pāyum paristhiti māṫṫān

When time turns upside down, the tail wags the dog. Trying to change our external situation is like fertilizing tree tops. It is futile.

5
duṣcintanattinde cēṫṫil – manam
durggandha-pūritam ākum
tānum samūhavum tānē duṣiccu pōm
hīnam manaḥ-sthiti māṫṫām

Our mind stinks when it revels in the muck of evil thoughts. Both we and society become depraved when our inner attitude is wrong.

6
vairam muzhuttāl phalattil – svanta

svairyam naśikkunnu tānē
ādyam duṣiccu pōm tan manam śēṣamāṇ-
ā-viṣaccūr-anyan ēlpū

When enmity gains strength it destroys our peace. It first poisons our own mind and then others also feel its poisonous heat.

7
vidrōha-cintakaḷ ponti – nīḷe
śatru-samhāram vitaykke
uḷḷil madikkunn-or-ātma-śatrukkaḷe
vellān karuttilla kaṣṭam

When hatred wells up in our mind, we may slay our enemies; but, we do not have the strength to vanquish our inner enemies.

8
krōdha-rāgaṅgaḷ tezhiccu – svayam
jētākkaḷāyi camaññāl
svantam manaḥ-śakti jīrṇṇiccu pōm garvvu
melle meticconn-aṭakkū

Anger and likes and dislikes, lead us on and proclaim victory for themselves. These drain away our mental strength. Let us subdue our pride.

9
vyarttha-mōhaṅgaḷ menaññu – svārttha
lakṣyaṅgaḷil kūṭu-kūṭṭum
'svatvam' maṙanna manuṣyan ninaykkāte
peṭṭu pōm kāla-kkeṇiyil

Those who weave vain dreams to gain selfish ends forget their true nature and fall into the relentless trap of time.

10
snēham curattunna hṛttil – daiva-
bhāvam uṇarnn-ennu vyaktam
daiva-snēhattinde srōtassu vaṫṫāte
dhyāna-anulīnam lasikkū

Divinity awakens in a heart overflowing with love. Let us delight in the bliss of meditation and the source of love will never dry up.

11
jīvitam puṣpicciṭaṭṭe – snēham
ārilum varṣicciṭaṭṭe
vairam veṭiññu veṇtārakam pōl manam
nēruttu śōbhicc-iṭaṭṭe

May the flower of our life blossom. Let us let go of hatred and rain down love on everyone. May our mind shine like a silver star.

12
kai-vanna saubhāgyam ellām – svanta
vaibhavam enn-ōrttiṭāte
daivam niyōgicca sandarbham ennōrttu
sēvanōtsāham pularttū

Let us not think that we make our fortunes. Let us know they are opportunities given by God to serve with enthusiasm.

13
pōṇam viṣāda-ātmakatvam – sadā

vēṇam prasāda-ātmakatvam
pūvum pulariyum pūñcōlayam pōle
nēṭām sthira-āhlādakatvam

Let us overcome sorrow and be joyful. Our mind should always be joyful like a flower, the golden dawn, and a grove of flowering trees.

14
saumyata māyāt-udāttam – makkaḷ
śānti-sandēśam muzhakkū
ātma-harṣattinde ārāma-ramyamām
tū-mandahāsam pozhikkū

Let us proclaim the noble message of peace and never lose our inner calm. Let us smile with the overflowing bliss of the Self.

15
nenmēni vākappū-pōle – saumyam
cārutayārnn-ōjassōṭe
mēvum mana-kkāmbil tānē sphurikkunnu
vēda-vēdānta-sugandham

The essence of the *Vedas* and scriptures, fragrant like *vakappu* flowers, glows radiantly in a mind filled with the beauty of pure consciousness.

16
snēhattin jvālayāy tīrū – svārttha
mōha-aṅkuraṅgaḷ erikkū
vidyayārnnum karma-śuddhi ārnnum, lōka
sad-gatikkāyi śvasikkū

Let us become a flame of love that burns selfish desires as they germinate in our mind. Gaining right knowledge and purity in action, let us live for the welfare of the world.

17

poy-ppōyat-ōrttu tapiccu – kāla
naṣṭam varuttāte makkaḷ
kai-vannatum kai-varān-uḷḷatum – kāla
naṣṭattil naṣṭam enn-ōrkkū

Children, do not grieve over the past. Know that reliving the past and worrying over the future is a great waste of time.

18

satyattin-okkeyum satyam – ātma
sattayenn-ātmāv-uṇarām
vēdaṅgaḷil kāṇmat-ātmāvil darśiccu
kāṇmatinn-appuṙam kāṇām

Awaken to the Self, the ultimate Truth. See within your own self what is written in the *Vedas*, that cannot be seen by the external eye.

19

duḥkham tapass-ākki māṫṫum – bhāva
śuddhi-naipuṇyam pularttū
poṭṭi-cciriyākki māṫṫuvin jīvitam
lakṣya-smaraṇayil makkaḷ

Children, be skillful enough to convert sorrow into spiritual penance. Become pure in thought, and laugh in the remembrance of your final goal.

20

ceytatu ceytupōy nammaḷ – innu
ceyyunnatil śraddhayūnnām
varttamānattōṭu nīti pularttukil
bhāviyum śōbhāya-mānam

We cannot change our past mistakes. Let us act in the present with awareness. If we do justice to the present, the future will be bright.

21

innu nām ceyyunnat-entum – cittil
maṅgāte vṛttiyāy nilkkum
innate janmattin-arttham kuṙiccu mun
karma-samskāram enn-ōrkkū

Our actions remain as clear impressions in the mind. This life is the result of the latent impressions formed by actions in previous births.

22

kārmukil mānatt-iruṇḍāl – māṙi
peytozhiyāt-irikkilla
ceyta karmattinde bhāva-samskāravum
peytozhiyāt-irikkilla

When dark clouds gather, it rains. Likewise, the results of our past actions also rain down on us.

23

kālacciṙak-ēṙi martyan – mṛtyu
lōkam gamikkān orukkam
karmārjjitaṅgaḷ tan māṙāpp-azhiccuḷḷu

kāṇān bhayakkunnu kaṣṭam

We travel on the wings of time to the land of death. We are afraid to look inward and open the heavy bundle containing the fruits of our karma.

24

āḷunn-ahantaykku pinnil – bhayam
māṙāt-irippuṇḍu śaktam
pūpōl minusam manassin-uṇḍēlatinn-
ādhāram ātma-samsarggam

Strong fear fuels the flaming ego, but the mind in constant union with the Self has the softness of a flower.

25

nāṭāke mālinyam ākkum – manō
mālinyam āruṇḍu nīkkān
tānē prayatniccu vēṇam manō-taṭam
mūṭum viṣajjvāla nīkkān

Who can clean the impurities of our mind? We ourselves must strive to douse the poisonous flames that hide our inner essence.

26

mitra-bhāvatte naṭiccu – uḷḷil
śatru-bhāvatte pularttum
martyanu nañcu pinn-entinnu jīvita
nāśattin-ā viṣam pōrum

If we pretend to be a friend while hiding enmity inside, we need no other poison to destroy lives.

27

kaṇḍāl-aṙiyātta bhāvam – karim
kallinnu cērunna dharmam
kallinde dharmam manuṣyan pularttukil
kall-āṇatil tellu bhēdam

A stone remains true to its own nature, but a stone-like human is untrue to his nature. He is worth less than a stone!

28

sēvana-hastaṅgaḷ nīṭṭām – kaṇṇil
kāruṇya-tīrttham niṙaykkām
ātmāvil ūṙunna snēha-anubhūti tan
mādhurya-vākkonn-uṙaykkām

Let's stretch out our hands in service. Let's fill our eyes with the sacred waters of compassion. Let the sweetness of the pure Self flow out through our words.

29

ajñāna-vairiyōṭ-ēṫṫu – ārum
pōril jayikkilla nēril
andhakārattōṭu malliṭān pōkēṇḍa
pontiri-onnu koḷuttām

None can defeat the enemy of dense ignorance in a straight battle. Let us not fight with darkness; rather, let us light the golden lamp of knowledge.

30

ālasyam-āḷēṇḍa makkaḷ – tellum-
ākular ākēṇḍa makkaḷ

ōmkāra-rūpan jagan-nivāsan hṛttil
ātma-svarūpam ennōrkkū

O children, do not be indolent and despondent. Remember that the Lord who pervades the universe, who is the essence of Om, resides in your heart.

31
satyattin niṣṭhar-ākēṇam – matam
satya-niṣṭhaykk-uḷḷupāyam
vyaktamāṇāyatin lakṣyam mahattāya
satyam teḷikkān upāyam

Religion is the path that guides us to the ultimate Truth. Let us stand firm in the Truth.

32
bhaktikku śuddhi uṇḍāvān – śraddha
tattvattil cūzhnnu nilkkēṇam
śraddhayillēl bhakti bhaktiyall-ātmāvil
niṣṭhayāṇ-ekānta-bhakti

Pure devotion is rooted in spiritual principles. To have true devotion, we must be aware of these principles. True devotion is being established in the Self.

33
pāṭunna pāṭṭinde-īṇam – mauna
śāntiyil cāliccat-eṅkil
kēḷkkuvōrkk-ātmāvil ātmā-utirkkunnor
ānanda-sāndra-anubhūti

If the melody of our song arises from deep silence, it transports the listener to the exalted heights of union with the Self.

34

satya-anubhūti tan śabdam – vēda
nistandra-tāra-svaraṅgaḷ
uccāritaṅgaḷām śabdaṅgaḷil vēda
śabdam samārāddhyam ennum

The sound of the *Vedas* resonates with the experience of Truth. The *Vedas* are always worthy of our worship.

35

ellā balattinnum mēlē – ātma
vidyā-balam ennaṙiyū
buddhiyil taṅgunna vidyayāl ātaṅka
muktar-āvill-ārum ōrkkū

Know that Self-knowledge is the greatest strength. Remember, no one will gain freedom from sorrow through mere intellectual knowledge.

36

dvēṣam manassil sphuriccāl – śānti
māyum, manō-dūṣyam āḷum
nām aṙiyīla nām ceyyunnat-entennu
cintakaḷ vyāmiśram ākum

When anger rises in our mind, peace disappears. Anger makes the mind impure. In anger, we lose awareness of our actions, and our thoughts become debased.

37

mālōkar okkeyum nērē – namme
māt̤rka ākkān kotikkum
nēriya kai-ppizha pōlum niyantrikkū
makkaḷē lōkam duṣikkum

People may look up to us as role models. So, children, be careful of even a small mistake. The world will blame us for every trivial error of judgment.

38

vaividdhya-pūrṇam ī lōkam – nammaḷ
vaikārya-jīvikaḷ ennum
snēhattāl ōjassiyaṫṫāykil okkeyum
krōdhattin cūrēṫṫu vāṭum

The world is full of diversity. Also, we are emotional beings. In love, our strength grows; and, in the heat of anger, we wither.

39

saundarya-pūrṇṇam ākkīṭām – snēha
kāntiyil vaividdhyam ellām
cētōharam varṇṇasūnaṅgaḷ cērtt-oru
pūcceṇḍ-orukkunna-pōle

With the radiance of love, let us create beauty out of diversity, like a fabulous bouquet of many-colored flowers.

40

tēṅgal oṭuṅgātta tīram – snēha
dāham śamikkātta tīram

tīmazha peyyunna mānava-cētassil
tēnmalar tūmazhayākām

We lament and long for love. Pour down as soothing rain in our ravaged hearts .

41
kaṇkaḷil āḷum kanalum – manō
granthiyil van viṣaccūrum
āṇava-jjvālaye vellum manassine
snēhānusēcanam ceyyām

Eyes burn with hatred and minds spew deadly venom. With the healing waters of love, let us cleanse our mind which can be more dangerous than a nuclear explosion.

42
sambhītar-ākēṇḍa makkaḷ – amma
tāṅguṇḍu samsāra-nīṫṫil
kāṫṫum tirakkōḷum ēṫṫēṫṫulayāte
kāttiṭām jīvita-nauka

Don't be frightened my children. Amma supports you in the ocean of samsara. She will protect the boat of your life from hurricanes and lashing waves.

43
āṭāt-iḷakāt-irikkū – lakṣya
bōdham tuzhayāy pīṭikkū
daiva-snēhattinnu pākamāy tanmanō
pāya nivarttuvin makkaḷ

Let not waves rock the boat of your life. Let awareness of the goal be your oars. Unfurl the sails of your mind and catch the wind of God's love.

44

anpiyann-ōmalkkiṭāṅgaḷ – lōka
bandhura-rāgam pozhikkū
lōka-kkuṭumbattil-angaṅgaḷ nām-ennu
cinticcu santuṣṭar-ākū

O my darling children, sing the song of Oneness to all beings. Know that we all belong to the universal family, and be joyous.

45

kāruṇyam-anpārdratayum – divya
snēha-vātsalyavum ellām
prēmānubhūti tan bhāva-sphulingaṅgaḷ
prēmam sadā svasvarūpam

Compassion, a tender heart, and humility are the expressions of glorious, divine love. Love is our true nature!

46

nalkiyāl tīrilla snēham – sadā
pūrṇṇatayāy-ttannirikkum
pūrṇṇatayonnāl eṭuttāl kuṟayātta
pūrṇṇata āṇatin dharmam

Love does not lessen when we give it away. Love always remains whole and perfect. Whatever is taken away from the whole never depletes the whole.

47

akṣaya-pātram manassil – snēham
nitya-nikṣēpamāyenkil
etra sammōhanam mānava-jīvitam
nitya vasantābhirāmam

If love becomes the everlasting wealth in the *akshaya patram* (inexhaustible source) of our mind, human life will ever be a wondrous spring season.

ōmkāra divya porūḷe 48 (Malayalam)

Disclaimer: The translations of certain verses are not literal; they aim at bringing out the essential meaning from the Malayalam verses in a way that is easily understandable.

ōmkāra-divya-porūḷē varū
ōmana makkaḷē vēgam
ōmanayāy vaḷarnn-āmayaṅgaḷ nīkki
ōmkāra-vastuvāy tīrū

Come quickly darling children, you who are the divine essence of Om. Remove all sorrows, grow dear and adorable, and merge with the Absolute.

1

cinni-tterikkāt-ozhukām – aikya
sandēśa-ccintukaḷ pāṭām
aikyattil ākunnu śakti nām onniccu
viśvattin-uḷvēv-akattām

Let us flow as a mighty river and sing the message of unity. Let us not shatter into countless small droplets. Strength lies in unity. Together we can soothe the burning heart of the world.

2

nēṭunnatil tṛptar ākū svanta
nēṭṭatte vāzhttāt-irikkū
nēṭṭam samūhattināyāl svadharmattil
kōṭṭam varillillor-āḷkkum

Let us be content with our gains and not boast about our successes. When our gains also benefit our fellow beings, we will not swerve from the path of *dharma*.

3

nēṭṭam varumbōḷ kutikkum marttyar-
ākāśa-mēlāppilōḷam
kōṭṭam varumboḷ kitaccu tāzhum perum
pātāḷa-garttattinōḷam

When we succeed, we leap up to the sky in happiness. When we fail, we plunge into the nether world of sorrow.

4

uḷḷatte uḷḷāl aṙiyū – uḷḷam-
ellārkkumāy tuṭikkaṭṭe
anyōnya-maitri tann-āhlāda-puṣpaṅgaḷ
eṅgeṅgum-ullasikkaṭṭe

Know your true Self. May you pulse with love for everyone. Let joyous friendship blossom everywhere.

5

mānasam mārddavam ārnnu prēma
mādhuryam-ōlunnatāyāl
dhyānam suvarṇṇam pōl mūlyam-ēṭṭum snēha
bhāvam sugandham curattum

When our hearts soften with the sweetness of love, meditation becomes as precious as gold made fragrant with the perfume of love.

6

paura-bōdhattinde kātal – veṟum
pūtalāy māṭṭāte makkaḷ
jīva-kāruṇyavum kaivalya-lakṣyavum
bhāricca dautyam-ennōrkkū

My children, be serious about your social responsibilities. Your two great goals in life are compassion for all living beings and the attainment of liberation.

7

kṣēmam samūhattin-ēkān – svārttha
mōham tyajikkuvin makkaḷ
svārtthattil-ūnnunna karmaṅgaḷ marttyande
mārggam pizhacc-ennu vyaktam

Let go of selfishness and thus bring prosperity to society. Children, know for certain that selfish actions lead you away from your path.

8

jñānam nilāvu-pōl hṛttil – svayam
vyāpanam ceykē, saharṣam

sādaram ennum svajīvitam anyarkku
mātṛkayāy ācarikkum

When knowledge dawns like silvery moonlight in your heart, it brings joy and humility. Then your life becomes a beacon for others.

9
poṭṭi ōr-ōṭakkuzhalāy – janmam
niṣphalam ākkāt-irikkū
nānā-svaraikya-śrutiyil svajīvitam
mēnmēl uṇarttu-pāṭṭākkū

Let us not be like a broken flute by wasting our life. Let harmony flow as a song of awakening and renewal through the flute of our life.

10
vēdanikkunn-avarkkāyi uḷḷam
vēpathu pūṇḍ-uzhalumbōḷ
māyunnu mānuṣa-garvvukaḷ mānasam
prēmārdram-ākunnu tānē

When our heart suffers for the sorrow of others, pride and ego are humbled and our heart becomes tender in love.

11
tēṅgum manuṣyande kaṇṇīr kāṇke
vēdanayillāykil-ōrkkām
uḷḷil timirkkunnu himsra-jantukkaḷ tan-
uḷḷam mahāraṇya-sāmyam

If our heart does not feel the pain of another's sorrow, know that vicious animals roam the wild forest of our mind.

12
anyaril teṫṫu kāṇumbōḷ makkaḷ
tannuḷḷilēkk-uṫṫu nōkkū
svantam manassinde ceppile nāṇayam
kaḷḷam allenn-uṙappākkū

My children, when you find fault in others, turn inward and introspect. Make sure there are no fake coins in your own heart.

13
kaṇ-turannīlōka-dainyam kaṇḍu
neñcam nuṙuṅgā yatīndran
unnata-jñānipōl kaṇṇaṭacc-andhanāy
entō kināvu kāṇunnu

If an ascetic closes his eyes to the suffering of the world, if sorrow does not grip his heart at its plight, then, even if his eyes are closed like a sage, he is really just a blind man dreaming futile dreams.

14
jīva-ttuṭippāṙuvōḷam – neñcil
āḷaṇam lōka-saubhrātram
sēvanōtsāham jvalikkum sirākēndram
ākaṇam-ōrō manassum

As long as our heart beats, let us feel the welfare of this world as a burning need. Every heart should burn with the eagerness of selfless service.

15
tuḷḷikaḷ vēṙiṭṭu ninnāl – svayam
dhanya-samudramāy tīrā

onnicc-ozhukiyāl śaktiyāṇāguṇam
martyan-uṇḍāyāl mahattvam

Isolated water drops will never become a mighty ocean. They gain strength as they flow together. We become great when we acquire this quality.

16
jīvita-grantha tuṙakkām – ōrō
pāṭhavum gāḍham paṭhikkām
tān tanne ōrunna pāṭhattōṭ-antyattil
jīvita-grantham maṭakkām

Let us open the book of life and learn each lesson well. Then, let us close the book of life having learned the lesson: "I am in everything."

17
ādarśa-hīnanām marttyan – lōka
vāzhcaykku pōlum vighātam
ārbhāṭa-bhaktiyum pēccu vēdāntavum
ātma-rakṣaykkum virōdham

A man without ideals impedes the flow of life. Lavish rituals in the name of devotion and mere book knowledge of *vedanta* are obstacles to liberation.

18
siddhānta-lōkattirikkum – marttyan
kallicca brahmamāy tīrum
maṇṇinde gandham kalarnnuḷḷa jīvitam
kallalla kalkkaṇḍam-ākum

We become like a rock when we live only in the world of theories about Brahman. We become sweet as rock-candy when we live in harmony with the fragrant earth.

19
prēma-svarūpam-āṇuṇma tanne
tānākki nirttunn-oruṇma
nannubhāvaṅgaḷ tan puṇya-srōtassukaḷkk-
ellām uṙavāy-oruṇma

The Truth is love. Our nature is love. Love is the source of all life's divine emotions.

20
uḷḷile snēham vṛthāvil – kallin-
uḷḷile tēn-tuḷḷi pōle
ullāsavāhiyām pūñcōla pōl atiṅg-
ellārkkumāy ozhukēṇam

Let us not hide our love like honey inside a stone. It should flow like the spring breeze laden with the fragrance of flowering orchards.

21
dharmam hanicc-arttha-kāmam – pulki
ātma-naṣṭam vismarikke
vyarttha-janmaṅgaḷkku mītē kutikkunnu
svārttha-lakṣyaṅgaḷ puṇarān

Forgetting *dharma*, we chase wealth and desire, and fail our true Self. We will take many more vain births to gain our selfish ends.

22

āṇavam neññēṫṫi nilkkē – svārttha
lābham namukk-ēka-lakṣyam
arttha-kāmattāl nikattāvatall-ētum
ātma-naṣṭattinde garttam

Our arrogant ego is like a loaded weapon aimed at gaining our selfish ends. But, wealth and desires will never fill the gaping void left from losing our true Self.

23

kāmārttha mātrānuśīlam – lōka
jīvitam bhāriccat-ākkum
dharma-anukūlam ennāyāl svajīvitam
śarmābhirāmamāy māṙum

Life spent chasing wealth and fulfilling desires is a heavy burden. Life becomes prosperous and beautiful when we live according to our *dharma*.

24

lābha-cētattinde trāsil – marttya
jīvitam tūṅgilla sūkṣmam
kālattin-appuṙam kāṇumbozh-allāte
kāṇillatin mūlyam ārum

The scale of profit and loss cannot measure the value of life. We can only realize its value when we are able to see beyond time.

25

cinticc-uṙaykkunnatalla – nammaḷ
ceyyān tuniyunnat-ennāl

collumbōḷ vēṙonnu – ceyyumbōḷ vēṙonnu
illonninum tammil bandham

If we make a decision then act contrary to it, we are saying one thing and doing something else. There is no relation between our word and our deed.

26
lakṣyattil ūnnātta cittam – sadā
vikṣubdham aṅgiṅgu muṅgum
tellonn-orēṭatt-irikkilla – kāṫṫupōl
taṅgāt-alayunnit-eṅgum

A mind not focused on the goal is always unsettled and pulled down by emotions. Never still, the unfocused mind wanders ceaselessly, like the wind.

27
mellennu vēṇam merukkān – allēl
tellonnum allatin śauryam
tantrattil snēhiccu mantrattil bandhiccāl
tañcattil tānē iṇaṅgum

We need to tame our mind slowly and gently; otherwise it resists ferociously. If we tie it to a mantra with loving ruses, then, gradually, it becomes our friend.

28
śraddhā-vivēkam vaḷartti – bhaktyā
citta-kavāṭam tuṙakkū
atyapūrvānanda-ratnam manassinde
ceppil uṇḍ-atyanta-ramyam

Let us foster deep faith and discernment and open wide the door of our heart with devotion. The treasure chest of our heart contains a jewel of unsurpassed bliss.

29

jīvita-saundarya-sāram – nēril
jīvicc-aṙiyāykil-ārum
klāviccu kānti keṭṭ-ārōrum-ōrāte
ādhāram ēlāte pōkum

If we are unable to experience life's beauty in its true essence, we are like vessels covered with green patina. Our life has no foundation, and no one cares for us.

30

satyamē nīṇāl jayikkū – svanta
dharmamē nīṇāḷ nayikkū
satya-dharmattin pratiṣṭha nēṭumbozhē
duḥkha-trayatte jayikkū

Ultimately, only Truth prevails and only *dharma* truly leads us. We vanquish the three types of sorrows when our thoughts, words and actions are grounded in Truth and *dharma*.

31

āmayādhāram tiraññāl – aham
dēham enn-anyathā-bōdham
mōcanōpāyam śarīrattil ñān enna
bhāvamaṫṫ-ātmāvabōdham

Our identification with our physical body binds us. Liberation happens when we identify ourselves with the eternal Self.

32

kaṣṭam meruṅgātta cittam – kṣudra
citraṅgaḷ neyt-ullasikkum
bhōga-pralōbhanam mūrcchicca mānasam
tāzhnn-aṭiññīṭum tamassil

An uncontrolled mind enjoys spinning evil pictures. Wanton pleasures plunge the mind into darkness.

33

āśakaḷ kōṭṭakaḷ tīrkkum – atil
ākāmkṣa vāykkum anantam
sāphalyam onnil uṇḍāyāl atinmīte
āyiram mōhaṅgaḷ vīṇḍum

Wishing builds castles in the air and we wait anxiously for them to materialize. If a single desire is fulfilled, a thousand more spring up.

34

santōṣa-santāpam ellām – vastu
tantratte āśrayikkunnu
vastu-samyōgam sukham viyōgam vyatha
cittam niyantrikka makkaḷ

Joy and sorrow depend on external objects. If our desires materialize, we feel joy; if they don't, we are miserable. My children, learn to control your mind.

35

kaiviṭṭu pōyatil duḥkham – pinne
kai-vanniṭātt-atil duḥkham

kaivannat-eṅgane kāttu-sūkṣikkum-
enn-ōrkkumbōḷ bhōgaṅgaḷ duḥkham

We are sad at what slips though our hands, and we are sad at what we do not gain. When we strive to protect our possessions, they become our sorrow.

36
jīvana-dharmam maṙannāl – ātma
mōcana-marmam pizhaykkum
mōhana-svapnaṅgaḷ neytuneyt-entinī
śōkānta-nāṭakam vīṇḍum

Forgetting the *dharma* of our life, we lose the chance to save ourselves. Why do we continue to weave sweet dreams that delude us, and repeat this sorrowful drama of life?

37
śōkattin duḥsvādiyaṫṫum – svargga
bhōgattil āśavaykkāte
citta-kuṇḍattil jvalikkum hutāgniyil
vṛtti-dravyaṅgaḷ yajikkū

Let us not desire heaven or material pleasures. Let us offer all our thoughts into the sacrificial fire of pure consciousness.

38
āśayāṇ-ētinum hētu – ātma
lābham koticcāl-atēkum
bhōgam koticcāl nizhal-pōle śōkavum
tānēyatōṭ-ottu kūṭum

Desire is the cause of everything. If we desire Self-realization we gain it. If we desire material pleasures, the shadow of sorrow inevitably follows us.

39

tyāgōjjvalam karmam eṅgum – puṇya
dēva-tīrttham pōle vandyam
svārttha-karmam viṣa-mālinyam ēṫṫunnor-
ōṭa-nīr ennapōl nindyam

Actions, lustrous with sacrifice, are worthy of worship, like sacred rivers. Selfish actions are like poisonous pollutants, repugnant as stinking drain water.

40

rāga-dvēṣatī keṭuttān – manam
snēha-tīrtthattil kutirkkū
lōka-jētākkaḷām tyāgikaḷ tan vazhi
tārayil dhīram carikkū

Soften your heart in a stream of love to quench the fires of desire and anger. Move forward with courage on the path shown by the great souls who have conquered the world.

41

uḷkkāmb-erikkilum duḥkham – nammil
utkṛṣṭa-bhāvam teḷikkum
andhakārattile kaittiri veṭṭamāṇ-
antarangattile duḥkham

Our heart may burn in sorrow, but grief can ennoble us. Our inner sadness becomes the little lamp that lights up the darkness.

42
ceṫṫaham muṫṫittiṇarttāl – pinne
teṫṫum śariyum tiriyā
illāttat-uḷḷatāy uḷḷatillāttatāy
vallātta mōhattil-āzhttum

When ego grows, we cannot discern right from wrong. We fall into delusion and imagine the real to be unreal, and the unreal to be real.

43
dharma-karmaṅgaḷkku tammil – bhinna
dharmam illenkilum tānāy
ceyyunnat-okkeyum karmam-āṇuḷḷ-uṇarnn-
ācariccāl atu dharmam

Actions performed with the notion of "I" become karma. The same action, performed with an awakened inner self, becomes *dharma*.

44
krōdhattāl bhinniccitāte – daiva
snēhattāl onnikka makkaḷ
svantam manassinde āndōḷanam svayam
tān tān niyantrikka makkaḷ

My children, do not divide yourselves in anger. Rather, unite in the love of God. Learn to control the pendulum swing of your mind.

45
āyussorālkk-etra tuccham – atin
mūlyam ōrttāl etra meccam

nēṭunnat-ittiri nēṭān orottiri
āśakaḷ etrayō miccam

Our life is short and its value is beyond compare; yet, we live only to fulfill desires. Then, we leave with many more yet to be fulfilled.

46
martya-svātantryam pradhānam – prēma
maitri-bandham supradhānam
mṛtyu-nirmuktamām ātma-svātantryamāṇ-
atyantam uttamam nūnam

Freedom is important; but, more important still are relationships forged in love. The highest ideal is the liberation that frees us from death.

47
rakṣippavan tanne namme – svayam
śikṣikkum enn-ōrttiṭēṇḍa
rakṣitāv-āyavan śikṣitāv-ennatu
durbala-nīti onnatre

God always protects. The Protector will never be the punisher.

48
snēha-hastattin taṇalil – ōrō
jīvanum śānti śvasikkām
snēha-svarūpanil cētass-aṇakkyukil
kēvalānandam svadikkām

Let everyone breathe in peace under the shade of a loving hand. Let us merge into the One who is the embodiment of love, and experience the infinite bliss of liberation.

ōmkāra divya porūḷe 49 (Malayalam)

Disclaimer: The translations of certain verses are not literal; they aim at bringing out the essential meaning from the Malayalam verses in a way that is easily understandable.

ōmkāra divya porūḷe varū
ōmana-makkaḷē vēgam
ōmanayāy vaḷarnn-āmayaṅgaḷ nīkki
ōmkāra-vastuvāy tīrū

Come quickly darling children, you who are the divine essence of Om. Remove all sorrows, grow dear and adorable, and merge with the Absolute.

1
uḷḷil guru-prēmam uṇḍēl – daivam
ennum namukkoppam uṇḍām
nērkkezhum-ōrō pratisandhiy-enkilum
vēgēne durggam kaṭakkām

When we love the *guru*, then God is always with us. We may face many difficulties, but we will be able to swiftly overcome every challenge.

2
bhūmikku gandham tyajikkām – jalam
tānē dravatvam tyajikkām
śiṣya-dharmattil carippavan tan guru
bhakti-bhāvam santyajikkām

The earth can never lose its earthy smell, and water always remains fluid. Likewise, the disciple who remains true to his *dharma* never loses his reverence for the *guru*.

3
ādaraśīlam pularttām – ātma
bōdhattāl āmayam nīkkām
svātantrya-sāram grahikkām, svajīvitam
lōkōpakār-ārttham ākkām

Let us cultivate reverence, and let Self-awareness cleanse us of all impurities. Let us grasp the essence of freedom and dedicate ourselves to helping others.

4
snēha-pīyūṣam ozhukkū – perum
dāhattāl lōkam trasippū
mōhattil vīzhāt-irikkū, vikārattin
kṣōbhattāl vāṭāt-irikkū

Let the ambrosia of love flow over this world burning in thirst. Let us not fall prey to delusion or wither in emotional storms.

5
snēham uṇḍuḷḷil ennōtum – ārkkum
ēkāykil illatil kāṛyam
kallinde uḷḷile tēn-tuḷḷi pōl atu
tellum prayōjanam ceyyā

The love that we claim is within us is like honey trapped inside a rock. Unless we share it with others, our love won't benefit anyone.

6

pūmaṇam pēṙunna kāṫṫin – nērttor-
ōḷam pōl saumyam carikkū
pūmazha tuḷḷi pōl nīḷe pozhikkuvin
tūmayil kāruṇya-tīrttham

Let us live gently like a breeze carrying the fragrance of flowers. Like showers of flowers, let us spread compassion everywhere.

7

lābham kotikkāte uḷḷam – snēha
dhārayāy eṅgum sarikkām
snēham śaratkāla candrika ennapōl
śōkā-tapatte akaṫṫum

The love of selfless hearts flows everywhere. Like the autumn moon, love soothes burning sorrows.

8

nīla-nilāvōḷi pōle – snēha
dhārayāl lōkam viḷakkām
snēha-śuśruṣayāl āṙāttorādhiyill-
āgōḷa-sīmayil eṅgum

Let our love light up this world like radiant moonlight. There is no sorrow in the universe that love cannot heal.

9

pāṇḍitya-mēnmayāl alla – nēṭṭam
bhautika-lābhattāl alla

dīnaril tūkunna kāruṇyam ākunnit-
ātma-samtṛptikk-upāyam

Neither learning nor material wealth has any real value. Only the compassion we show to the suffering can bring contentment.

10
snēha-samvādam naṭattām – ātma
maitri tan kāhaḷam-ūtām
uḷḷattil-āḷunna krōdhāgni-jjvālakaḷ
divya-snēhattāl keṭuttām

Let us have loving dialogues, and let true friendship be our clarion call. Let divine love extinguish the flames of anger.

11
addhyāpakan yantram eṅkil – innu
vidyārtthi kalmatil pōle
uḷḷam tuṙannuḷḷa samvādam illeṅgum
ellām orācāram-allo

If a teacher is like a machine, then the student will be like a wall of stone. Unless hearts are shared, learning becomes mechanical.

12
vidya ārjjippatin lakṣyam – veṙum
vitta-lābham mātramāyi
vidya koṇḍ-uḷkkaṇ tuṙakkēṇḍā – vēṇḍatu
vidyaykk-orudyōga-nēṭṭam

Nowadays, our learning is only for professional success and accumulating wealth. We do not desire to open the inner eye of Truth through knowledge.

13

ādarav-ētilum illa – ētum
nērē grahikkayumilla
tannōḷam ārum varillenn-ahantaye
vandikkayill-unnatanmār

We respect nothing and have no correct understanding. We claim greatness, but the truly great do not flaunt an inflated ego.

14

vāḷināl ēlkkum kṣatatte – vēṇēl
auṣadhattāl uṇakkīṭām
vākku koṇḍ-ēlkkum vraṇappāṭ-uṇaṅgilla
cīrkkum hṛdantattil ennum

Medicines can heal sword wounds, but wounds inflicted by our words never heal. They fester in the heart forever.

15

samgharṣa-vēnalil vāṭi – manam
sankōcicc-īṭāte vēgam
tann-antarangatte viśvēśa-śaktikku
naivēdyam ākkuvin makkaḷ

Children, do not let the heat of conflict wither and narrow your mind. Without delay, offer your heart to God, the universal power.

16

eyyān tuṭaṅgunn-orastram – vēṇēl
eyyātirikkām, maṭakkām
vēṟonn-eṭukkām, kulakkyām atallenkil
vēṟoru lakṣyattil eyyām

We can either shoot an arrow at a specific target, or we can remove it from the bow string. Then we can pick up another arrow, aim, and shoot at the same target; or we can change direction and aim at another target.

17

karmavum avvidham ceyyām – allēl
ceyyātirikkām yathēṣṭam
maṟṟoru rūpattil ceyyām niyantriccu
ceytāl mahattvam varikkām

Likewise, we may either perform an action, or refrain from it, or perform it in another manner. Self-control makes actions great.

18

lābhacētam ninaykkumbōḷ – karmam
ētum namukk-attalākum
pūjā-manōbhāva-karmam nirāmayam
nērdiśābōdham teḷikkum

When we calculate the profit and loss of each action, it brings us grief. Actions offered as worship are pure and shed light along the path.

19

dharmam pizhaykkāte makkaḷ – sūkṣma
karmaṅgaḷ ācarikkumbōḷ

cittam teḷiññ-ātma-sūryōdayam varum
satya-sākṣātkkāra-sajjam

Children, when your thoughts are good and ethical, your heart becomes clear. Then Truth will dawn, and the Self will awaken like the rising sun.

20
dhyānam vicāramall-ōrkkū – manō
līnata āṇ-ennaṙiyū
yātonnil āzhavē cētass-aliññu pōm
āyatāṇātma-yāthārtthyam

Know that meditation is a merging of the mind, not a stream of thoughts. In deep meditation, the mind dissolves in the Self (Reality).

21
sthūlattil ninnum manassu – sūkṣma
lōkaṅgaḷil vyāparikke
kāṇātta kāzhcakaḷ kaṇḍu rasiccitām
keḷkkātta nādaṅgaḷ kēḷkkām

As our mind travels from the physical to the subtle worlds, we may see wondrous sights till now unseen, and hear music till now unheard.

22
āmagnam ākāte vīṇḍum – manam
āzhattil sūkṣmata ārnnāl
uḷḷil tapōvahni āḷum manōvṛtti
onn-ozhiyāte dahikkum

Instead of becoming immersed in the world when your mind reaches the subtle realm, let the fire of tapas (penance) consume all your thoughts and impressions.

23
vṛttikṣayam vanna cittam – nīla
niścalākāśa samānam
kāṇāte kāṇunna kēḷkkāte kēḷkkunnōr
ānanda-lōkam uṇarum

A quiet mind is like a still, clear blue sky. There, a blissful world can awaken—a world seen with the inner eye and heard with the inner ear.

24
udbuddhar-ākuvin makkaḷ – manō
nidrālasyam viṭṭuṇarū
ujjvalikkunn-uṇḍu sūryan cidākāśa
citram teḷiññ-onnu kāṇū

Children, the sun is shining! Wake up from your mental lethargy and behold the vast light of consciousness.

25
āgraham ētum tyajikkū – makkaḷ
ātma-yāthārtthyam grahikkū
mōham nivartticcu jñānam prakāśiccu
lōkam jayicc-uḷḷaṭakkū

Children, renounce your desires and realize the Truth of the Self. Be free of delusion, conquer the world, and remain established in the effulgent light of the Self.

26
dhyānam-entākilum lakṣyam – manō
nāśam phalam śōkaśānti
ātma-svātantryam hanikkum manassinde
māyikā-lōkam jayikkū

There are many kinds of meditation, but the goal is the dissolution of the mind and relief from sorrow. Conquer the illusory world of the mind that veils the pure, free Self.

27
ātma-saṅgītam pozhikkām – manō
vīṇayil nādam korukkām
mandānilan tande cintupāṭṭennapōl
uḷḷil muzhaṅgaṭṭe or-īṇam

Let us sing the song of the Self and play the *veena* of our mind. May melody resound within like sweet music floating on the gentle breeze.

28
mūṭi kiṭakkunna cāmbal – uḷḷāl
ūti teḷikkān kazhiññāl
agnikkanal dīptam ākum teḷiññatil
svasvarūpam dṛśyam ākum

When we blow away the ash that covers the Self, the embers will burst into flame. In that light, we will behold our true Self.

29
ikkaṇḍa kāzhcakaḷ ellām – manō
sṛṣṭiyāṇ-enn-orāḷ ōrttāl

akkināvalliyil ūyalāṭīṭāte
'svatva' bōdhattil ramikkum

When we realize that everything we see is a projection of our mind, we will revel in pure consciousness instead of swinging on those dream-vines.

30

mithya ennōtum īlōkam – ārkkum
arttha-samphullam ākkīṭām
satya-sākṣātkkāra-dṛṣṭiyāl īkṣikke
immaṭṭil allennu mātram

This illusory world reveals its meaning when seen through eyes that have realized the Truth.

31

vairāgya-niṣṭhaykku vēṇḍi – lōkam
mithya enn-ācāryan ōtum
mithya ennāl nityam allennu mātramām
illāttat-allennu vyaktam

To instill dispassion and discipline, the *guru* teaches us about the illusory nature of the world. "Illusory" does not mean "does not exist"; it means that the world is impermanent.

32

arttham grahikkāte nammaḷ – vṛthā-
jalpanam ōrōnnu ceyyum
sthūla-sūkṣmaṅgaḷām arttham nirūpikkil
āśayabhēdam nissāram

We make hollow statements without knowing their meaning. Once we understand the common and subtle undertones of words, we can convey meaning clearly.

33

āzhattil vēru kaṇḍettām – bāhya
lōkattin nēṛu kaṇḍettām
lōka-vṛkṣattinde tāyvēril ettiyāl
tān enna kāmbu kaṇḍettām

We can find our roots deep within, and the true nature of the outer world. When we reach the central root of the world tree, we will find the inner core of our being.

34

arppaṇa-bhāvam uṇḍenkil – ellām
īśvarākāramāy kāṇām
kaypum kavarppum kalarnnat-āṇenkilum
okkeyum svāduṫṫat-ākām

When we have an attitude of surrender, we see God in everything. Though a mix of bitter and sour, everything becomes delicious.

35

uḷkkāzhca kaivannuveṅkil – sṛṣṭi
etrayum saundarya-pūrṇam
vaikṛtam kāṇumbozh-ōrkkaṇam tanmanō
vaikṛtam-āṇat-ennārum

How beautiful is creation when seen with the inner eye! Let us remember that imperfections we see in others are reflections of imperfections in ourselves.

36
nērāya kāzhca uṇḍāyāl – ellām
cāruta ārnnatāy kāṇum
sṛṣṭiyum tānum abhēdam āṇantaram
kāṇunnat-ajñāna-dōṣam

When we have insight, everything is beautiful. We see creation as separate from our Self because of our ignorance.

37
uḷḷuṇarnn-īkṣicciṭumbōḷ – kāzhca
onnāke vēṙonnāy māṙum
ceyta karmaṅgaḷ tuṭarnn-ācarikkilum
artthavum bhāvavum navyam

Inner awareness lets us see everything in a new light. Though we perform the same actions, they become more meaningful.

38
bandhicciṭāt-antarangam – lōka
bandham pularttān paṭhikkū
duḥkhatte ātmāvil andhakārattile
neyttiri-veṭṭam ennōrkkū

Learn to establish worldly relationships without getting attached, and to interact with the world without being bound by it. Know that sorrow can be a lamp that illumines the darkness.

39
nērāyatin nēṛkkaṇaññāl – pinne
nēraṫṫatil manam paṫṫā

nityam allāttatu satyam āvillatil
ceṫṫum manaḥpaṫṫu vēṇḍa

When we are close to the Truth, our mind does not attach itself to the impermanent. The unreal will never become the Truth. Let us quit all attachment to the impermanent.

40
tēn-kani enn-ōrtt-aṭuttu – manam
mōhiccu nēṭum phalatte
nañc-ennaṙiyukil taḷḷān kṣaṇam mati
santāpam illatil tellum

We eagerly choose a fruit expecting it to taste like honey; but when we realize it is poisonous, we instantly throw it away without regret.

41
kaikōrttu nīṅgunnit-eṅgum – sukha-
duḥkhamat-ennōrttiṭāte
vēṇam sukham, vēṇḍa duḥkham – manōgati
ōrttāl atēṫṫam vicitram

We want to experience joy and we do not want to accept sorrow. We should realize that joy and sorrow are intertwined. What a wonder that the mind does not understand this truth!

42
arttham illāttatinnāyi – ōrō
arttham menayunnu vyarttham
arttham illāttatinn-arttham tirakkunna
tikkum tirakkumāṇ-eṅgum

We concoct meanings for meaningless things. Then, we race and jostle each other searching for meaning in the meaningless.

43

vēṇḍennu vaykkāte entum – vīṇḍum
vēṇam ennārttiyāṇ-ārkkum
bhōgam bhujicc-ārtti tīrum enn-ōrkkēṇḍa
kālam kaṇakku māyccālum

Without self-restraint, we will always chase after our desires. Even as our time runs out, our endless desires will remain unsatisfied.

44

kaiviṭā sandēham ētum – manō
sankalpa-lōkam vicitram
ellām niṣēdhikkum onnum uḷkkoḷḷilla
tan manam vēdi viṭṭāṭum

This illusory world is always confusing, and our thoughts become impure. Then, we reject everything and cannot imbibe reality.

45

nalpu-tilp-ōrāte entum – manam
bhakṣippū vāya tōrāte
andhakārattinde santati eṅkilum
ellām aṟiyunna bhāvam

Our mind feeds insatiably on everything, good or bad. We are children of ignorance, but we think we know everything.

46
hṛttilēkk-āzhnnu nōkkumbōḷ – kāṇām
okke svīkāryata mātram
ellā samasyayum māyum viśvāsyata
hṛttin mukha-mudra āvum

If we dive deep inside, we find total acceptance. Our doubts fade and trust becomes the emblem of our heart.

47
dharma-mārgattil cariccu – niṣṭha
kaivannu, 'svatva'prakāśam
eṅgum paratti uṣassu-pōl śōbhikke
cittam ātmāvinnu mitram

When we walk steadfastly on the path of goodness, our inner light spreads like a golden dawn, and our mind befriends the Self.

48
illāttat-uṇḍākkiṭēṇḍa – uḷḷil
uḷḷatonn-āviṣkarikkām
anyadikkil cennu nēṭēṇḍa – tān tannil
kaṇḍettaṇam mōkṣa-dhāmam

Let us not make up what is not there. Let us manifest what truly is within. We must find the abode of the Self within. We will not find it anywhere else.

49
āśa tan keṭṭ-azhiyumbōḷ – mōkṣa
vātil malarkke tuṙakkum

muktikku mōhicc-uzhaṙēṇḍa mōhanir-
mukti tān – muktikk-upāyam

When the knot of desire is untied, the door to Self-realization opens wide. We need not wander in search of liberation. Renouncing desire is the way.

ōmkāra divya porūḷe 50 (Malayalam)

Disclaimer: The translations of certain verses are not literal; they aim at bringing out the essential meaning from the Malayalam verses in a way that is easily understandable.

ōmkāra divya porūḷe varū
ōmana-makkaḷē vēgam
ōmanayāy vaḷarnn-āmayaṅgaḷ nīkki
ōmkāra-vastuvāy tīrū

Come quickly darling children, you who are the divine essence of Om. Remove all sorrows, grow dear and adorable, and merge with the Absolute.

1
pūrṇa-tējassōṭe vāzhām – maṇṇil
pūvupōl saumyarāy tīrām
pūritānanda-hṛdantam mahēśvara
pūjaykku pūvākki māṫṫām

Let us live vibrant lives and attain the calm beauty of a flower. Let us offer our blissful hearts to the Lord.

2
kaivalya-rūpan kaniññāl – ārkkum
kaitavam ellām-oṭuṅgum
snēhattāl lōkam jayiccuḷḷ-aṭakkuvōrkk-
īśvaran dāsanāy tīrum

When God, the embodiment of pure consciousness, showers His compassion upon us, all our sorrows cease. God is the servant of those who control their minds and conquer the world with love.

3
śītaḷam nīhāra-dharmam – tāpam
tīyin tanatāya dharmam
ānandam ākunnit-ātmāvin dharmam enn-
ōruvōn ānanda-rūpan

The nature of water is wetness; the nature of fire is heat. God, who is infinite bliss, tells us that bliss is the nature of the Self.

4
nērkkezhām vighnaṅgaḷ nīḷe – lakṣya
lābhattin-ārjjavam vēṇam
ātma-sākṣātkkāra-vīthiyil pātāḷa
garttaṅgaḷ uṇḍām anēkam

We need enthusiasm and energy to overcome the obstacles that hinder our reaching the goal. There are many deep ditches on the road to Self-realization.

5
ōmkāra-bījākṣarattil – mūnnu
kālavum lōkavum līnam

kaivalya-muktikk-anuṣṭhāna-sādhanam
abhyāsa-naipuṇyar ākū

The three times (past, present and future) and this universe merge in Om. Let us meditate on Om to attain liberation.

6
tān tannil ārenn-uṇarū – svayam
tannil ēkāntam tirayū
tanne aṙiyumbōḷ tānē aṙiyunnu
tānāṇu kāṇāyat-ellām

Let us seek the Truth within and awaken to our true Self. When we realize the Self, we will know that everything is nothing but our own Self.

7
śōkam śamikkān upāyam – śōka
hētu entenn-ōrttu nōkkū
svāṛttham āṇenkil nissāram āṇ-āgraha
tyāgattāl tāpam taṇukkum

To become free of sorrow, let us discover its cause. Selfish desire is the cause of sorrow. When we renounce selfish desire, then we will be free.

8
nissvārttha-sēvanōtsāham – śraddhā
bhakti, viśvāsam, vinayam
anyūnamāy irikkaṭṭe – tapōtkarṣa
nairmalyavum snēhavāypum

Let us be enthusiastic in service and become pure and loving. Let faith, devotion and humility flow ceaselessly.

9
mōha-nirmuktar ākumbōḷ – ārum
śōka-vimuktar ākunnu
bhakti ennāl bhāva-śuddhi āṇ-ōrkkukil
mukti-lābhēcchayum vighnam

We will be free of sorrow when we are free of desire. True devotion is purity of heart. If our heart is selfish, even the desire for liberation becomes an obstacle on our path.

10
niṣkāma-bhāvattilūṭe – pūjā
puṣpamāy uḷḷam viṭarnnāl
tān enna tēn-kaṇam tūmaññu-tuḷḷi pōl
prēmārṇṇavattil layikkum

When our heart is free of desire, it will bloom as a flower for the Lord. Then we will be like a honey drop that merges in the ocean of love.

11
sārasa-patram kaṇakke – karma
lēpam puraḷāte makkaḷ
jīvande udgatikkāyum jagattinde
sadgatikkāyum śramikkū

Children, do not allow karma to sully your soul. Strive for the welfare of the world and for your own upliftment. Do not let desire for the fruits of karma stain your heart.

12
ācāra-niṣṭhar ākēṇam – pakṣē
ācāra-baddhar ākolla

ātmaikya-lakṣyattil ūnnāttor ācāram
kālccaṅgala-kkeṭṭu tanne

Let us perform rituals and follow traditions, but not get trapped in them. Any ritual not rooted in longing to merge with the Self becomes a binding chain.

13
dhyānattin neyttiri nīṭṭām – hṛttil
jñāna-prakāśam teḷikkām
kēvalānandam svadikkām, svajīvitam
snēhātmakam śōbha ēṫṫām

Through meditation, let us light the lamp of knowledge in our hearts and experience pure bliss. Then our life will be full of love and light.

14
innallēl nāḷe nām vēṇam – tannil
tan bhāgadhēyam tirayān
nērvazhi kāṭṭuvān amma uṇḍenkilum
nēr-aṙiyēṇḍavar makkaḷ

If not today, then tomorrow you will have to search for your inner essence. Amma will show you the right path, but you children must seek the Truth on your own.

15
kāmanayil ninn-uṇarnnāl – lōkam
ādarikkum daiva-tulyam
kōri coriyunnor-audārya-vāypināl
ārilum ādarav-ēṫṫum

The world reveres the desireless one as equal to God, and bows down before the love and care that flow from him.

16

kaiviṭān uṇḍ-ēṙe yatnam – dēham
ñān enna mithyābhimānam
janmāntaraṅgaḷāy onnenn-uṙaccu pōy
tānum śarīravum tammil

Let us renounce pride and identification with the body. The delusion that we are the body has strengthened over many lives.

17

bhautikōpādhikaḷ tēyum – sthirōt-
sāham keṭum svaram tāzhum
kālamām tēr-uruḷ-kīzhil peṭumbōzhum
pōkilla bhōgāśa tellum

The senses through which we perceive the world will deteriorate. Our enthusiasm will wane and our voice will grow weak. But even when the wheels of the chariot of time crush us, our desires will remain strong.

18

ādarśa-bōdham pularttū – atin
nērvara nōkki carikkū
īśvarādēśam grahikkū – vinamrarāy
śāśvata-ānandam svadikkū

Let us always be true to our ideals and walk the straight path of *dharma*. Let us understand God's intentions for us. When humility dawns within, we will be able to savor eternal bliss.

19

satyam vacikkunn-avarkkum – sadā
dharmam carikkunn-avarkkum
mithya-abhimānamaṫṫ-ātmāvabōdhattil
nityam pratiṣṭha nēṭīṭām

Those who always speak the truth and walk the path of *dharma* are able to abandon their false ego. They become established in the Self.

20

ōti paṭhippippat-ellām – innu
bhōga-samskāra-pradhānam
tyāga-samskārattil ūnnal ezhikkilō
lōkattinn-āpatt-aṇakkyum

Today, the purpose of education is the attainment of material wealth. Such education, not rooted in the spirit of sacrifice, is dangerous for the world.

21

nandanōdyānatte vellum – uḷḷil
ponmaṇiddvīp-onnu kāṇām
lōkaṅgaḷ okkeyā lōkattu dhūḷikaḷ
mēḷiccu kūttāṭimāyum

Within us is an island of gems that rivals the garden of the gods. In that wondrous inner land, all the worlds are mere specks that play together and fade away.

22

bāhya-lōkattinnu vēṇḍi – ātma
lōkam maṫakkāt-irikkū

bāhya-lōkam mařann-ātmalōkam mātram
nēṭān kotikkāt-irikkū

Let us remember the inner world of the Self for the sake of the world. At the same time, let us not reject the external world thinking to gain the world of the Self.

23
onnum niṣēdhicciṭēṇḍa – uḷḷat-
uḷḷapōl kaṇḍ-ādarikkām
taḷḷān iṭam pōrā koḷḷān iṭam pōrā
uṇmayāl pūrṇamāṇ-ellām

Let us not reject anything. Remember that everything is perfect in its essence. Let us know and respect the true nature of everything. Then there will be no place inside for likes and dislikes.

24
bāhya-nētram koṇḍu mātram – kāṇum
kāzhcakaḷ ellām apūrṇam
ātma-nētram tuřann-īkṣikkil darśikkām
sīmayaṫṫ-ēkātma-lōkam

The knowledge we gain through our sense organs is always imperfect. When we see with the inner eye, we behold the world as the One all-pervading Self.

25
anyaril nyūnata kāṇān – kaṇṇor-
āyiramāṇ-ārkkum eṅgum
tannile nyūnata kāṇilla kāṇkilum
kāṇātta bhāvam naṭikkum

We have a thousand eyes to see the faults of others, but we are blind to our own faults. Even when we do see them, we fail to acknowledge them.

26
vāḷalla vajrāyudham tān – kaṭum
vākk-ennat-ārōrttiṭunnu
kāṇillayeṅkilum vāṭā-vraṇam pōlat-
āzhattil viṅgum, tiṇarkkum

We do not realize that our cruel words cut as sharply as a blazing sword and leave hidden wounds that fester and do not heal.

27
vīṇayil tatti tuḷumbum – nāda
vīcipōl prēmārdramāyi
lōkattin-ākeyum hṛdyata tōnnunna
vākkum pravṛttiyum nēṭū

Let us learn to speak and act with love as tender as gentle music arising from a *veena*. Then the whole world will welcome our deeds and words.

28
śānti-tēṭunnavar ennum – tēṭum
āgamōdātta-sandēśam
ārāma-vāṭiyil pūnilāvenna pōl
jīvitam pālamṛtākkum

Those who search for peace always look to the exalted message of the *Vedas*. Their lives are beautiful as a flower garden bathed in moonlight.

29

vidyaye vittam kavarnnu – vidya
vittam enn-ārōrttiṭunnu
pāṭṭi kozhicc-eṭutt-āṭṭil kaḷaññu nām
ārjjicca samskāra-mūlyam

Now, knowledge serves wealth. No one realizes that knowledge is the true wealth. We have thrown out, like chaff, the noble *samskara* passed down from our ancestors.

30

agnikkanal kāññukatti – uḷḷil
addhyātma-dāham tiḷaykke
muktikk-orāḷāy avan tēṭi ettunnu
satya-dṛkkām sadguruvil

When the thirst for Self-knowledge burns within, the seeker of liberation searches for the *Satguru*, the Seer of Truth.

31

nīrccālu nīnti kaṭakkām – mahā
sāgaram nīntān prayāsam
īśvara-anugraham sāddhyamām eṅkilum
klēśam guru-prēmalābham

Fording streams is easy, but crossing an ocean is difficult. God may grant boons, but gaining the loving grace of the *guru* is difficult.

32

sadguror-ājñaykk-adhīnam – manō
vṛttikaḷ vērāṭṭiṭumbōḷ

tattvamasyādi-vicāram vazhikk-aham
śuddha-caitanyam ennōrām

Actions in obedience to the *guru's* words uproot all distractions from our mind. Let us contemplate the great truth, "You are that," and realize that we are pure consciousness.

33

vāsanā-bījam manassil – melle
āzhattil āzhnnu vēr-ūnnum
mēlē paṭarppēṙi mūṭum, nizhal vīśi-
pāṭē iruṇḍū pōm māṟgam

Our latent tendencies are like seeds that set down deep roots in our mind and grow into the thick shrubs of desires. They cast a dark shadow and conceal the path to our goal.

34

ñaninde tāyvēru kāṇān – dēham
ñān enna mithya māyēṇam
ñān-āyirunna ñān ñānalla –jñānikaḷ
ñān ennu kāṇunnu sarvam

To find the root of "me", we must break free of the delusion that "I" am the body. The 'me' that I know is not my real essence. Knowers of the Truth see themselves in everything.

35

mēghaṅgaḷ garjjicciṭaṭṭe – mahā
sāgaram kṣōbhicciṭaṭṭe
parvatam-pōle uṙapp-ārnn-ezhum cittam
allilum lōkam jayikkum

The clouds can thunder and the ocean can rage, but the heart that remains firm as a mountain will conquer the world.

36

ceytiṭṭu cinticciṭāte – svayam
cinticcu ceyyēṇam entum
cinticcu ñān enn-ahantayaṫṫ-ācaricc-
ennāl phalam nūṙumēni

When we think only after we act, it's too late. Before we act, we must think for ourselves and act without ego. Then we reap fruits a hundred fold.

37

mānikaḷ māniccitāññāl – ceytat-
ētum kṛtārttham ākilla
'ñān' ennu kunticc-ezhum cintakaḷkk-antyam-
ākumbozh-ārāddhyar ākum

Our life is fulfilled when the great ones are happy with our work. They find our actions worthy if they are done without arrogance and selfishness.

38

sattayil jīvikkum-eṅkil – attal
okkeyum astamiccīṭum
duḥkha-saukhyam manōvṛttikaḷkk-āspadam
sattayil taṅgaṭṭe cittam

When we are established in our true essence, all our troubles disappear. Joy and sorrow depend on the turbulence of our mind. Let us always remain established in our true Self.

39

vastukkaḷ kāṇunna kaṇṇāl – vastu
sattaye kāṇill-orāḷum
sattaye kāṇunna kaṇṇonnu vēṙeyāṇ-
akkaṇṇu kāṇāykil andham

Our sense organs can never perceive the Reality that sustains the universe. We can see the Truth only with our inner eye, and our life is futile if our inner eye is closed.

40

uḷḷuṇarnn-uḷḷat-ōtēṇam – naṙum
veṇṇilāv-ōlunna pōle
satyattin saurabhyam ēlātta vākkukaḷ
cappum cavaṙum enn-ōrkkū

We must awaken within and discover the Truth, radiant like moonlight. Words without the fragrance of Truth are meaningless.

41

kaṇḍāl aṙaykkunna dhārṣṭyam – pūṇḍu
tān allāt-ākolla makkaḷ
munnē paṭhikkēṇḍa pāṭham maṙakkukil
kallicc-iruṭṭilām uḷḷam

Children, do not be proud and obstinate. Be true to yourselves. If you forget these lessons, your hearts will become dark and hard.

42

koṫtum kuṭiyum illāte – tēṅgum
paṭṭiṇi-pāvaṅgaḷ cuṫtum

nāykkaḷe pōṭṭunna cētōvikāravum
marttyar ōṭillāttat-entē?

We see the starving and homeless poor around us. Why do we, who are kind even to dogs, have no compassion towards them?

43
sadyaykkilakaḷ niratti – atil
tattva-vēdāntam coriññāl
kāḷum vayaṙinde tī keṭill-ārttaril
ātmōpadēśam nirarttham

Vedanta philosophy does not fill the hungry stomachs of the starving poor. Without appeasing their hunger, teachings about the Self have no meaning for them.

44
ūṇalla lakṣyam ennālum – veṙum
vēdōktikaḷkk-entu mūlyam?
ānanda-lābhattin ātmā-anusandhānam
kāyum vayaṙukaḷkk-annam

Preaching *Vedanta* has no value unless we help to meet the needs of the poor. We contemplate on the Self for inner bliss, but the body requires nourishing food.

45
kāññ-eriyum karaḷ-tāpam – tiṅgi
nīrāvi kaṇṇunīrāyi
tāzhnn-aṭiyunn-avarkk-āśvāsam ēkāykil
jīvitam ennatē vyarttham

The burning sorrow of our heart should be transformed into acts of consolation for the downtrodden. Otherwise, our very life is futile.

46

dēvatōpāsanayālum – melle
ātmīya-bōdham uṇarum
ēkānta-bhaktiyum bhāvanā-śuddhiyum
tānatāy tīrān sahāyam

Even through the worship of *devatas*, Self-knowledge can slowly dawn within. Our pure-hearted faith and devotion reveals our oneness with the Self.

47

svatam pitāvinde citram – veṙum
citram ennalla nām kāṇmū
vigraham kāṇke smarikkunnat-avvidham
svasvarūpātma-caitanyam

For each of us, the picture of our father is not a mere photo. It brings alive his memories. Similarly, the idol before us makes us contemplate the all-pervading consciousness that is our true Self.

48

satyam advaitam ennālum – dvaita
bhāvam niṣēdhicciṭēṇḍa
ōrātirikkunna nērattu nēṛāṇat-
ōrumbōḷ satyam advaitam

Though the Truth is non-dual, it does not refute God with name and form. Until we realize the Truth of *advaita*, duality exists for us.

49
kṛṣṇa-pakṣattile candran – pōle
āśakaḷ lōpiccu pōkām
vīṇḍum 'sitēndu' pōl varddhicciṭām āśa
pōṇam manō-vṛtti pāṭē

Our desires might disappear like the sliver of the waning moon. But when the flow of our thoughts continues, our desires return like the waxing moon. Let us become free of all selfish desire and, thus, subdue our thoughts.

50
āśaykk-adhīna peṭumbōḷ – śakti
hīnanāy tīrum manuṣyan
āśa varjjikkukil śakti ārjjicciṭum
śaktanē mukti ārjjikkū

When desire enslaves us, we lose all inner strength. When we renounce desire, we gather strength. Only the strong can attain liberation.

ōmkāra divya porūḷe 51 (Malayalam)

Disclaimer: The translations of certain verses are not literal; they aim at bringing out the essential meaning from the Malayalam verses in a way that is easily understandable.

ōmkāra divya porūḷe varū
ōmana-makkaḷē vēgam
ōmanayāyvaḷarnn-āmayaṅgaḷ nīkki
ōmkāravastuvāy tīrū

Come quickly darling children, you who are the divine essence of Om. Remove all sorrows, grow dear and adorable, and merge with the Absolute.

1

satyam vadikkān paṭhikkū – makkaḷ
dharmam carikkān śramikkū
satyattōṭ-ābhimukhyam varum buddhikku
dharmam viḷakkāy bhavikkum

Children, learn to speak the truth and act according to *dharma*. Your intelligence will be trained to speak the truth, and *dharma* will guide your way like a lamp.

2

satyam svayam śvasikkunnu – satya
hīnan svayam naśikkunnu
satyattināy koṇḍu jīvipp-avan svayam
mṛtyu-lōkam jayikkunnu

Truth lives on. The untruthful ones bring destruction upon themselves. Those who abide in Truth conquer death.

3

āṭi-timarkkunnu lōkam – bhōga
lālasarāy iṅgu mūḍham
svantam mukhattin kariñcēṙu kāṇāte
kāṇunnit-anyande dūṣyam

Mankind is caught in the grip of hollow entertainments and sensory pleasures. We miss the dark stains on our own face and see only the faults of others.

4

neñcakam tiṅgunna snēham – jīva
sañcayattinn-arghyam ākkū
puñciri-ppūkkaḷāy bhūmukhōdyānatte
añcitam ākkuvin makkaḷ

Our loving hearts should be an offering for the welfare of the world. May our smiles be flowers that light up the garden of this world.

5

tēṅgum manassukaḷkk-ennum – snēha
dhārayāy tīruvin makkaḷ
vāzhttuvin makkaḷē, sānandam eppozhum
snēhāpadānaṅgaḷ eṅgum

Children, be a stream of healing love for sorrowing hearts, and sing joyfully in praise of loving deeds and words.

6

nindikka śīlam-uḷḷōrē svantam
tinmakaḷ nindiccikazhttū
vandikka samskāram uḷḷappozh-anyande
nanmakaḷ vāzhtti stutikkū

Before we criticize others, let us first correct our own faults and become free of them. Let us always praise the good qualities and deeds of others.

7

kāla-dōṣatte pazhikkum – ceyta
karma-dūṣyam vismarikkum

karmānusāriyām harṣa-viṣādaṅgaḷ
kālam kaṇḍāgamiccīṭum

We blame the time and say it is unfavorable, but we fail to recall our bad actions. Time brings both joy and sorrow and all are the fruits of our past actions.

8

anyaney anyanāy kāṇkē – tānum
anyanāy tīrunnu tānē
anyanum avvidham kaṇḍāl samūhattil
anyar ākunnu nām ellām

When we see others as "others," we also become "the other," and everyone in society becomes "the other."

9

onninōṭ-iṣṭam varumbōḷ – varum
pinn-onninōṭ-iṅg-aniṣṭam
ajñāna-buddhi ñān ende enn-ōrkkumbōḷ
antaram kāṇunnit-eṅgum

When we like certain things, we naturally dislike other things. Our ignorance causes us to see everything as "me and mine," and to find differences.

10

onnukil dēhōhabhāvam – pinnat-
allenkil ātmāvabōdham
raṇḍil ētenkilum onnil ākunnu nām
raṇḍum kalarnnat-āvilla

When we think, "I am the body," the Truth of "I am the Self" is hidden. We can only be in one of these states at a time, never both at the same time.

11

narttanam ceyyunna nēram – nṛttam
narttaki tann-ātmabhāvam
sṛṣṭiyum sraṣṭāvum raṇḍalla taṅgaḷil
raṇḍattat-āṇātmasatyam

The dance emanates from the Self of the dancer. Similarly, the creator and the creation are not two. This knowledge leads us to the Truth of the Self.

12

mithyaye satyamāy kaṇḍāl – manō
duḥkhattin-illazhiv-ētum
svapnattil mṛṣṭānnam uṇṇunna martyannu
jāgrattil kṣutt-eṅgan-āṙum?

When we believe this illusory world is real, we always experience sorrow. Even if we feast in our dreams, we remain hungry upon waking.

13

mōhattāl kaṇṇukaḷ andham entum
svāyattam ākkān tiṭukkam
tyāgattil ānandam āsvadikkunnavar
bhōgattil āsaktarākā

Desire blinds us! We crave to own everything, but those who discover the bliss of renunciation never hanker after pleasures of the world.

14

yōgattil āsakti illēl – manam
bhōgattil āsaktam ākum
bhōgattil āsaktamāyāl mahāmāya
mārgatil vanmatil tīrkkum

If we are not eager for union (yoga) with God, we will crave worldly pleasures. And if we are greedy for such pleasures, the great *maya* (divine illusion) builds a big wall across our path to the divine.

15

bhōgattil āsakti māññāl – manam
yōgattil āsaktam ākum
yōgattil āsaktamāyāl mahāmāya
mārgattil pūmetta tīrkkum

When desire for worldly pleasure disappears, we will long for union with God. When we desire God, the great *maya* transforms our path into a bed of roses.

16

yōgam samatvam atallo – raṇḍu
cērnnatall-ēkatayallo
ēkātma-bōdhattoṭ-ācarikkum karmam-
āreyum yōgasthan ākkum

Yoga is equality; it is Oneness. When we perform actions with the knowledge of Oneness, we become established in yoga.

17

māykkilum māyilla mēnmēl – manō
vṛttikaḷ 'svatvam' maṙaykkum

niṣkāma-bhāva-samśuddhiyāl ajñāna
vṛttikaḷ tēññ-astamikkum

Our turbulent thoughts can never be erased. However hard we try, they veil our inner essence. When our actions become pure and desireless, our mind ceases its turbulence and thoughts disappear.

18
mudraṇam ceyyunnu cittil – ōrō
ceytiyum cintayum sūkṣmam
māññu pōkillatin svādhīnam etrayō
bhāvi-janmaṅgaḷkku hētu

Each subtle thought and action leaves an imprint on the mind. These remain as latent impressions and become the cause for future births.

19
nanma-tinmaykk-āke bījam – pūrva
karma-samskāram enn-ōrkkū
samskāram evvidham avvidham ākunnu
jīvitam ennōrkka makkaḷ

Remember, past actions and latent tendencies are the seed for both good and bad in our present life. My children, know that your life will unfold according to your previous karma *samskara*.

20
ātmīya-mūlyam tyajikke – uḷḷil
āsuravṛtti tezhikkum
āyōdhanattil madikkum, malarvāṭi
pōlum maruppaṙamb-ākkum

When we betray our spiritual values, evil thoughts take their place. Then we delight in warfare and make a charnel field of a flower garden.

21

tankaiyil ākunnu nañcum - divya
pīyūṣavum ennaṟiyū
onnil uṇḍām mṛtyumaṭṭatil jīvitam
raṇḍilonn-āhariccīṭām

Know that both poison and divine ambrosia are within us. One brings our destruction, and the other a fulfilling life. We can choose to partake of either one.

22

tattva-anuyōjyam-alleṅkil - ceyyum-
ētor-ācāravum vyarttham
ācāra-yōgyam alleṅkil mahattāya
siddhāntam ētum nirarttham

Traditional rituals are vain if they are not in harmony with spiritual principles. Similarly, any great principle becomes meaningless if we cannot practice it.

23

kaṇṇināl kāṇunnat-ellām - nēru
tannennu nām naṇṇiṭēṇḍa
kānaljalam nammaḷ kāṇunnu enkilum
pādam nanaykkillat-ētum

Let us not indiscriminately accept as true everything that we perceive through our senses. We may see drainage water, but we never use it to wash our feet.

24

cintaykku tāṅgāy vivēkam – vēṇam-
allēl niṣedhikkum ellām
svīkārya-bhāvam nadikkuṇḍat-okkeyum
āvahicc-āzhiyil cērum

Insight and discernment should support our logical thinking; otherwise we refute what is not within its realm. Our broad vision should be like the river that accepts everything as it flows to its final destination.

25

pērum pratāpavum māyum – bāhya
mēnmakaḷ lōkam maṙakkum
ācandra-tāram smarikkum mahattāya
tyāgam bṛhattāya lōkam

Power and fame fade away, and the world forgets external pomp and glory. Great sacrifices remain written in the stars for eternity.

26

buddhiyekkāḷum pradhānam – ātma
śuddhi tan divya-prakāśam
neñciṭippēṙiyāl mātramē ōrttiṭū
svantam hṛdayatte nammaḷ

The radiance emanating from a pure heart gives more clarity than mere intelligence. We seek to know our own Self only when faced with our mortality.

27

kūṭe naṭapp-uṇḍu mṛtyu – ōrō
śvāsa-niśvāsavum eṇṇi

kālam pizhaykkill-arakṣaṇam pōlum ā
kaittalam nērkk-iṅgu nīḷam

Death walks beside us counting each of our breaths. We can never delay the moment when death stretches out its hands to take us.

28
jīva-ttuṭipponn-aṭaṅgān – mātra
nēṛam mati ennirikke
tammil kalahiccum anyare drōhiccum-
entē svayam tān naśippū?

Our life can end in one second; then why do we self-destruct by quarreling and harming others?

29
tān ennu tān tān uṙaykke – āru
tān ennat-āruṇḍ-aṙivū
nērāya tān dēhabāhyam-āṇānanda
rūpamāṇ-ēkātma-sāram

We keep saying "I". Does anyone know the real "I" beyond the body and mind? The real "I" is the pure bliss of the oneness of the Self.

30
nī enna samjñaykkor-ūnnāy – bāhya
mānaṅgaḷ illāykil appōḷ
ñān enna samjñaykkum ādhāramilla pinn-
āruṇḍ-anantata mātram

Stripped of its external moorings, the ego sinks. Then, the sense of "I" has no foundation and no-one exists. Only the eternal and infinite remain.

31
dēham tyajiccu pōm dēhi – dēha
nāśattil ātapikkilla
dēhi vēṟpeṭṭatām dēhattin-illazhal
śōkam ārkk-entinnu pinne?

The self that departs from the body does not grieve. Neither does the body grieve at its separation from the self. Then why does anyone else grieve?

32
bhōgādhipatyam phalattil – ātma-
lōkādhipatyam hanikkum
śāśvatamāyatē śānti nalkū svayam
ātmāv-anaśvaram allō

When we focus on external pleasures, we neglect the kingdom of the Self. We can find peace only by realizing the everlasting eternal Self.

33
mālinyam ēlāt-uṣassin – bhāva
dīpti coriññ-uḷḷ-uṇarnnāl
tāvunnat-ētāṇat-ākunnu ñān enna
sāram – cidānanda-bōdham

When our hearts awaken in the light of purity, we realize our true essence, *satchitananda* (existence, consciousness, bliss).

34

satyam mar̆aññu nilkkunnu – dr̥śyam
dr̥kk-ennu nām bhramikkunnu
darśanam draṣṭāvu dr̥śyam enn-antaram
illēlat-ākunnu satyam

We identify ourselves with the world around us, so the Truth remains hidden. When we understand that the one who sees, the seen, and the act of seeing are One, then we realize the Truth.

35

bhinna-dēhaṅgaḷ āṇēlum – makkaḷ
onnāṇ-anādi-caitanyam
bhinnata kāṇunnat-ajñāna-buddhiyāṇ-
ajñāna-gēham ī dēham

My children, though your bodies are separate, you are the One, all-pervading consciousness, without beginning or end. Your body is the seat of the ignorance that causes you to see everything as separate.

36

aikyamall-ēkatayallō – aikyam-
ātmāvil illaṅgat-ēkam
cārccayil ninn-ezhum cērccayall-ēkata
kēvalam raṇḍat̆t̆a-bōdham

The Self is One. This Oneness is not a union of two. Realize that there is no "two." There is only the non-dual Self.

37

kāṇumbōḷ nann-ennu tōnnum – tōnnal
mār̆umbōḷ kāzhcayum mār̆um

sankalpa-valliyil pūtt-ullasikkunna
varṇasūnaṅgaḷ āṇellām

We like something for a while; then that liking abates and we like something else. Our likes and dislikes are the colorful flowers that bloom on the vine of our imagination.

38
onnuviṭṭ-onnilēkk-ōṭum – manam
taṅgāte eṅgatil śānti?
śānti tēṭunnavar ādyam manassinde
bhrānta-sañcāram taṭukkū

Our mind runs from one thing to another. Unless it stands still, how will it find peace? To find peace, we must first stop this mad travel of the mind.

39
ōṭum manassine ārum – balāl
rōdhicciṭēṇḍ-ennu collum
'cēkku-vṛkṣattile pakṣipōl tirye
vannīṭum annēram piṭikkām'

Some say we should not forcibly restrain the wandering mind. Like the bird that comes to roost in its own nest, we can subdue the mind when it comes on its own.

40
kēṭṭāl atetrayum yuktam – pakṣē
ōrttāl atetrayō mauḍhyam
addhyātma-sādhanā-niṣṭhar ā jalpanam
atyukti ennōrttu taḷḷum

The above lines may seem logical, but, on reflection, we realize their foolishness. Those who are steadfast in their spiritual practices know those words are a fallacy.

41

keṭṭaṙutt-ōṭum paśuve – nalla
paccappul kāṭṭi iṇakkām
nāma-rūpattil bhramikkum manassine
nāma-mantrattāl iṇakkām

Give a bolting cow green grass and you can tame it. Like this, a mantra can tame our wandering mind.

42

kīrttanālāpanam kēḷkkē – uḷḷam
ārdram ākkīṭunnu bhakti
kōri tariccitum bāṣpam pozhicciṭum
śvāṣam kramādhikam nīḷum

Singing *bhajans* can make our hearts tender with devotion. We yearn for the Lord with tears of love and longing.

43

kīrttanam pāṭunn-avarkkum – bhakti
pūrvam śravikkunn-avarkkum
āsura-vṛttikaḷ māññ-aham tēññu tan
ātmīya-dugddham curattum

Bhajans quiet the turbulent mind of both the singers and the listeners. The "I" fades away and the milk of spirituality flows.

44
tāzhma kaṇḍ-aunnatyam ōrām – tāzhma
uḷḷōriḷam tennal pōle
ellām aṙiyām tanikkenn-ahambhāvam-
uḷḷōr koṭunkāṫṫu pōle

Humility makes us noble like a gentle breeze. But if we consider ourselves to be all-knowing, we are like a destructive whirlwind.

45
kaṇṇaṭacc-uḷḷam caliccu – svapna
lōkam menaññatin śēṣam
dhyānikkay-āyirunn-ennu tān bhāvikke
kāpaṭyam tannōṭu tanne

If we close our eyes and pretend to meditate while dreaming rosy dreams, we deceive ourselves.

46
bāhya-cihnaṅgaḷāl ārum – mahā
yōgiyum tyāgiyum-ākā
jñāna-vairāgyēṇa lōkam jayikkāykil
jñānikaḷ mānikkukilla

Robes alone do not make a great *yogi* or *tyagi*. Their wisdom and dispassion have to win over the world.

47
jñānikaḷ mānicc-iṭāññāl – ceyti
ētum kṛtārttham ākilla

dharmatte ādaricc-ācarikkunn-atē
śarmamāy mānikaḷ kāṇū

We do not find fulfillment if our actions are not accepted by the great ones. The knowers of the Self honor only those actions that are true to *dharma*.

48

dhairya-śauryaṅgaḷ uṇḍēlum – dharma
carya illennāl anarttham
laṅghikkān śaktan-āṇēlum svadharmatte
laṅghikkukillilla dhīran

Courage and valor are useless unless we tread the path of *dharma*. The courageous ones always perform their *svadharma*. They never willfully abandon their responsibility.

49

nērām virāgam varāykil – nēril
ōrilla nērāyat-ārum
rāga-dvēṣattinn-aṭippeṭṭa jīvitam
ñāṇaṫṫa villinnu tulyam

Without true dispassion, we never walk the right path. Enslaved by likes and dislikes, our life is useless, like a bow without a string.

50

vāṙaṫṫa vākk-ōtiṭāte – dharmam-
ācaricc-arttham kuṙikkū
ādarśa-niṣṭharkk-orāzhi tan gāmbhīryam-
ōrō vacassilum tiṅgum

Instead of merely mouthing words, make life meaningful through obedience to *dharma*. Each word spoken by those who are steadfast in *dharma* has the power of the mighty ocean.

51
nallatē cinticciṭāvū – makkaḷ
nallatē collāvu nityam
uḷḷatāy-uḷḷatil uḷ-uṇarnnīṭukil
nallatē nāvil viḷaṅgū

Children, always think good thoughts and perform good deeds. When your heart awakens to the Truth, you will speak only auspicious words.

ōmkāra divya porūḷe 52 (Malayalam)

Disclaimer: The translations of certain verses are not literal; they aim at bringing out the essential meaning from the Malayalam verses in a way that is easily understandable.

ōmkāra divya porūḷe varū
ōmana-makkaḷē vēgam
ōmanayāyvaḷarnn-āmayaṅgaḷ nīkki
ōmkāravastuvāy tīrū

Come quickly darling children, you who are the divine essence of Om. Remove all sorrows, grow dear and adorable, and merge with the Absolute.

1
aihika-karmaṅgaḷ pōlum – bhāva
dīptiyāl daivikam ākkām

dēvatvam ārnniṭām – puṇya-lōkattu pōy
ākulam ēlāte vāzhām

Worldly actions become divine if performed with pure intention. Our divinity takes us where we can live free of sorrow or misfortune.

2
puṇyam kṣayikkum ādēvan – tāzhnnu
vannī manuṣya-kulattil
vīṇḍum janikkām – manassu vaccāl brahma
sāyujya-lakṣyam varikkām

Even celestial beings exhaust their merits and fall down to earth to be reborn as a human. If we fix our mind on the goal, we merge with the Absolute (*Brahman*).

3
īśvarādēśām enn-ōrttum – makkaḷ
sāmūhika-āśvāsam ōrttum
ātmārtthamāy uṇarnn-ācarikkum karmam-
ātma-lābhattinn-utakum

My children, perform your actions sincerely, as the will of God, and in the service of society. Thus purify your mind.

4
ellām tyajicc-enn-uraykke – ārum
onnum tyajiccilla tanne
illāttat-uṇḍenna tōnnal onnallāte
illa maṫonnum tyajikkān

We say that we have renounced everything, but, in fact, we have nothing to renounce except the misconception that the transient is eternal.

5

tyāgam svatantrar ākkunnu – karmam
āyāsahīnam ākkunnu
ñān ende ennuḷḷa bhāvattil uḷḷattil
bhāram cumakkunnu nammaḷ

Sacrifice frees us and makes our actions effortless. The burden we carry is the feeling of 'I' and 'mine'.

6

karmattil āśanka vēṇḍa – kartṛ
bandhamē bandhanam ākū
ceyta karmattinde pinnile prēraka
bhāvam phalam nirṇṇayippū

Let us not fret over the fruit of our actions. The attitude behind our actions determines the result. The sense of doership is what binds us.

7

kollēṇam ennorāḷ ōrkke – konna
pāpam patiyunnu neñcil
konnilla bāhyamāy eṅkilum himsicca
pāpam bhujikkēṇam appōḷ

If we desire to kill someone, that thought leaves an impression in our mind. Even though we do not actually commit murder, we will suffer punishment for the cruel thought.

8

vannu cērunna daurbhāgyam – ōrttu
khinnar-āyīṭēṇḍa makkaḷ
bhāgya-daurbhāgyaṅgaḷ āgamāpāyikaḷ
ōrttāl svayam sāntvanikkām

My children, do not feel sad over the misfortunes in your life. Know that both joy and sorrow come and go.

9

bhūmikku bhūmitan dharmam – svarga
lōkattināy-atin dharmam
dēvakaḷ bhūmiyil vāzhān kotikkavē
svargam kotikkunnu martyan

While we long for the pleasures of heaven, the *devas* long to live on earth where they have the opportunity to realize the Self.

10

nērkku-nēr kāṇunna nēram – svargam
ārkkum matipaṫṫat-ākum
tan sṛṣṭiyāṇatu tan karma-puṇyattin
bhōjana-śāla enn-ōrkkū

As we advance on the spiritual path, we realize that heaven is not such a perfect place. It is our own creation, the dining hall where we eat the fruits of our own merits.

11

sammōhanam sāmagānam – pōle
anyōnya-sallāpam ellām

santōṣa-dāyakam ākumeṅkil lōka
vāzhv-etra samskāra-dhanyam

If our conversations are as joyful and melodious as the songs in the *samaveda*, the *samskara* of our lives in this world will noble.

12
akṣara-lakṣam japiccu – mantra
siddhi ārnnāl entu puṇyam?
siddhippat-okkeyum śuṣkicc-oṭuṅgiṭum
siddham allātmāvu nityam

Where is the merit in chanting a hundred thousand mantras to acquire special powers? After a while, special powers decline. Only the *atman* is eternal.

13
ippōzh iviṭe allenkil – pinne
eppōzh eviṭe nām tēṭum
daiva-sānniddhyam cidākāśa-raṅgattil
ākunnat-āviṣkarikkū

If not now and here, when and where will we seek Him? Knowing that God resides in the inner skies of our heart, let us realize Him.

14
vēṣam nissāram āṇēlum – bāhya
vēṣatte mānippu lōkam
vēṣa-pradhānikaḷkk-ātma-lāvaṇyatte
īkṣippatinn-illa nēṭram

The world hankers after external finery. Those obsessed with external appearances never experience the beauty of the *atman* beheld by the inner eye.

15

anya-lōkattalla śānti – dēśa
kālāśraya-adhīnam alla
śāntam śivam sundaram, sva-svarūpattil
āmagna-cētassu śāntam

Peace is not in another world or time or place. Peace, auspiciousness and beauty are our very being. Peace dawns when we are absorbed in our own true nature.

16

śuddham allātuḷḷa cittil – dhyāna
citram viḷaṅgilla vyaktam
klāvicca pātrattil pāl enna pōl atum
kēṭāyi māṟunnu tānē

The form of meditation cannot shine clearly in an impure heart. Like milk that curdles when poured into a moldy pot, such meditation does not uplift.

17

dēha-dharmaṅgaḷe nammaḷ – ātma
dharmamāy kāṇmat-ajñānam
kṣut-pipāsādikaḷ dēha-dharmam – pakṣē
vērtiriccōr-illellārum

Due to ignorance, we superimpose the attributes of the body on the Self. Hunger, thirst etc. are attributes of the body. Not everyone discerns the difference.

18
ātmāvil anyatayilla – dēha
bhēdattāl tōnnunnu bhēdam
jīvātma-bhinnata yāthārtthyam allatu
kēvalam śābdika-bhēdam

The Self is One. Our identification with our body causes us to see others as separate from us. The one Self pervades everything.

19
kāṫṫatt-iḷakunn-ila pōl – tuḷḷi-
āṭāt-avadhāna-pūrvam
antaraṅgatte orambākki nēṭaṇam
brahma-sāyujya-phalatte

Let our mind not sway like a leaf in the wind. With discernment, let us transform our mind into an arrow, carefully aimed, and gain the fruit of Self-realization.

20
nirmala-ākāśatte vīṇḍum – ārō
veṇmēgha tuṇḍāl tuṭappū
pankilam ākāte uḷḷavum annannu
dharma-bōdhattāl tuṭaykkū

Every day white clouds polish the pure blue sky. Like this, let us clean our mind every day with the awareness of *dharma*.

21
ātmīya jīvitārambham – svārttham-
ēlāttor-audārya-bhāvam

sēvanam sādhanayāy aṙiññ-āhlāda
lōkam camaykkuvin makkaḷ

Selfless humility is the beginning of spiritual life. Service is a spiritual practice that creates a world of happiness.

22
svārttham tyajikk-ennatallō – ādya
pāṭham – maṙakkāte makkaḷ
sāhacaryattinde sammarddam ēlāte
sēvā-pathattil carikkū

My children, remember that the first lesson in spirituality is to renounce selfishness. Do not let circumstances turn you away from the path of service.

23
snēham samastar āśikkum – buddhi
bhēdam veṭiññ-ēkiṭāykil
kallicc-uṙaññatu vidvēṣa-lāvayāy
ellām dahippikkum ōrkkū

Love and compassion have to resolve differences created by our intellect. Otherwise, they become as destructive as an all-consuming lava flow.

24
abhyasicc-ārjjippatalla – snēham
niṣkāma-hṛttin nivēdyam
snēhippat-ārennum āre ennum bhēda-
mōham ārnnāl atum svārttham

Love is a spontaneous offering of our heart; but, love becomes selfish when it is offered only to some and not to others.

25

dhyānam sugandham pakarnnum – nīḷe
jñānam prakāśam coriññum
ātmā-anubhūtiyil nīnti āṙāṭunna
cētassil snēham curattum

Meditation radiates fragrance and knowledge radiates light. Love overflows from a heart that swims in the bliss of the *atman*.

26

ātmā-anubhūti tan svādil – maṫṫu
svād-okke duḥsvādāy tōnnum
ñān ende ennuḷḷ-ahamvṛtti māyumbōḷ
māyayaṫṫ-ātmāv-uṇarum

In the bliss of the *atman*, all other tastes become distasteful. When the "I and mine" sense fades, the pure *atman* awakens.

27

ālasyam ēlātirikkū – mada-
mātsaryam dūre tyajikkū
ānanda-sāndrāvabōdham enn-ōruvōr
ārum nirādhārar-alla

Renounce unhealthy competition. Consciousness and bliss are the substratum of every one of us.

28

santāpam-āṫṫunna mēgham – koṭum
santāpam-ēṫṫām cilappōḷ
sarva-lōkārāddhyar ākum mahātmākkaḷ
sanmaṅgaḷam mātram ēkum

The same cloud that pours down healing rain can also wreak havoc. The revered mahatmas can only bless and bring auspiciousness to the world.

29

tān ennat-ārenn-uṇarān – jñāna
vāridhi sadguru vēṇam
sūryōdayattil tuṣārōdgamam pōle
māññu pōm ajñāna-dhūmam

To awaken to the knowledge of the Self, the grace of the *satguru*, who is pure Consciousness, is essential. As dew drops disappear in the morning sunshine, the *satguru* dispels ignorance.

30

dāham keṭuttām jalattāl – agni
śaityam keṭuttān sahāyam
nērē tiricc-orāḷ svīkariccāl phalam
jīva-nāśattil kalāśam

Water quenches thirst; fire dispels the cold. We should have the discernment to know their attributes and use them as such.

31

ārādhanattinde puṇyam – citta
rāgādi-vṛtti-kṣayam tān

mōkṣattinum sarva-nāśattinum manam
mātram āṇōrttāl upādhi

True worship quiets our desires and emotions. Our mind can lead us to salvation or drag us down to self-destruction.

32
krōdham śamicc-ennu vannāl – śatru
lōkam jayicc-ennu vyaktam
ārāṇu śatru tann-antaraṅgattile
āsura-vṛttikaḷ enye?

When our anger subsides, we have conquered the enemy. Our only enemy is the negative thoughts and tendencies of our mind.

33
mitra-bhāvam pularttumbōḷ – illa
śatru-bhītikk-arttham ētum
bhītiyum śōkavum dvaitānusārikaḷ
dvaita-hīnan śōka-hīnan

When we are friends with everyone, we have no enemies to fear. Fear and sorrow arise from duality. Freedom from duality brings freedom from sorrow.

34
svīkārya-bhāva-pradhānam – hṛttil-
ūṟunnu daiva-kāruṇyam
prēmattāl uḷḷam kuḷirnnāl anāyāsam
ācariccīṭām svadharmam

When we bring acceptance into our lives, we feel the grace of God in our heart. When love awakens, we perform our duties and responsibilities wholeheartedly.

35

ātma-harṣattinnu vēṇḍi – viṅgum
klēśa-nāśattinu vēṇḍi
mānasa-ponmaṇi-vīṇayil mīṭṭuvin
daiva-saṅkīrttanam makkaḷ

My children, play the songs of God on the *veena* of your hearts, and thus be blissful and destroy all sorrow.

36

neññēṫṫi lāḷiccatallē – ārṣa
dharmamām viśva-samskāram
nālu kāśinn-atinn-īṭu vecciṭuvān
nāṇicc-iṭunnilla – kaṣṭam

The noble *samskara* of our ancient land has been protected and passed down through the generations. Now we pawn it for trivial wealth.

37

pāramparyattinde pēril – andhamāy
entum ācarikkēṇḍa
ādarśa-dautyattil ālasyam ēlāte
kālānukūlam carikkū

There is no need to follow rituals blindly in the name of *samskara*. Let us live in tune with the times, but maintain our enthusiasm to attain our noble goal.

38
kaivanna saubhāgyam ellām – kāla
cakram ñericc-amarttīṭām
kālamām paitalin kālkkal kaḷikkōppu
mātramī kāṇāyat-ellām

The wheels of time may trample our abundance. Everything in the world is just toys under the feet of the child called time.

39
nidrayil kālam marikkum – vīṇḍum
jāgrattōṭ-oppam janikkum
cittam calikkāykil kāla-dēśātīta
satyatte sākṣāt-karikkum

Time dies in sleep and is reborn in the waking state. A still mind transcends time and space and attains the ultimate Truth.

40
kāzhcaykku sūkṣmata vannāl – lōka
vāzhcaykku vīzhca vannīṭā
sthūla-nētraṅgaḷāl kāṇmat-all-ātmani
kāṇmatē kāṇmatāy tīrū

When our vision is subtle and clear, we make the right decisions. With insight, we know Truth as it is.

41
ātma-nētram tuṙannīṭān – gurōr-
ājña-anuvarttiyāy tīrū

śraddhā-vinamrarāy nityam gurōr-ājña
tattva-anusandhānam ākkū

Let us accept the words of the guru and gain insight. Let us know that the guru speaks the Truth of the scriptures, and follow the *guru's* words with faith and humility.

42
durjjana-samsargam ēṫṫāl – uḷḷam
durggandha-vāhiyāy tīrum
sajjana-samsargam uḷkkāmbil ēṫṫiṭum
candanālēpa-sugandham

When we associate with base people, our thoughts become degraded. When we associate with noble people, our thoughts have the fragrance of sandalwood.

43
arttha-bōdhattōṭe makkaḷ – daiva
kīrttana-ālāpanam ceykil
vēda-mātāv-ent-uraykkunnatil poruḷ
tānē teḷiññ-uḷḷ-uṇarum

My children, if you appreciate the meaning when you sing the songs of God, slowly the Truth of the *Vedas* will dawn within you.

44
āyiram nāmattāl vāzhtti – hṛttil-
ādarikkām śaktibhāvam
yōgastham ākunna kūṭastha-śaktiye
tāḷam ēḷattōṭ-uṇarttām

Let us adore *shakti*, the primal energy with a thousand names. Let us awaken, with song, the divine life force lying dormant within us.

45

kāla-dēśa-āśraya-atītam – buddhi
vyāpāra-sīmaykk-atītam
vēdārttha-sāram svayam svapramāṇena
vēdiccu varttikka makkaḷ

The Truth revealed in the *Vedas* is beyond time and space, and the transactions of the intellect. Children, know and live in the truth of the *Vedas*.

46

mṛtyu-lōkatte kaṭakkān – manō
vṛtti-kṣayam vanniṭēṇam
vṛtti-kṣayam vannu ennāl manam cuṭṭu
bhasmam dharicc-ennu vyaktam

To transcend death, our thoughts must end. Thoughts end only with total renunciation.

47

muḷḷine muḷḷāl eṭukkām – jñāna
karmattāl karmam keṭuttām
cummāt-orēṭatt-irunnāl manōvṛtti
illāte āvill-orāḷkkum

A thorn can remove another thorn. Action born of right knowledge can negate the fruits of ignorant action. Refraining from action does not result in the cessation of thoughts.

48

kaikārya-kartṛtvam uṇḍēl – karma
lēpam puraḷum manassil
dhārṣṭyam veṭiññ-avan karma-lēpam nīṅgi
nēṭunnu kaivalya-lōkam

If we claim ownership of our actions, the effects of karma tarnish our mind. If we act with humility, abandoning our ego, we become free of the binding nature of karma and gain liberation.

49

sthāna-mānam dhana-lābham – tēṭi
ōṭunnu nāṭāke mēḷam
ātmāvu hōmiccu nēṭunna svārtthaṅgaḷ
sārtthakam all-ennaṙiyū

We search frantically for wealth, name and fame. We should know that all selfish gains are worthless if we overlook our true essence, the *atman*.

50

prāṇan naśiccāl sahikkām - dravya
nāśam ōrkkumbōḷ ñeṭukkam
dāna-dharmam veṙum durvyayam ennōrttu
pāpam paliśa ēṫṫunnu

We can handle the thought of death but not the loss of wealth. We consider giving charity to be a waste of money. This turns us away from our real essence.

51

ellārkkumāy koṇḍu vēṇam – makkaḷ

ullāsamōṭ-iṅgu vāzhān
vyakti nām eṅkilum satta-tannāgōḷa
vyāptiyil ōrkke – nām onnām

My children, live happily in this world for the sake of everyone. Even though we appear to be individuals, we are truly only one cosmic, all-pervading Consciousness.

52
mujjanmam ār-āyirunnō – entō
janmāntaraṅgaḷum ēvam
martya-janmattin mahattvam ōrtt-anvaham
makkaḷē, lakṣyam teḷikkū!

Who knows what we were in previous lives? Let us be thankful and understand the greatness of this human life we have been granted. Let us strive to attain the goal!

ōmkāra divya porūḷe 53 (Malayalam)

Disclaimer: The translations of certain verses are not literal; they aim at bringing out the essential meaning from the Malayalam verses in a way that is easily understandable.

ōmkāra divya porūḷe varū
ōmana-makkaḷē vēgam
ōmanayāy vaḷarnn-āmayaṅgaḷ nīkki
ōmkāra-vastuvāy tīrū

Come quickly darling children, you who are the divine essence of Om. Remove all sorrows, grow dear and adorable, and merge with the Absolute.

1
lōka-hitēratar-āyi – manō
mālinyamaṫṫ-avarāyi
kāt-iṇakkattōṭe kālōcitam dharma
sārōpadēśam pozhikkū

For the good of the world, with a pure heart, let us speak words that are true and right for the times, and pleasing to the ear.

2
ellām aṙiyunnu daivam – ennu
collum namukk-entaṙiyām?
ellām aṙiyunnu ennall-aṙivennu
collām azhivaṫṫa jñānam

When we say that God knows everything, what do we know about that? The realized ones tell us that God is Knowledge itself.

3
pērāyiram koṇḍu vāzhttām – ennāl
pērinn-atītam āsatyam
prēmamāy-uḷḷil tuḷumbumbozhum svayam
lōkam kaviyumā satyam

We can praise Truth with a thousand names, but it transcends all names. Truth overflows into our world when it fills our heart as love.

4
buddhi koṇḍ-ōrāvat-entum – sūkṣma
buddhi koṇḍ-ōtān kazhiyum

astitvam ennatin tattvārttha-grāhyattil
buddhi-sāmartthyam vṛthāvil

What the gross intellect cannot understand can be understood by the subtle intellect. Intelligence alone cannot grasp the principle of existence.

5
ātma-svātantryam pradhānam – atil
ānayikkunnatē dharmam
sadbhāvanakaḷām veṇpūkkaḷāl ennum
arccana-arādhanam ceyyām

Self-realization is of utmost importance. Seeking it is our dharma. Let us adore the Self with the white flowers of pure thoughts.

6
yāthārtthya-bōdham maṙannu – entum
ācariccīṭarut-ārum
pārambaryattinde nāḷvazhi eṇṇiyāl
āyussu jīrṇṇicc-oṭuṅgum

When we follow observances, we should remember their underlying principles. Empty rituals are a waste of our life.

7
cētōvikāraṅgaḷ ētum – balāl
gōpanam ceyyarut-ārum
sāttvikōpāsanā-tīrtthattil āṭiyāl
svāntam sutāryam ākkīṭām

No one should subdue their emotions forcibly. When we worship in the sacred waters of *sattva*, our hearts become free and receptive.

8

kālōcitam lōka-dharmam – nēre
ācarikkumbōzh-uḷḷil
tān ennat-ārenn-aṭisthāna-dharmatte
ārumē vismarikkallē

While performing the dharma of our times, let us always remember the fundamental reality of the pure Self.

9

ācāra-viśvāsa-mānam – mātram
ādhāram ākkāte makkaḷ
ātmīyatayil uṇarnnāl matattinde
ātmāvu kaṇḍetti nammaḷ

My children should not just listen to their teachers. Only when spirituality awakens will we find the essence of religion.

10

tellonnu cintikkum eṅkil – ātma
hantākkaḷ āvill-orāḷum
mujjanma pāpakkaṙaykk-āzham ēṫtunna
duṣkarmam āṇatenn-ōrkkū

If we reflect even a little, we will never try to take our own life. Suicide never ends our misery. We only carry it forward to our next life.

11

āḍambarattil bhramiccu – kaṭam

vīṭān gatiyaṫṫ-oṭukkam
ātmahatyā-munamb-āśrayiccīṭāte
hōmikka mithyābhimānam

Obsessed with luxury and drowning in debt, some reach the brink of suicide. Instead we must learn to be content with what we have.

12
śraddhayonn-alpam bhramikkām – ceṫṫu
kayya-baddhaṅgaḷ bhavikkām
teṫṫil ninn-eppozhum teṫṫilēkk-āzhāte
teṫṫum guṇa-pāṭham ākkām

We may lose our discernment for awhile and commit a few mistakes. Instead of going from wrong to wrong, let us learn valuable lessons from our mistakes.

13
kārmukil mānatt-iruṇḍāl – ūzhi
cūzhum nizhal atu pōle
uḷḷil ajñānakkariṅkāṙu mūṭiyāl
karmaṅgaḷ ellām iruḷum

Dark shadows cover the earth when rain clouds darken the sky. When the darkness of ignorance covers our heart, all our actions also become dark.

14
bhāvanayāl onn-uzhiññāl – ellām
cētōharamāyi māṙum
lāvaṇya-bōdham palarkkum palat-atin
srōtass-āṇ-ādicaitanyam

Our imagination can make everything beautiful. Beauty is different for each person, but the source of beauty is the eternal Consciousness.

15

uḷḷil virōdhāgni cūzhnnāl - svantam
āyuss-eriññ-amarnnīṭum
āgōḷa-maitriyil ātmāv-aliyukil
ārārōṭ-īrṣya pularttum?

The flames of hatred torch our very lives. When our hearts melt in friendship for the whole world, we feel enmity towards no one.

16

śaktan vivēkiyāy-illēl - śakti
vidrōhamāy kalāśikkum
śaktande dharmam āṇārtta-samrakṣaṇam
mātsaryam śakti-vairūpyam

If the strong are not wise, their strength becomes a threat. The dharma of the strong is to protect the weak and helpless. Rivalry turns strength into ugliness.

17

tinmakaḷ tannu ennālum - tiryē
nanmaye nalkāvu nammaḷ
nalkunnatin bhāva-māhātmyam anyatra
nanma viḷayikkum ārkkum

Even if others harm us, let us return only goodness. In giving we attain greatness and sow the seeds of goodness.

18
tōḷōṭu-tōḷoṭṭi-ninnu – sarva
lōkattinum nanma nērnnum
ācarikkunnatin ārādhanā-phalam
nūṙu mēnikkum atītam

Standing together to do good for the world is worship that yields fruits a hundredfold.

19
sāntvanam tēṭunn-avarkkāy – tellu
svāntam kuḷirkkum vacassāl
bhāvukam nēruvōrkk-āyiram tīrtthaṅgaḷ
āṭiyāl enna pōl puṇyam

When we console the grieving through our words and actions, we become as pure as if we bathed in a thousand sacred springs.

20
anyanall-īśvaran ennāl – nammaḷ
anvēṣikkunn-anya-dikkil
anyamāy-anvēṣiccāl ennum apporuḷ
anyamāy tanne ninnīṭum

God is not a stranger, but we search for him in strange places. If we search for Him as someone different from us, we will never find Him.

21
bōdhikka ennat-allāte – tēṭi
nēṭēṇḍatall-ātmasatyam

anvēṣicc-anyam onnillāte ākumbozh-
entu śēṣikkum atuṇma

The Truth of the Self is to be realized, not attained. The Truth dawns when we realize that what we seek is not separate from us.

22
satyam piṙappu koḷḷunnu – ōrō
cittavum cuṭṭu tapikke
satya-jijñāsayāl antarangam sadā
yajña-kuṇḍam pōl jvalikke

Truth is born in the heart that blazes like a sacred fire in search of Truth.

23
uḷḷāl samarppaṇam illēl – illa
tellum guruprēma-vāypum
veṇṇīṙil vīzhunna veṇṇilāv-ennapōl
maṅgum kṛpā-dīpti uḷḷil

If we are not sincere, we cannot receive the love of the guru. The light of grace becomes dull within us, like silvery moonlight shining on ash.

24
svantam guruviṅkal ētum – bhakti
śraddhakaḷkk-ūnam varāykil
sadguru-prēmam-akakkāmbil dīptamāy
satya-avabōdham uṇarttum

When we are full of faith and devotion to our *satguru*, our love for our *satguru* awakens the knowledge of Truth within us.

25
cittam viḷakki teḷiccu – jñāna
sadyōdayam kāttirikkām
puttan pularikku pūcceṇḍumāy pṛthvi
kāttirunnīṭunna pōle

Let us clean and burnish our hearts, and wait for knowledge to dawn as the earth awaits the arrival of a new day with a bouquet of flowers.

26
kōlāhalam viṭṭ-ozhiññu – dūra-
dēśattu pōy tapam ceytāl
antarangattile kōlāhalaṅgaḷkk-or
antam uṇḍāvilla tellum

If we go to meditate far from the noise and furor, the noise and furor within us will never cease.

27
sāhacaryattinde pēril – ceyta
hīna-samskāraṅgaḷ pōlum
rēkhīya-citram kaṇakk-antaraṅgattil
ālēkhanam ceyyum ōrkkū

Remember, when we blame circumstances for our bad actions, they remain as impressions in our minds, as clear as hand-drawn pictures.

28
vīṇāl eṇīkkāt-irunnāl – vīṇḍum
vīzhilla ennuḷḷa bhāvam
bālarkku pōlum illānayam uḷkkoṇḍu

pōyāl jayam kaivarikkām

Let us not think that by staying on the ground after a fall, we can avoid another fall. Even small children know that is not so. Let us get up and try again, and victory will be ours.

29

dvandva-bōdhattin nivṛtti – ātma
svātantryam enn-ōrkka makkaḷ
kaittalattāl orāḷkkāvill-orikkalum
māykkuvān bhēda-samskāram

Only the notion of duality constrains the freedom of the Self. The notion of duality cannot simply be rubbed away with our hands.

30

dhyānam onnatrē sahāyam – citta
durvāra-vṛttikaḷ māyān
sadguṇōpādhiyāl ujjvalippikka nām
nityam cidagni-kuṇḍatte

Meditation removes the bad impressions in our mind. Let good thoughts light the fire in the sacred fire pit of our heart.

31

āzhipōl āzha-pparappil – vēda
sāhitī-tīrttham lasippū
āzhi nīrāviyāy, mēghamāy māriyāy
tūvumbozh ārkkum sahāyam

The sacred *Vedas* are as deep and vast as the ocean. They nourish the world as the water in the ocean nourishes the earth when it becomes vapor, forms a cloud, and then falls as rain.

32
vēda-kṣīrābdhi kaṭaññum – sāra
pīyūṣa-dhāra nukarnnum
tēṭunna pātrattil ēkum mahātmākkaḷ
nāṭinn-anugraham ennum

When the great ones churn the milky ocean of the *Vedas* and drink their ambrosial essence, they are a blessing to humanity. They impart knowledge to those who seek spiritual knowledge.

33
jñāna-dānattin caritram – vīṇḍum
bhāva-lāvaṇyam coriyum
bāhya-sampattil bhramikkāte jīvitam
tyāga-sampūrṇam ākkīṭām

When knowledge is given, the beauty of the Self is revealed. Let us not get trapped in the desire for wealth. Let us lead lives of great sacrifice.

34
tānē muḷaccu pontilla – nanma
tān tān vitaccu koyyēṇam
dharma-jijñāsayō mōkṣa-jijñāsayō
uḷḷōrkk-atātinde jñānam

We can only reap the goodness that we sow. Only those who seek knowledge and liberation reap the benefits of their quest.

35
kaṇṇ-onnu cimmi tuṙakke – kaṇḍat-
ellām kināv-ennu tōnnām

minnalppiṇar pōle minni poliññiṭām
unnata-saubhāgyam ellām

As it changes in the blink of an eye, this world seems like a dream. Even great fortunes can disappear in a flash, like a brilliant streak of lightning.

36
svārttha-sampūrtti tann-ārtti – kaṇḍāl
cīrttezhum pāmbum bhramikkum
svantam viṣappallu naṣṭappeṭēṇḍ-ennu
cinticcu tan phaṇam tāzhttum

The evil we will do to fulfill our insatiable greed shocks even a poisonous snake rearing up to strike. It will concede defeat and decide to save its poison fang.

37
jīvanam ēkunnu kūpam – tellum
ēkunna bhāvam illētum
kōriyāl pinneyum ūṙūnna pōle – nām
ēkiyāl ūṙunnu nanma

We have the nobility to share the waters from the well of life. Just as well-water replenishes itself from an underground source, goodness increases when we give to others,

38
nalkuvān allāte nēṭān – onnum
illātta kāruṇya-śīlar
manniṅkal ennum apūrvam āṇenkilum
illāt-irikkilla nūnam

The compassionate ones only give; they have nothing to gain. Such noble ones do exist, though they are rare in this world.

39
dēśa-bhēdaṅgaḷāl eṅgum – bhinna
samskāra-bhēdam uṇḍēlum
snēhānubhūti tan svādonnu tanneyām
pālveṇma pōl aṅga-bhinnam

Though different countries have different cultures, love is the same for all, like churning milk always produces butter.

40
lōkam ennāl kāṇmatallo – dṛśyam-
āyat-ellām naśvaraṅgaḷ
naśvara-lōkatt-anaśvara-satyam onn-
anvēṣicc-eṅgu kaṇḍettum?

The changing sights are what we call the 'world'. Where can we find the imperishable Truth in this perishable world?

41
sattābhiṣiktar ākāte – tellum
śaktar alluḷḷāl orāḷum
ātmīya-śaktiyāl ānītam ākumbōḷ
hā! labdham ākunnu satyam

We become strong only when we desire the Truth. When we gain strength in spirituality, the Truth is revealed to us.

42
uḷḷōṭṭu nōkkān paṙaññāl – manam
vallāte nāṇicc-ozhiyum
āvātta kāryattin ādēśam ēkiyāl
ā vazhikk-ārum varilla

When asked to look inside, our mind is ashamed and refuses. When advice is against our liking, we reject it.

43
vyatyasta-lōkattu mātram – kāla
baddham calippatē śīlam
kāmya-viṣayaṅgaḷ illāte ākukil
illāte ākum manassum

We use our mind to travel in the time-bound, impermanent world. But when desire ends, the mind ceases to be.

44
āstikya-buddhi uṇartti – makkaḷ
ātma-sandhānam tuṭarū
ātmā-avadhānamām śraddhayāṇ āstikya
buddhi enn-ōrkkuvin makkaḷ

My children should have faith and seek to realize the Self. Know that faith is awareness and insight into the Self.

45
āstikya-bōdham uṇarnnāl – bhāva
lāvaṇyamāy tīrum ellām

ōḷavum tīravum pōle parasparam
rāgārdramāy tīrum ellām

When faith awakens, everything is beautiful. It is like a wave and the shore that are in love with each other.

46
kaṇṇīru pōlum varaṇḍu – bhūmi
viṅgi karayunnu dīnam
ārōṭ-ennillāte – pāvam! dayā-vadham
yācippatinde vilāpam

The earth is sobbing even though its tears have dried up. It laments for its lost glory, and seeks mercy.

47
cūṣaṇōpādhiyāy kāṇke – bhūmi
ūṣaram ākunnu vēgam
dōhanam ceyyukil pinneyum mēdini
vēṇḍa pōl ellām curattum

When we exploit the earth it quickly becomes arid; but if we milk it with love, the earth becomes bountiful.

48
drōham vitaccu munnēṙi – svāsthyam
āke takartt-āṭi nēṭum
nēṭṭaṅgaḷ eṇṇi madicc-aṅg-irikkavē
kōṭṭa takarkkum niyati

When we sow the seeds of harm, we destroy the wellbeing of this world. As we gleefully count our ill-gotten gains, justice will demolish our fortress.

49

munpokke jātyābhimānam – sthūla
bhāvattil āyirunneṅkil
sūkṣmam āṇ-innatin śaktiyum vyāptiyum
tīrppu kalpikkān prayāsam

In the past, the pride of different castes was expressed outwardly. Now it is subtler, and it is more difficult to estimate its hold and breadth.

50

vyaktiyāṇ-annatte śatru – nērkku
nēr-ninnu pōr-viḷiccīṭām
unmūlanam ceytu munnēṙum innatte
śatru ār-ennārkk-aṙiyām

In olden times, the enemy was a known individual, and we fought face-to-face. Today, we annihilate anything in our path without knowing whether it is the enemy.

51

mūlyaṅgaḷ ellām agaṇyam – innu
lābha-kaṇakk-āṇu gaṇyam
snēha-nūlaṫṫāl parasparam marttyare
kōrttiṇakkān ent-upāyam?

We no longer appreciate values; we only count the value of our profits. If the thread of love is broken, how will mankind be united?

52

nētram nimīlitam ākki – cuṭṭum
āndhyam āṇenn-uraykkāte
antarangattōṭu bandham pulartti ninn-
anpum prakāśavum tūkū

Let us not close our eyes and proclaim that only darkness exists. Let us connect with our Self and spread love and light all around!

53

jāti-mata-atītar-āyi – sarva
bhūta-hitaiṣikaḷ-āyi
śāntarāy ārdrata cōrāte, kartavya
nīti-bōdhattil carikkū

Let us become well-wishers of all creation. Rising above religion and caste, let us know our responsibilities and live with peaceful and tender hearts.

ōmkāra divya porūḷe 54 (Malayalam)

Disclaimer: The translations of certain verses are not literal; they aim at bringing out the essential meaning from the Malayalam verses in a way that is easily understandable.

ōmkāra divya porūḷe varū
ōmana-makkaḷē vēgam
ōmanayāy vaḷarnn-āmayaṅgaḷ nīkki
ōmkāra-vastuvāy tīrū

Come quickly darling children, you who are the divine essence of Om. Remove all sorrows, grow dear and adorable, and merge with the Absolute.

1

svātantryam ēṫṫam pradhānam – ārum
ā varadānattin arhan
svanta-svātantryam vila-matikkum pōlat-
anyanum kalpicciṭēṇam

Everyone deserves the blessing of freedom; therefore, we must value the freedom of others as much as we do our own.

2

kaiveḷḷayil vaccu nalkām – amma
kaivalya-mukti ennālum
mōha-nirmuktar āyillēl atinnoru
mūlyavum kāṇikk-orāḷum

Amma can place liberation in our hands; but, unless we are free of all desire, we will not value it.

3

kiṭṭaṇam kaivalya-mukti –atu
peṭṭennu kiṭṭiyāl nannu
muṫṫatte mullayil pūviṙukkum pōle
kiṭṭaṇam āyāsa-hīnam

Everyone wants immediate liberation; but, they only want to make as much effort as it takes to pluck a jasmine flower from the garden.

4

pālinde bodham illeṅkil – pālu
kāṇunn-avarkk-entu tōnnum?
satkalā-bōdham illeṅkil kathakaḷi
kaikāl iḷakkamāy tōnnum

If you don't know what milk is, you will not drink it even when it is placed before you. The *Kathakali* dance form will seem like mere hand and leg movements to those who do not know how to appreciate it.

5

bandhitan tān, enn-aṙiññāl – pinne
bandha-nirmukti tān mukhyam
janmārham ākunnu svātantryam eṅkilum
niṣkriyanmārkk-entu puṇyam?

When we know that we are bound, freeing ourselves becomes of utmost importance. Though freedom is our birthright, what good is it unless we claim it?

6

sattayil pūrṇṇar āṇēlum – dēha
buddhiyil bhēdamē kāṇū
svantam mahattvam maṙannāl sthalakāla
buddhikku kīzhppeṭṭu pōkum

Though everyone is complete and perfect in their essence, our dissecting intellect sees only differences. Forgetting our greatness, we become slaves of space and time.

7
aru ñān? ārāññ-aṙiyum – vidya
yātonnat-addhyātma-vidya
ātmāvil ātmāv-aṙiññāl anātmāvil
tōnnum aham-buddhi māyum

We seek the spiritual knowledge that answers the question, 'Who am I?' When the self merges in the Self, the ego that is superimposed on the Self disappears.

8
rāvinde andhakārattil – pāta
kāṇāt-uzhanniṭām ennāl
sūryōdayam varum kāṭu pinniṭṭiṭām
vēṇam śubhāpti-viśvāsam

We may wander in search of the path in the pitch-black night. Let us have faith that the forest will be behind us at sunrise.

9
cāru-centāmara-ttāru – kāṇke
cāritārtthyam varām hṛttil
tārinde tyāgōjjvalamāya jīvitam
ārum ōrkkārilla pakṣē

Seeing a beautiful lotus fills our hearts with delight. We forget the great sacrifice made by the plant.

10
pūmaṇam kāṫṫ-ēṫṫu vāṅgum – varṇṇa
kāntiyō, kaṇṇukaḷkk-arghyam

neññētti sūkṣicca tēn tuḷḷi vaṇḍinnu
sanmanō-bhāvattōṭ-ēkum

The breeze carries the fragrance of the flowers, and our eyes worship their beauty. The flowers joyfully offer the honey dew in their hearts to the bees.

11
nāsikā-jīrṇṇam uḷḷappōḷ – maṇam
āsvadikkān āvukilla
pūvine kuṫṫam paṙaññāl budha-janam
mūkkattu kaiviral vaykkum

Without a sense of smell, we cannot enjoy the fragrance of flowers. Wise folks pity us when we blame the flowers for that.

12
samsāra-lōkattu makkaḷ – citta
cāñcalyam ēlātirunnāl
maññin malamīte ēṙi tapam ceyta
puṇyam nissāram ennōrum

My children, if your minds remain equipoised in the midst of this world, your purity will be greater than if you had performed austerities on a mountain-top.

13
mārgam pizhaykkāt-irikkān – vēṇam
ācārya-śikṣaṇam mēnmēl
duṣcaritanmārkku duṣprāpyamāy varum
addhyātma-vidyānubhūti

We constantly need the *guru's* discipline that we may not stray from the path. The bliss of spiritual knowledge is beyond the reach of the wicked.

14

ēkānta-vāsattilūṭe – nalla
cētō-vicāram vaḷarttām
krodha-kāmaṅgaḷ kariññ-ennu kāṇkilum
rōgabījam nāmb-ezhikkām

Living in solitude can awaken and strengthen noble thoughts. But even when desire and anger seem burnt up, they can still sprout anew.

15

tan karma-dūṣyam maṙakkum – kuṫṫam
anyaril cārtti koṭukkum
ōrō vipattum ninaykkāte nērkk-ezhum
vīṭu kaiyēṙi timarkkum

We forget our bad deeds and blame others for our setbacks. Unannounced, misfortune enters our homes and takes over our lives.

16

karmattil uṇḍ-ābhimukhyam – ennāl
āsaktanalla āḷeṅkil
āyatil ninn-ezhum ānanda-satphalam
lōkōpakāramāy tīrum

When we are free of desire yet are willing to act, the favorable fruits of our actions benefit the world.

17

mūlyavatt-ākum ā karmam – eṅgum
ārkkum atāvēśam ēṫ˙þum
samtṛptiy-uṇḍatil sandēśam-uṇḍatil
janmattin-artthavum siddham

Such actions are precious and an inspiration everywhere. They bring contentment and the message of the meaning and fullfilment of life.

18

ceyyām svārtthamāy ellām – sadā
ceyvatin sākṣiyāy taṅgām
bandhanam ākumenn-andhamām cintayāl
bandhiccu-nilpavan mūḍhan

There is nothing wrong in performing actions; however, always do them as the witness. It is foolish to refrain from actions due to fear that they will bind us.

19

ācariccīṭunnu sarvam – bhāvam
śrīkṛṣṇa-prēmattil magnam
gōpī-janattinde rāgārdra-bhakti pōl
bhāvātmakam ākkām karmam

Let our actions be soaked in our love for Lord Krishna. Then they will be like the tender devotion of the *gopis* (milk maids) of Vrindavan.

20

prēmavāy pōlum hṛdantam – jīva
rāśiyil kāṇilla bhēdam

prēmam tuḷumbiyāl bhēdam janikkilla
pūraṇam āṇ-atin dharmam

A heart full of love is never biased by the differences amongst living beings. Oneness and perfection are the nature of a heart overflowing with love.

21

jaiva-sākalyam ī lōkam – ellām
ōtavum prōtavum atre
cittum jaḍavum vivēcicc-aṙiyumbōḷ
satta onn-atrē samastam

This world is Truth (Brahman) alone. When we come to know the substratum of both the sentient and insentient, we know the divine essence that pervades everything.

22

kaikārya kartṛtvamōṭe – nammaḷ
ceyyunnatin pēru karmam
kartṛtva-bhāvam veṭiññ-ātma-niṣṭhayil
ceytāl atin pēru yōgam

When we feel we are the doer, our actions become karma. When we renounce doership and perform our actions while established in the Self, our actions become yoga.

23

āravam illāte ceyyum – karmam
ārilum ādarav-ēṫṫum
nālāḷu kāṇēṇam ennōrttu ceyyukil
rājasādhīnamāy tīrum

Actions performed quietly, without public show, earn the respect of everyone. Actions performed with a desire for praise are *rajasic*.

24
ātmārpaṇattinde pēril – ārum
ārkkum aṭima āvilla
nitya-svātantryattil ettān utakunna
siddhi, bhāvātmaka-cittam

Surrendering your heart and mind to the enlightened master does not make you a slave. A trusting and discerning heart gains eternal freedom.

25
garvinde vēr-aṫṫiṭāte – ōtum
sarvam samarppiccu pōlum
arddha-manassu koṇḍ-arppaṇavum pāti
svārtthavumāyāl anarttham

Without uprooting our ego, we sing, "I have surrendered everything." It is fruitless to surrender half our mind and harbor selfishness in the other half.

26
ceṫṫu ceṫṫ-āgraham muṫṫi – namme
teṫṫennu teṫṫilēkk-untum
vēnalil vāṭum tṛṇam kaṇakk-uḷḷavum
māya tan cūṭēṫṫu vāṭum

When desires overtake our mind, we are pushed from wrong to wrong. Just as a blade of grass withers in the heat, our hearts wilt in the heat of *maya* (illusion).

27

ākarṣakatvam varumbōḷ - vastu
mūlyavatt-āṇennu tōnnum
āsakti illēl vikarṣaṇam tōnniṭum
mūlya-sankalpavum māyum

We attribute value to what attracts us. Without attraction towards it, we see no value.

28

pālaṭa-pāyasam munnil - onnu
svādu nōkkān āśa uḷḷil
āsakti-muktarkku pālaṭayum kaññi
nīrum paśikk-auṣadhaṅgaḷ

When sweet rice pudding is before us, we long to taste it. When we are free of desire, both sweet rice pudding and rice gruel are only food to appease our hunger.

29

vārmazhavill-onnu kaṇḍāl - manam
kōri tarippatu nyāyam
mārivill-eṅgō maṙaññāl manas-tāpa
mēlarut-ennatē vēṇḍū

A rainbow naturally delights our heart, but we should not feel sad when the rainbow vanishes.

30

mārgam vyati-calippikkān - taram
pārtt-irippuṇḍ-arivṛndam

dhīran manassinde dāsyam takarttu tan
vāgdatta-lakṣyam varikkum

Many enemies are waiting to tempt us. The courageous break free of slavery to the mind and reach the promised goal.

31
garjjiccu pāyunna mēgham – kaṇḍāl
nirgamiccīṭilla sūryan
mēgham maṙaykkilum māññ-ozhiññīṭilum
māṫṫattam arkkan illētum

The sun does not leave the sky when a dark cloud rushes thundering at it. The sun remains the same whether hidden behind clouds or shining bright in a clear blue sky.

32
ajñāna-kālattu nammaḷ – svayam
mithyaye satyamāy kāṇum
satyatte avvidham mithya enn-ōrkkilum
satyattin illazhiv-ētum

In our ignorance, the false seems to be true. Even when we are under the delusion that the false is true and the Truth is false, the Truth remains changeless.

33
pūvine darśiccu nilkē – atē
pūvāyi māṙum manassum
uḷḷam praphullam ākumbozh-anātmāvum
illa 'tān' tanne āṇellām

When we enjoy a flower, our mind becomes the flower. When our hearts become effulgent, there is nothing anywhere but our own Self.

34

sarvēśvaran tan prabhāvam – viśvam
sarvatra vyāpanam ceyvū
sadguru-rūpanām īśvaran tan kṛpā-
pātramāyālē aṙiyū

The glory of God pervades the entire universe. We realize this Truth only when God's grace appears in the form of the *Satguru*.

35

āṙu śāstrattinnu nīḷe – vēṇēl
nūṙu vyākhyānam camaykkum
nūṙu kāṇillavaykk-onnum; vazhi pōle
nūṙil onn-ācarikkilla

We can write a hundred commentaries on the six scriptures. If they omit the essence of the teachings, no one will practice even one of them.

36

vēda-vijñānam muzhuvan – ōti
svāyattam ākki ennālum
jīva-kāruṇyam curattāykil āgrantha-
bhāram tala tazhamb-ēṫṫum

Even if we can chant the *Vedas* by heart, they are just an intellectual burden unless they fill us with the milk of compassion towards all.

37
koccu kocc-āśayaṅgaḷkkāy – nammaḷ
vanpada-śrēṇikaḷ tīrkkum
alpākṣaraṅgaḷāl tīrkkum mahattukkaḷ
vanpiccor-arttha-prapañcam

We construct elaborate sentences to convey trivialities, but a few words of the great ones convey a world of profundity.

38
nindicc-ikazhttarut-ārum – nammaḷ
munnamē ārjjiccat-onnum
prācīnam-āyatu prākṛtam āṇennu
śāṭhyam piṭikkarut-ārum

Let us not insult and dismiss our ancient knowledge and rituals as barbaric.

39
'sṛṣṭiccat-entinnu daivam – śōka
saṅkulam ākum ī lōkam?'
kuṫṫam ārōpiccu nilkkāte paṫṫukil
teṫṫennu maṫṫonnu tīrkkū

Some ask, "Why did God create this sorrowful world?" Instead of finding fault with God, let us strive to live meaningful lives.

40
tinma kāṇān ent-eḷuppam – svanta
tinma kāṇill-ennu mātram

nanma kāṇum kaṇṇu vēṙe āṇ-akkaṇṇu
maṅgāte sūkṣikka makkaḷ

We never see faults in ourselves, but we easily find faults in others. There is a third eye that sees goodness in all. My children, take care that this eye never dims.

41
nōkkunnat-eṅgane ennāl – nammaḷ
kāṇunnat-aṅgane mātram
yāthārtthyan eṅgan-enn-ārkk-aṙiyām, svayam
yāthārtthyamāy māṙuvōḷam

Our outlook colors all that we see. We never understand reality until we 'see' reality.

42
sajjana-samsargam ēṫṫāl – ārkkum
tat-svabhāvam kai varikkām
anyāyamāyatil vyāparikk-illavar
satyam kalarppaṫṫu kāṇum

By association with noble people, we can acquire their character. Their mind is never deluded and they see only the Truth.

43
kāṫṫum veḷiccavum pōlum – ceṫṫum-
ēlkkāte śraddhā-vihīnam
ātma-hṛttil paṇḍu paṇḍē vasippuṇḍu
ēkākiyām oru dēvan

Since time immemorial, God resides in our heart but we neglect God within. We have locked out the sun's rays and the fresh breeze.

44
eḷḷil uṇḍ-eṇṇa ennālum – yatnam
illēl labhikkillat-ārkkum
ātma-caitanyam tuṭikkunna hṛttil ninn-
āviṣkarikkān paṭhikkū

The oil in the sesame seed can be released only with great effort. We must put effort to realize the divine Consciousness that fills our heart.

45
kāṇi-nēram kaḷayāte – makkaḷ
kālōcitam pravarttikkū
kai-vanna jīvitam caitanya-pūrttiyāl
cāritārtthyam kai-varikkū

Without wasting a single moment, you should act in harmony with the times. Children, fulfill your life by realizing the Divinity within.

46
nalla vākk-ōti paṭhikkām – nanma
kai-varicc-uḷḷam kuḷirkkām
andhakāratte bhayakkāt-akakkaṇṇil
indu-lāvaṇyam tiḷakkām

Let us speak noble words and bathe our hearts in the waters of goodness. Let us not fear darkness, but let the radiant moonlight give sight to our eyes.

47
sadgurukkanmār uraykkum – vākkil
sajjanam satyamē kāṇū
vyarttha-vākk-ōtilla; satya-dharmattinde
vyaktata āṇavar ennum

Good people see the Truth in the words of the *satguru* who never speaks empty words. The words of the *satguru* always have the clarity of Truth and *dharma*.

48
tāmara-nūlāl cilappōḷ – matta
vāraṇattēyum taḷaykkām
mūrkha-cittatte anunaya-vākkināl
ārkkum merukkāvat-alla

It is possible to gather together the wandering tendrils of a creeping vine, but diplomatic words cannot tame a wild and wicked mind.

49
kūttāṭi ōṭum manassu – alpa
nēratt-orēṭattu taṅgām
teṫtennu pinneyum maṫtonnil ōṭunnu
māṫtattam āṇatin śīlam

The mind may rest for a while, but soon it runs unrestrained after something else. Its nature is change.

50
satya-dṛkk ākum guruvil – manam
svārtthamaṫt-arppikka makkaḷ

satya-sākṣātkāra-yōgyataykkā-vara-
siddhi onnatrē sahāyam

My children, unselfishly offer your hearts to the guru who sees the Truth. By the blessing of the guru you attain the Truth.

51
tattvam maṙannuḷḷa bhakti – pinne
śraddha illātta tapassu
niṣkāmam allātta karmavum jñānavum
vyarttham enn-ōrkkuvin makkaḷ

My children, remember that devotion without principles, and spiritual austerities without faith and awareness, are all in vain. Actions and knowledge only for fulfilling desire are in vain.

52
dēvata-ārāmamāy māṙum – bhūmi
prēmavāyp-anyōnyam uṇḍēl
ādara-śīlavum anyonya-maitriyum
daivika-lōkam racikkum

If we love each other, this world becomes a garden. When we respect each other and are friends with everyone, the world becomes divine.

53
śrīkōvil ākkām hṛdantam – karmam
ārādhana ākki māṫṫām
kāruṇya-pūrṇā-vacassukaḷ mantraṅgaḷ
sad-vicāraṅgal sumaṅgaḷ

Let us make our hearts into shrines, and our karma into acts of worship. Let compassionate words be our mantra and noble thoughts the flowers of our worship.

54
ippōl viṭarnna hṛtsūnam – nūṙu
centārinotta lāvaṇyam
ñeṭṭaṙukkāte ammaṭṭil samarppiccu
janma-dautyam nirvahikkām

The heart that has blossomed is as beautiful as a hundred lotuses. Let us not pluck it, but offer it as it is, and attain life's goal.

ōmkāra divya porūḷe 55 (Malayalam)

Disclaimer: The translations of certain verses are not literal; they aim at bringing out the essential meaning from the Malayalam verses in a way that is easily understandable.

ōmkāra divya porūḷe varū
ōmana-makkaḷē vēgam
ōmanayāy vaḷarnn-āmayaṅgaḷ nīkki
ōmkāra-vastuvāy tīrū

Come quickly darling children, you who are the divine essence of Om. Remove all sorrows, grow dear and adorable, and merge with the Absolute.

1
tāḷātmakam-āṇu kāṫṫum – śvāsa
dhārayum āzhi tirayum

hṛt-spandanam, māri, āgamōccāraṇam
okkeyum tāḷātmakaṅgaḷ

Wind and breath, ocean waves and heartbeats, rain and *Vedic* chanting — all have rhythms.

2
uḷḷam tuḷumbi kaviyum – sarga
saṅgītam ākaṭṭe janmam
tārāṭṭu pāṭṭupōl āsvādana-ātmakam
ākaṭṭe jīvitam ennum

Let our life be a song, spontaneously overflowing from our heart. Let our life be a lullaby forever.

3
satkatha ellām śravikkū makkaḷ
satkarma-mārgē carikkū
sadguruviṅkal ninn-ātmōpadēśaṅgaḷ
sadbhāvamōṭ-ēṭṭu vāṅgū

Children, listen to auspicious stories and tread the path of auspicious actions. With an auspicious mind, imbibe the teachings of the *satguru*.

4
sadgurukkanmār uraykkum vākku
nityam ārādhyam āṇ-ārkkum
vyartthamāy pōkilla, satya-draṣṭākkaḷ tan
satya-vākk-ennum navīnam

The *satguru's* words should be worshipped forever. The sayings of the knowers of Truth are not in vain. Their words are Truthful and ever fresh.

5

nanma mātram vitaccālum - entē
tinma mātram labhikkunnu
mujjanma-pāpa-karmattin phalam tānē
ñeṭṭaṭṭu vīzhunnat-āvām

Why do we reap bitter fruits even if we do only good actions? Remember, the fruits of selfish actions from previous lives ripen in the present.

6

karmāvasānam varekkum - ārkkum
janmāvasānam varilla
janma-karmaṅgaḷkk-orantyam bhavikkunnu
brahma-avabōdhōdayattil

We are destined to take birth as long as our karma remains. When the awareness of the Absolute dawns within, both birth and karma come to an end.

7

vṛttikaḷ ēṟum ennōrttu - karma
rathya veṭiyarut-ārum
śuddhāntaraṅgattil ātma-svarūpatte
nityam upāsikka makkaḷ

Children, action alone doesn't clutter the mind; therefore, don't abandon the path of action. Always meditate on the Self in your pure heart.

8
vēda-samskāra-arṇṇavattil – nīnti
sānandam unmattar ākām
ātmānubhūtikk-anujña ēkum vēda
vāṇikku kātōrkka makkaḷ

Let us blissfully swim in the ocean of *Vedic* culture. Children, listen to the *Vedic* sayings that point us to Self-realization.

9
ātmīya-śakti uṇarnnāl – dautya
bhāravum lāghavam ākum
dēha-balam balamalla – kaittōṭine
āzhiyōṭ-ādarikkāmō?

Spiritual power lightens the burden of life. Physical strength is not true strength. Spiritual power is vast as the ocean. Mere physical strength is only a small stream.

10
pāzhvēla ceyyarut-ārum – vṛthā
pāzhvākk-uraykkarut-ārum
āyiram kaṇṇināl āyiram kātināl
īśan nirīkṣippū namme

Don't perform futile deeds or utter vain words. God watches over us with a thousand eyes and ears.

11
dēha-kāryārttham allōrkkū – janmam
dēva-kāryārtthavum alla

ātma-lāvaṇyattil āṙāṭi mōdiccu
jīvitam sārtthakam ākkū

Birth is not for worldly existence. Neither is it to worship a god high up in the sky. Immerse yourself in the beauty and bliss of the Self, and fulfill your life.

12
dēha-lāvaṇyam smarikkum – martyan
ātma-sāram vismarikkum
puṣpa-saundaryattil ākṛṣṭar ākumbōḷ
vṛkṣatte ōrkkātta pōle

We forget the tree when fascinated by the beauty of its flowers. Like this, we see physical beauty and forget the essence, the Self.

13
durjjanam namme duṣikkām – lōka
sajjanam vāzhti stutikkām
raṇḍilum vaikārya-bhāvam pularttēṇḍa
janma-dharmam nirvahikkām

The wicked may condemn us, and the pious may praise and glorify us. Let us carry out the dharma of our birth and not be affected by either.

14
āḷdaivam enn-andhalōkam – connāl
āśankayārkk-entin-ōrttāl
marttyan mahēśanāy māṙunna vidya
ī nāṭinde uḷkkaruttallē?

The ignorant ones cannot see that God can manifest in a human body. The strength of this land is that it uplifts man to union with God.

15

daivam manuṣyanāy tīrām – vēṇēl
marttyan mahēśanāy tīrām
daiva-manuṣyare sṛṣṭiccu pōrum ī
nāṭin caritram varēṇyam

God can be born as a human, and a human can merge with God. Noble is the history of this land that has witnessed many divine incarnations.

16

pāl-niṙam śōṇam ennārō – nūṙu
nāvināl ārttalaccālum
śanka viṭṭ-ōtaṇam kṣīra-varṇam sadā
śvētam enn-ārjjavattōṭe

Even if a hundred tongues assert that milk is red, we should confidently affirm that milk is white.

17

vāg-vāda-śīlam tyajikkū – nalla
vāṅmādhuryam kai-varikkū
vāg-dēvataykkuḷḷor arccanayāy kaṇḍu
vāg-arttha-lōkam teḷikkū

Let us not speak harshly, but learn to speak sweet and true words. Let us shed the light of knowledge on the world as an offering to Saraswati, the Goddess of Speech.

18
vācālar ākāt-irikkū - vākkil
aucitya-bōdham pularttū
ākarṣakamāy vacikkum vacassukaḷ
ādarikkum lōkam ennum

Let us be aware of our words, and see that our speech is right for the situation. The whole world respects graceful words.

19
ābharaṇaṅgaḷāl mātram - ārkkum
ākarṣakatvam varilla
samskāra-sambanna-vākkāṇ-alaṅkāram-
āguṇam svāyattam ākkū

Ornaments alone do not make us attractive. Noble words are the real ornaments that we should display.

20
sādhakam ceyyātirunnāl - vidya
svāyattam-ākilla-ētum
ellāttinum tellu sāvakāśam vēṇam
allēl vaśappeṭill-onnum

Knowledge becomes ours only through its application. Unless we take careful and measured steps, we cannot master knowledge.

21
munn-orukkaṅgaḷ illāte - ārkkum
unnata nēṭṭam varilla

svārtthattin-allāte ācarikkum karmam-
āyāsam-āvilla tellum

Without adequate preparation, no one can achieve great success. Selfless actions can be performed effortlessly.

22
nēṭunnatalla variṣṭham nammaḷ
ēkunnatallō mahattvam
ārṣa-lakṣyam, phala-tyāga-rūpattilūṭ-
ārjjippat-ēkuvān mātram

Greatness lies not in what we gain for ourselves but in what we give to others. The tradition of our land is to dedicate the fruits of our good actions for the benefit of society.

23
ramya-harmyaṅgaḷ camaykkum – dravyam
ellām kṣayippicc-oṭukkum
paṭṭiṇiyum ṛṇa-bādhyatayum cērnnu
śiṣṭa-kālam kayyaṭakkum

If we spend all our wealth building mansions, then a heavy debt will burden us, and we will live a life of poverty.

24
kālkkāśu kayyil illēlum – kaṭam
nēṭiyum mōṭi kāṭṭunnu
vīṭān kazhiyāte āśrayam tēṭunnat-
ātma-hatyā-munamb-atre

Some penniless people indulge in pomp, and show off with borrowed money. Unable to repay the debt, they commit suicide.

25

lakṣaṇam keṭṭat-āṇēlum – tande
ceṫṫamāṭam tanne svargam
koṭṭāravum paṭṭu-mettayum kiṭṭiyāl
nidra kiṭṭēṇam ennuṇḍō?

Our home can be our haven even if it is a hut. Sleep can elude us, even if we live in a palace and lie on a silk mattress.

26

āsakti-āyuss-oṭukkum – kīrtti
nāśavum klēśavum vāykkum
āḷunna tīyilēkkiyal pōl bhōgattil
ākṛṣṭar-ākarut-ārum

Insatiable greed can shorten our life and destroy our name and fame. Don't run after sense pleasures like moths rushing to the fire.

27

tījjvāla pōl uḷḷil āḷum – bhōga
kāmkṣaykk-adhīnarāy tīrnnāl
nanmaye nañc-enna pōle veṙuttiṭum
tinmaye neñcōṭ-aṇakkyum

If we succumb to the flames of sense enjoyments, we will embrace evil and hate goodness as if it were poison.

28
āsvadicc-āśa tīrilla – āśa
tīrātazhal-āṙukilla
āśvāsa-jīvitam āśaykk-adhīnamall-
ātmā-aśrayatvattil atre

Enjoyment does not quench desire. Sorrow ends only when desires cease. Life becomes calm and peaceful when we depend on the Self!

29
jīvāvasānam varekkum – tṛṣṇa
tōḷattu kayyiṭṭu nilkkum
sādhu-prakṛtiyāy tōnniyālum – tande
tōḷattu māṙāppu tūkkum

Until the very end of life, desire keeps its hand on our shoulder. It might appear as a harmless friend, but, really, it lays a bundle of burdens on our back.

30
jīrṇṇicc-azhiññu pōm dēham – tṛṣṇa
jīrṇṇicc-oṭuṅgilla tellum
vārddhakya-kālattum ālasyam illatinn-
āḷum yuvatvam āṇ-ennum

The body may fail and become decrepit, but desire does not diminish. Desire knows no fatigue even in old age; it remains ever young and vigorous.

31
antimānattinde cantam – kaṇḍu
santuṣṭarāy-aṅgu nilkkē

andhakārattinde munnōṭi āṇat-enn-
antarangam smarikkilla

Our mind looks happily at the beauty of the evening sky, and forgets that sunset is the forerunner of darkness!

32
bhōgaiśvaryattil muzhukum – manam
mōha-pāśattāl muṙukum
āgraha-tyāgamē ātma-svātantryattin
orttāl upāyam onnuḷḷū

Indulging in sense pleasures binds our mind with the rope of desire. Renounce desire and walk the path to the freedom of the Self.

33
ālmarattai onnu naṭṭāl – taṇal
āyiraṅgaḷkk-utakīṭum
ālin-cuvaṭṭil tapass-irunnāl mahā
tyāgiyāy ennāṇu bhāvam

If you plant a banyan tree, it will offer shade to thousands. We should not imagine ourselves as selfless as the banyan tree just because we meditate under it.

34
āpaṇa-sthānattu pōlum – manam
āravam ēlātirunnāl
yōga-pradhānanām ā mahānārilum
jñāna-prabhā-raśmi tūkum

When our mind remains equipoised even in the market place, we can shed the light of union with the Divine in the hearts of everyone.

35

svantam manassāṇu śatru – ārkkum
svantam manassāṇu mitram
mitra-bhāvam koṇḍu śatru-lōkam jayicc-
etrayum śaktarāy tīrū

Our mind is our enemy, and our mind is our friend. Let us win over the enemy with friendly tact, and thus become strong.

36

aikyam prasaṅgattil mātram – cēri
māṫṫam kulattozhil pōle
antaraṅgam sadā samgharṣam eṅkilum
vākkinde ūkkonnu vēṙe

Unity exists only in speeches. As our inclinations change, we also change sides. Though the mind is always in conflict, our rhetoric is always of Oneness.

37

veṇtārakam pōle uḷḷam – mēnmēl
minni tiḷaṅgaṭṭe nityam
keṭṭ-aṭaṅgīṭaṭṭe vṛttikaḷ, bhakti tan
śubhra-nīhāra-prabhayil

Let our hearts shine like the morning star forever. May our thoughts cease in the pure light of devotion.

38

nanmakaḷ taccuṭaykkāte – svanta
tinma tan tāyvēr aṙukkū
āsurōnmādam tyajikkū, parasparam
ārjjava-snēham curattū

Let us protect the goodness of the world, and uproot the evil within us. Let us discard demonic tendencies and spread real love and affection.

39

manda-hāsānvitam makkaḷ – manam
centāmaraykk-ottatākkū
cañcalar ākāte samtṛpta-cittarāy
svanta-dharmam nirvahikkū

Children, keep smiling and make your mind like a lotus flower. Perform your duties unwaveringly and be fully content.

40

lōkam camaccat-ārennum – pinne
vēdam raciccat-ārennum
cinticcu vādiccu kālam kaḷayāte
raṇḍilum nanma kaṇḍ-ettām

Who made the world? Who wrote the *Vedas*? Such questions and arguments waste our time. Let us find goodness in both.

41

vēda-vēdāntaṅgaḷ ellām – vēṇēl
cēlārnn-udīraṇam ceyyām

antaraṅgam koṇḍu sākṣātkariccatē
svantam ennōtān kazhiyū

We may recite the *Vedas* and *Vedanta* beautifully. Yet only when we have realized it in our own heart can that knowledge be said to be our own.

42
śāstrīya-mānattoṭ-ārum – sūkṣmam
ātma-nirīkṣaṇam ceytāl
kāṇāyatinn-okke ādhāram āṇennu
kāṇām svayam, śuddha-bōdham

If we search with the help of the scriptures and inquire subtly into our own self, we will see that the basis of everything is our own pure Awareness alone.

43
dēha-vaḷarccaykku vēṇḍi – bhakṣya-
pēyaṅgaḷ ennatu pōle
ātma-vikāsattin ācariccīṭaṇam
dhyāna-japādikaḷ nityam

Just as we eat and drink for our body's growth, let us practice daily chanting and meditation to realize our Self.

44
janmāntarattin tapassāl – māññu
pōkilla māyā-pralōbham
jñāna-vairāgyaṅgaḷ illēl niṙam keṭṭu
pōkum tapassinde mūlyam

Maya's temptations don't go away even with the tapas (austerities) of several life times. Tapas has no value if it does not give us knowledge and dispassion.

45

bhinna-dēhaṅgaḷil taṅgi – etra
janmaṅgaḷ eṇṇi kazhiññu
nanmakaḷ ceyyuvān daivam kaṭākṣicca
puṇyamāṇ-ī narajanmam

We have lived so many lifetimes in diverse bodies. Now, God has blessed us with this human birth for doing good to all.

46

nannāy anuṣṭhikkum eṅkil – bāhya
karmavum dhyānam ākkīṭām
dhyāna-yōgam sarva-karma-sannyāsattinn-
ādhāram ākum ennōrkkū

If done with the right attitude, our actions can also be meditation. Remember, meditation is the basis for the renunciation of all actions.

47

ceyyunna bhāvam illāte – makkaḷ
ceyyunnu karmaṅgaḷ eṅkil
niṣkāmam ākum ā karma-yōgam vazhikk-
ātmāv-uṇarnn-āramikkum

Action is selfless if done without sense of doership. Such karma-yoga (path of action) awakens the blissful Self.

48
ātmā-anusandhāna-pūrvam – bhakti
bhāva-nairmalyam tuḷumbi
lāvaṇyam ārnnantaraṅgattil addhyātma
sūryōdayam varav-ēlkkām

Let us constantly contemplate on the Self, with overflowing purity and devotion. Then we will welcome the dawn of the spiritual sun in our beautified inner world.

49
innate duḥsthiti ellām – tīrum
nāḷatte sūryōdayattil
ittham śubhāpti-viśvāsam vaḷarttukil
duḥkham taḷarttilla namme

All of today's miseries will end in tomorrow's dawn. If we practice such optimism, weariness won't overwhelm us.

50
innale ceyta teṫṫ-ōrttu – vṛthā
khinnarāy nīṙēṇḍā makkaḷ
ceytat-entākilum ceytupōy, teṫṫini
ceyyātirikkān śramikkū

Children, don't brood and suffer over yesterday's mistakes. Whatever has been done is done. Just try not to repeat your mistakes.

51
ōti paṭhippicca tattvam – makkaḷ
ōrmmayil sūkṣicciṭāykil

vīṇa teṫṫil ninnu mēlēkku pontilla
tāzhum ceḷikkuṇḍil vīṇḍum

Children, if you forget the principles of spirituality, you will never escape the pit of your mistakes. You will only fall again and get trapped in that mire.

52

anyamāy kāṇarut-onnum – ātma
bhinnamāy kāṇarut-onnum
brahma-anubhūti kaivann-avar connat-ōrtt-
anyata kāṇāt-irikkū

Let us not see anything as separate from us. Let us not see anything apart from the Self. Recall the words of those who have realized the Self, and try to see oneness alone.

53

ārṣa-vijñānam muzhuvan – amma
āṫṫi kuṙukki uraccāl
'sōham' ennākum, gurōr-ājña ādaricc-
ācariccāl atāy tīrām

Amma's words contain the entire scripture and reveal its essence — 'so-ham' (That I am). If we heed the *guru's* teachings, we will realize we are "That."

54

śōka-śāntikkuḷḷ-upāyam – aham
deham enn-andhataykk-antyam
mōha-pāśattin kurukkazhiññāl uṭan
dēhōhabhāvattin-antyam

When we loosen the knot of ignorance, the delusion that 'I am the body' comes to an end. Then suffering goes and peace dawns.

55
janmāvasānam varekkum –karmam
ācarikkām tyāga-pūrṇam
'tyāgam uṇḍenkilē jñānam uṇḍāku'uḷḷ-
āvēda-vākyam smarikkū

Let us serve the world selflessly until the end of our life. Let us remember the *Vedic* teaching that Knowledge arises only with sacrifice.

ōmkāra divya porūḷe 56 (Malayalam)

Disclaimer: The translations of certain verses are not literal; they aim at bringing out the essential meaning from the Malayalam verses in a way that is easily understandable.

ōmkāra divya porūḷe varū
ōmana-makkaḷē vēgam
ōmanayāy vaḷarnn-āmayaṅgaḷ nīkki
ōmkāra-vastuvāy tīrū

Come quickly darling children, you who are the divine essence of Om. Remove all sorrows, grow dear and adorable, and merge with the Absolute.

1
cittam calikkāt-irutti – makkaḷ
satya-mārgattil carikkū

kāla-koṭunkāṫṫil āṭiyulayāte
nērinde tīratt-aṇayū

Children, keeping the mind still, take the path of Truth. Remain poised in the buffeting storm of time and reach the shore of Truth.

2
vēdam ahārṇṇavam nīntān – svayam
āvatillātt-avarkk-ennum
gītāmṛtam nukarnn-ātmaikya-bōdhattin
tīram karēṙān-eḷuppam

Those who cannot navigate the great ocean of the *Vedas* can easily reach the shore of Self-realization by drinking the nectar of the Bhagavad Gita.

3
vēdārṇṇavam kaṭaññ-atre – divya
gītāmṛtam namukk-ēki
vēdasāram tanne vēṙe prakārattil
ōti paṭhippiccu kṛṣṇan

Krishna churned the *Vedic* ocean to extract the essence of the *Vedas*. Thus, He bestowed on us the divine nectar of the Bhagavad Gita.

4
vēda-purāṇaṅgaḷ ellām – nāvil
oḷam tuḷumbum ennālum
ātma-lābhattinn-utakāykilō, tāḷi
ōlayum nāvum samānam!

No matter how glibly we recite the *Vedas* and *Puranas*, unless we use that knowledge to realize the Self, our words remain as dry writings on a palm leaf.

5

sandēśam uḷkkoṇḍiṭāykil – ārum
śankāvihīnar ākilla
ēkalōkattinde ātmāvu kāṇumā
vēda-sārārttham grahikkū

Without imbibing the message of the *Vedas*, we can never be free of doubt. To realize the non-dual Self, we must grasp the essence of the *Vedas*.

6

svānta-antarīkṣam teḷiññāl – jñāna
sūryan svayam prakāśikkum
prastāvayōgyam-allāttōr-udāttamā-
satyatte sākṣāt-karikkum!

When our mind becomes clear, the sun of Knowledge shines in all its glory. Then we realize the ineffable, supreme Truth.

7

lōka-hitaiṣikaḷ ākū – tyāga
jīvitānandam nukarū
svābhāvika-prēma-dīptiyāl nalloru
lōkam camaykkuvin makkaḷ

Be benefactors to the world and relish the blissful life of renunciation. Children, create a noble world with the light of your spiritual effulgence.

8

santōṣam ēṫṫunnat-entum - nammaḷ
śankaviṭṭ-ādariccīṭum
santāpamāyāl at-ārkku vēṇam? pakṣē
raṇḍum viḷambunnu kālam

We cherish whatever brings unconditional joy. Who wants what brings grief? Yet time dispenses both joy and grief.

9

vēdiyil uccastham ōtum – "nammaḷ
ēkātma-sōdarar-allō!"
vēdiviṭṭāl-anyan ātmāvum alla, tan
kaṇṇil nikṛṣṭanāyi māṙum!

We publicly proclaim, "We are kindred souls!" But in private, we consider others as separate, and we may even think them contemptible!

10

tānum prapañcavum tammil – dēha
bhāvattil bhēdam illētum
pañca-bhūtātmakam raṇḍum enn-ōrkkuvin
ātma-bhāvattilum ēkam

Ultimately our body and the universe are made of the same substance. Let us remember that everything is created from the five elements. The Self is one.

11

pinn-entin-anyata kāṇmū – lōkam
immaṭṭil āyirunn-ennum

mōcanam kāmkṣippat-ārākilum bhēda
bhāvam nivartticciṭēṇam

Why do we see others as separate? The world has been this way for eternity. Whoever aspires to liberation must relinquish the sense of difference.

12
baddhan āṇenn-ōrttiṭumbōḷ – svayam
baddhanāy tīrunna pōle
muktan-āṇennōrtt-azhal veṭiññīṭukil
muktanāy tīrum taniye

We are bound when we believe we are bound. When we break the delusion of bondage, we are spontaneously liberated.

13
ceyyum japadhyāna mūlyam – illa,
tellatum naṣṭappeṭilla
janmāntaraṅgaḷilūṭ-atin samskṛti
nanmaykk-uṙavāyi nilkkum!

Chanting and meditation are always of value. The refinement of our character gained through lifetimes of such practice leads us to goodness.

14
nitya-prakāśam āṇēlum – ātma
satyam tamō-hṛttin anyam
naṭṭucca nērattum andhande kaṇṇukaḷ
andhakārattil cuzhaṫṫum!

The Self is eternally effulgent. The Truth is not revealed in a *tamasic* (lethargic) heart. Even in full daylight, the blind cannot see.

15

darśanam raṇḍennu kāṇām – satyam
ennum 'bhramam' ennum ōrkkū
ēkātmamāy-uḷḷat-ārāddhya-satyavum
nānātvam ennāl bhramavum!

Know that the world has two aspects: It is both reality and illusion. The non-dual nature of the Self is the worshipful reality; diversity is the illusion.

16

āsakti āpatt-aṇaykkām – nāṭor-
ākṣēpa-hāsyamāy māṙām
andhakārattōṭ-iṇaṅgum manassinnu
tinmayum nanmayāy tōnnām!

Desire breeds sorrow. A society driven by desire becomes an object of ridicule. A mind habituated to the darkness of ignorance sees even evil as good.

17

tāmasa-vṛttikk-adhīnar – tānē
ālasya-śīlarāy māṙum
svantakāryam viṭṭu-cintayillātt-avar
nindārhar-ākunn-iteṅgum!

The nature of those enslaved by *tamas* (lethargy) is indolence. Those who pursue only their own selfish needs and gains drag themselves down.

18
rājasam durvṛttar ākkum – anya
drōhattinn-āvēśam ēṙum
svanta-kāryattinn utakātirikkilum
anyarkku svairam keṭuttum!

The quality of rajas (passion) leads to wrong deeds and incites us to hurt others. Thus, we are useless to ourselves and also disturb the peace of others.

19
sātvikam nanmayē kāṇū – ārkkum
kṣēmaika-tatparar ākum
svanta-kāryam maṙann-anyarkk-orudgati
cinticcu prāṇan tuṭikkum!

The *sattvic* (calm and peace-loving) one sees only the good, and is keen on the welfare of all. Forgetting himself, his mind pulsates with thoughts of how to uplift others.

20
lakṣyam guṇātītam ennāl – mārgam
entum sutāryam ākēṇam
sātvika-vṛttikk-adhīnamām rājasam
lōka-nanmaykk-ūṇarv-ēkum

If our goal is to rise above all attributes, the path we take must be open and clear. Action that arises from pure thoughts benefits the world.

21
svantam manassinde śatru – ennum
svantam manass-onnu mātram

śatruve mitra-bhāvattāl jayikkunna
sajjanam lōkaika-mitram!

The enemy of our mind is always our own mind. The noble one who conquers the foe with friendship is friend to the whole world.

22
snēha-rāhityam āṇ-eṅgum – dīna
rōdanam kātin tazhambāy
kāmana naṭṭu vaḷarttiya krōdham ī
nāṭine cuṭṭerikkunnu!

Love is absent everywhere. Our ears are numb to the cries of the distressed; and the fire of anger born of desire is scorching the world.

23
neñcakatt-anpiyalumbōl – bhēda
cintakaḷkk-antyam ākunnu
cellakkiṭāṅgaḷē, śanka-viṭṭ-amma tan
collukāḷ kāt-ōrttu kēḷkkū!

When love fills our hearts, all differences vanish. Darling children, shrug off all doubts and heed Mother's words.

24
strīkaḷkku 'śrī' ēṭṭiṭunnu – śuddha
śālīna-saumyamām bhāvam
pauruṣam vākkilall-ātmāvil āṇennu
pūruṣanmārum grahikkū!

A pure and calm nature is the mark of a noble one. We should know that real courage is not in words but in the integrity of the Self.

25

cēlezhum cillīvilāsam – kaṇḍu
cētassu cāñcāṭiṭāte
nāriye dēvatayāy ninaccīṭukil
māyaykk-atītarāy tīrām

Let not physical beauty tempt us away from the spiritual path. When we see divinity in the physical form, we will be able to transcend *māya*.

26

jaivō›rjjam ōlunnat-ellām – svayam
saundarya-āsvādanā-sajjam
saundarya-āsvādanam daivika-siddhi āṇ-
āvaram hṛttil veḷiccam

All that pulses with life invites you to reflect on your own beauty. Appreciating beauty is a divine art, and it manifests the radiance in your heart.

27

yantram niyantriccu nammaḷ – svayam
yantramāy tīrum taniyē
nallor-udyānam uṇḍ-ummaṙatt-eṅkilum
tellonnat-āsvadikkēṇḍē!

Even as we have gained control over machines, we ourselves have become automatons. When a beautiful garden is right before us, can't we appreciate it at least a little?

28

ātmānubhūti nukarān – cittam-
ātmāvil ēkāgram ākkū

nūṙu sankalpaṅgaḷ kūṭikkuruṅgukil
nūṫṫeṭukkān entu yatnam?

To experience the bliss of the Self, let us turn our one-pointed mind inward towards the Self. How else can we untangle our thoughts that are inextricably linked to each other?

29
pālpāyasam nannu, pakṣē – atin
svād-aṙiññ-āsvadikkēṇam
kūṭṭi kalartti kazhiccāl atin mēnma
vēṙiṭṭ-aṙiyilla tellum

Milk pudding is delicious, but we should know how to relish it. If we mix it with other dishes, how can we savor its unique sweetness?

30
kṣīra-nīrattinde nyāyam – sadā
pālikkaṇam jīvitattil
nanmayum tinmayum kaṇḍ-aṙiññeṅkilē
raṇḍinnum appuṙam pōkū!

In life, always honor the principle of separating milk from water. Only when we discern good from bad can we rise above both.

31
māṙi maṙiyum ī lōkam – manō
māyā-bhramattinn adhīnam
nērāyatil ninnu māṙāt-irikkunna
cētassu nērinn-adhīnam

This changing world is captive to the fallacies of *māya* (cosmic delusion). The mind that does not swerve from the path of righteousness adheres to Truth.

32
ātmaikya-cinta ceyyumbōḷ – makkaḷ
ātmārttha-bhakti uḷkkoḷḷū
cittatār utphullam-āyeṅkil allāte
tattva-bōdham tuḷikkilla

Children, reflect on the Oneness of the Self and practice true devotion. Awareness streams forth only from a fully blossomed heart.

33
cinta viṭṭōrōnnu ceyyum – teṫṫu
kuṫṫaṅgaḷ anyaril cārum
akṣara-teṫṫ-onnu vannāl tiruttiṭām
āśaya-teṫṫ-entu ceyyum?

We err when we act without thinking, and then blame others. We can correct a spelling mistake, but what can we do about a misconception?

34
sādhū-karikkāt-irikkū – teṫṫu
dūrīkarikkān paṭhikkū
bhāvi entākum enn-āśanka vēṇḍa, sad-
bhāvamē bhāvikk-utakū

Let us not rationalize a wrong action. We should just refrain from repeating it. We need not fear the future, as a noble attitude will protect us.

35

mānava-rāśikku vēṇḍi – mahā
tyāgaṅgaḷ ācarikkumbōḷ
antarangattil aṅg-āyiram svargīya
bhāvaṅgaḷ pīli-viṭarttum!

When we make sacrifices for humankind, our mind becomes pure and exalted.

36

mujjanma-pāpa-kaṙakaḷ – māyān
satkarmam ācariccīṭām
āreyum ātmāmśamāy kāṇukil appozhē
pāpaṅgaḷ bāṣpī-karikkum!

Let good deeds cancel the negativities of our previous births. Only when we see everyone as our Self will our sins be washed away.

37

kālam kaṭannu pōkumbōḷ – tānē
dēham kozhiññu pōkunnu
kāla-dēśattin niyantraṇam māṙāte
māṙilla pāpa-apahāram!

With the passing of time comes the passing of our body. We cannot escape the consequences of our bad thoughts and actions until we transcend time and space.

38

viṇṇ-ēṙiyuṇṇunna puṇyam – tīrnnāl
kiṇṇam kazhuki kamazhttām

viṇṇ-ēṙiyālum maṭaṅgi vann-ī maṇṇil
kiṇṇam tarappeṭuttēṇam

We go to heaven and enjoy the fruits of our good deeds; but once the merits are exhausted, we are born on earth again. Then, again we fill our bowl with the fruits of our good and bad actions.

39
puṇya-lōkam kṣayikkumbōḷ – vīṇḍum
karma-lōkam tanne rakṣa
ārjjita-samskāram appozhum pāzhalla
sūkṣma-dēhattil nilīnam!

When our merit is exhausted, we must return to the world of action. Once again we will acquire merit through good deeds. The purity of character we have gained is not lost but remains latent in the subtle body.

40
uṇma kaṇḍettān śramikkū – śāstra
lakṣyam phala-pradam ākkū
śāstraṅgaḷ buddhikk-orannamāy tīrāte
hṛttinn-uṣassākki māṫṫū

Strive to attain the Truth, and thus fulfill the goal of scripture studies. Scriptures are not just food for our intellect. Let them bring spiritual dawn in our heart.

41
kāraṇam tēṭunnu buddhi – satyam
kāraṇātītam ākunnu

kaivilaṅg-āṇenn-aṙiyumbōḷ buddhikku
kai-nīṭṭam ākunnu satyam!

The intellect seeks causes, but Truth is beyond reason. When we realize that the intellect can be a shackle, Truth becomes a gift to the intellect.

42
matsaram vēṇḍa vēṇḍ-oṭṭum – buddhi
matsaram satyam maṙaykkum
buddhiyum hṛttum parasparam nallayal
bandham pularttēṇam ennum

We should not try to prove the supremacy of one path over the other. Such intellectual debate can obscure Truth. The intellect and heart must always maintain a healthy relationship.

43
bāhya-pravṛttiyall-unnam – atin
āntara-bhāvam pradhānam
'śatruta kūṭāte yuddham nayikk'enna
tattvōpadēśam smarikkū!

What matters is not outward action but inner attitude. Heed the spiritual counsel to "fight without enmity."

44
karmatil kānām akarmam – kaṇḍāl
kānām akarmattin marmam
kartṛtvam illāte ceytāl akarmamāy,
karmayōgam tān atōrkkū!

There is inaction in action. When we understand this, we know the essence of inaction. Acting without the sense of doership is inaction. Know this to be karma yoga!

45

pālikkaṇam dharma-nīti – allēl
jīva-lōkattinn-aśānti
pālikkaṇam kṣamā-śilam, parasparam
snēhikkaṇam vāg-atītam!

If dharma is not honored, there will be strife in the world. Patience must prevail. We must love each other, and not merely in words!

46

munn-orukkaṅgaḷ illāte – onnum
nannāy kalāśikkayilla
ādariccitēṇḍa tattvam nirantaram
dhyāniccu sākṣāt-karikkū!

Without adequate preparation, the result might not be what we expected. Constantly meditate on the supreme principle and realize the Self.

47

karmattin-ottapōl janmam – vīṇḍum
janmattin-ottapōl karmam
karmam tirutti kuṙiccuḷḷ-uṇarukil
janmattin-antyam bhavikkum

Our life is the sum result of our actions, so our fate depends on how we live. When we set our actions right and awaken within, the cycle of rebirth ends.

48

kāla-dēśattin talattil – nammaḷ
kāṇunnat-ellām asatyam
kāladēśam māññu kāzhca munn-ēṙiyāl
kāṇunnu sarvatra satyam!

Everything in the realm of time and space is unreal. When our perception transcends time and space, everything we see is Truth.

49

ñān-bhāva-hīnamāy illēl – stuti
gītaṅgaḷ niṣphalam ākum
daivahitatte aṙiññ-ācarikkātta
karmavum niṣphalam ākum

Without rising above egoism, singing the praises of God will not bear fruit. Actions done while ignorant of God's will cannot bear fruit either.

50

kāzhcaykkī kaṇṇalla mukhyam – vastu
kāzhcakaḷ kāzhca āvilla
ātma-lāvaṇyam tiḷaṅgunna kaṇṇinde
kāzhcayē kāzhcayāy kāṇū!

Just seeing objects with our eyes is not the real seeing. Only eyes shining in the beauty of the Self truly see.

51

ādariccīṭēṇḍa tattvam – ādyam
ālōcanam ceyt-uṙaykkū

pinnatil tanne uṇarnn-irunnīṭukil
cemmē atāy māṙum ārum

Reflection roots us firmly in principles worthy of reverence. Thereafter, anyone who awakens to the truth of those principles will gracefully embody them.

52
ādarśa-śāli ennālum – onnum
ācarikkāt-aṅg-irunnāl
āṙi taṇutt-uraññ-ādarśam okkeyum
āke karikkūna ākum

Ideals that are not practiced are as useless as a heap of cold embers.

53
satyam paṙayuvān nāṇam – okke
veṭṭattu vaccāl veḷukkum
ōrkkāt-orāḷ oru satyam vacikkukil
kēḷkkunna āḷ vismayikkum!

Reticence to speak the truth vanishes in the light of the Truth. Even if we utter the Truth inadvertently, the audience will marvel.

54
ellā bhayattinum śānti – daiva
snēham onnāṇ-ennaṙiyū
bhīti allādhāram ānanda-bhaktikku
prēmam onnāṇ-ennaṙiyū!

Know that divine love alone calms our fears. Love alone is the source of blissful devotion, not fear.

55
sāmūhya-nanmaykku nammaḷ – namme
sādaram nēdikkum-eṅkil,
lōkattinn-aiśvarya-bhāga-dhēyaṅgaḷkku
bhāga-bhākk-āṇennu vyaktam!

When we offer ourselves for the welfare of society, we realize that our deeds lead to a brighter world.

56
sampattu kunnu pōlāyāl – ātma
samtṛpti nēṭumō martyan?
samtṛpti ātmāvil ātma-sākṣātkāram
onnu tān śāśvata-śānti!

If we amassed a heap of wealth, would we gain contentment? Contentment and eternal peace lie in the Self alone.

ōmkāra divya porūḷe 57 (Malayalam)

Disclaimer: The translations of certain verses are not literal; they aim at bringing out the essential meaning from the Malayalam verses in a way that is easily understandable.

ōmkāra divya porūḷe varū
ōmana-makkaḷē vēgam
ōmanayāy vaḷarnn-āmayaṅgaḷ nīkki
ōmkāra-vastuvāy tīrū

Come quickly darling children, you who are the divine essence of Om. Remove all sorrows, grow dear and adorable, and merge with the Absolute.

1

bhakti-vairāgyam varāte – jñāna
siddhi uṇḍākān prayāsam
jñānam illēl buddhi māyā-nibaddhamāy
mōcanōpāyam maṙakkum

We cannot attain knowledge without devotion and dispassion. Without knowledge, *maya* deludes the intellect, and we forget the means to obtain liberation.

2

dharma-bōdhattōṭe ceyyum – karmam
karma-nivṛtti varuttum
vidyayāl ātmīya-buddhiyāl niṣkāma
śuddhiyāl ā varam nēṭām

Dharmic action exhausts karma. We gain such a blessing through scriptural knowledge, disciplined intellect and the renunciation of desire.

3

sampradāyaṇgaḷil mātram – makkaḷ
samprītar-ākātirikkū
ācāra-niṣṭhakaḷ nannu tann-eṅkilum
ācāra-baddhata nindyam

Children, don't be satisfied with traditional observances alone. Religious observances are good, but you should not be bound by them.

4
uḷvilaññ-oṫṫapeṭāte – makkaḷ
uḷḷattil ēkāntar-ākū
ātmāvil ēkāntam-āyirikkumbozhum
lōkōpakārikaḷ ākū

Children, don't withdraw into yourself and become isolated. Instead, enjoy the solitude of the *atman*. Even when alone in the *atman*, continue to serve the world.

5
bandhaṇgaḷ bandhanam ākum – manam
andhakārattil tuzhayum
bandhanam tan manass-anya-kāryaṅgaḷil
andham nibandhippat-allō

Bondage is like rowing the boat of the mind in darkness. Relationships easily become bondage if our mind gets attached.

6
saṅga-rāhityam varumbōḷ – onnum
anyamāy kāṇilla nammaḷ
bhēdamaṫṫ-ātma-santuṣṭarām sādhukkaḷ
ōti tarum saumya-mārgam

When attachment ends, we see nothing as separate from our self. This is the gentle path taught by the masters who have risen above duality and remain ever blissful.

7
sādhu-samsargēṇa ārkkum – bhēda
bhāvattin antyam bhavikkum

dēha-tādātmyam āṇ-ātma-svātantryattin
ōrttāl taṭassam onn-ārkkum

The company of the wise (*satsang*) dissolves the sense of duality. Our identification with the body hinders our salvation.

8
nityam namaskṛti ceyyū – bhaktyā
satyābhidarśitan kālkkal
tṛccēvaṭittāril cittam uṙaykkukil
mṛtyuve pōlum jayikkām

Let us daily prostrate with devotion at the holy feet of the Seers of Truth. When our mind is firmly attached to their holy feet, we can conquer even death.

9
nāṭakam nirmicc-avan tān – svanta
nāṭakam nēriṭṭu kāṇke
bhāvi entākum enn-utkaṇṭha kāṇilla
bhāvi-raṅgam manaḥ-pāṭham

When the scriptwriter himself watches the play he has written, he has no anxiety about the future because he knows for sure what the next scene is.

10
satya-draṣṭākkaḷ ī lōkam – kāṇmū
hasta-amalakam kaṇakke
santōṣa-santāpam onnum ill-utkaṇṭha
sambhāvyam ent-enn-aṙiyām

For the Seers of Truth, this world is like a gooseberry in their palm. They are neither sad nor happy nor anxious. They know the future.

11

svatvam svatantram ākāte – lōka
satyatte darśikkayilla
satyattin ādara-pūrvam samarppiccu
svatvam svatantram ākkīṭū

To know the Truth of the world, we must know the Truth of the Self. Let us surrender reverently to the Truth, realize our true nature, and be free.

12

ājanma-śuddhar āyīṭum – puṇya
śālikaḷ ennum ī maṇṇil
jīvitam koṇḍ-avar ālēkhanam ceyta
tyāga-sandēśam smarikkū

Mahatmas are holy from birth, and such holy ones have always lived in this land. Their life is a teaching on sacrifice!

13

lōkam tyajikk-ennatalla – mithyā
bōdham tyajjippatē tyāgam
tyāga-samskāram ī nāṭin ñarambukaḷkk–
ōjassum vīryavum ēkum

We should renounce our illusions, not the world. The culture of renunciation gives vigor and splendor to this land.

14
tyāgamē samtṛpti ēkū – dhairya
śāliyē tyāgiyāy tīrū
dhīra-karmaṅgaḷe mānikkum ī lōkam
dhīrata tyāgam onnatrē

Renunciation alone gives contentment, but only the brave can renounce. The world respects brave deeds, and renunciation is true bravery.

15
cōṭukaḷ nīṭṭi caviṭṭām – neṭum
pātayil kāzhca kāṇāte
jīvitam pūrva-pitākkaḷ teḷiccor-ā
pātayil bhavyam nayikkām

Ignoring the sights and sounds on our way, let us take long strides, and lead an auspicious life on the path illumined by our ancestors.

16
satyam manō-janyam alla – anya
vastu pōl utpannam alla
satyam manuṣyande hṛt-spandanattinde
sarga-pracālaka-śakti

Truth is not a creation of the mind, nor is it an external object. Truth is the creative energy that pulsates in our heart.

17
mṛṇmayam āyatil ninnum – makkaḷ
cinmayarāy māṙiṭēṇam

koḷḷalum kiḷḷi koṭukkalum illeṅkil
mṛṇmayam ākunnu janmam

Without give and take, life becomes inert. Children, shrug off your lethargy and live with enthusiasm.

18
satkarmam ācaricc-ennāl – phalam
nalkṛpayāy bhaviccīṭum
karmam vidhikkum vidhikk-anyamām phalam
vannu cērillatu nūnam

When we do good actions, their fruits come back to us as grace. The destiny determined by our deeds is inevitable.

19
sātvika-adhīnam rajassāl – karmam
sargātmakamāyi māṙum
rajasam tāmasa-adhīnamāyāl manam
nārakīya-andhyattil āzhum

When knowledge and purity control ambition and energy, our actions become creative. When darkness and ignorance control ambition and energy, our mind becomes evil.

20
karmatin mūlyam nissvārttham – svārttha
karmam manaḥ-śānti cōrttum
kaṇṇil taṙaykkēṇḍ-orambum kṛpā-lēśam
uṇḍēl lalāṭam taṭukkum

Selflessness determines the value of karma (action). Selfish action destroys our mental peace. When we perform selfless actions, grace flows into us. By grace, even an arrow aimed at our eye can get deflected and leave only a scratch on our forehead.

21

varjjicciṭām svārttha-lakṣyam – hṛttil
ārjjicciṭām nirbhayatvam
prārtthicciṭām lōka-nanma ellāyppozhum
kīrtticciṭām dharma-tattvam

Let us abandon selfish goals and attain fearlessness in our heart. Let us always pray for the welfare of the world and celebrate *dharma*.

22

prārtthanā-nirbhara-cittam – puṇya
tīrtthattin okkeyum mēle
snēhārdram ākum manassu nūṙ-āyiram
dēvā-layattinum mēle

A prayerful heart is more exalted than all the holy rivers. A mind soaked in love is superior to a hundred thousand temples.

23

snēham koṭuttāl phalattil – svarga
lōkam tanikk-iṅg adhīnam
duḥkham grasikkātta svargam, parasnēha
magnam manass-onnu mātram

When we give love, we create heaven on earth for ourselves. A mind absorbed in love for others is a heaven untouched by sorrow.

24

ippōzh-iviṭalla eṅkil – pinne
eppōzh eviṭ-āṇu svargam?
yuddhōtsukam koṇḍu svargam paṇiññatil
etra pēr ārūḍharāyi?

When and where is heaven if not here and now? Has anyone attained heaven by an aggressive pursuit of war?

25

ūzhi viṭṭ-ōṭēṇḍ-orāḷum – svarga
rājyam ī maṇṇil āṇ-ennum
anyarkku duḥkham koṭuttiṭṭu svargattil
santuṣṭiyōṭ-āru vāzhum?

Let us not run from this world. Heaven has always been here on earth. No one will live peacefully in heaven after causing sorrow for others on earth.

26

āyōdhanam ceytu nēṭān – svarggam
uṇḍēl atin pēru 'mauḍhyam'
pātakam ceytiṭṭu svargam labhikkukil
bhēdam narakam atallē?

A heaven gained by war is named 'folly'. Isn't even hell better than a heaven gained by committing atrocities?

27

alleṅkil martya-hṛdantam – svargam
ennu kaṇḍ-ādariccīṭām

iṣṭa-dēvan tande vāsa-sthalam atil
nityam upāsiccu vāzhām

We can transform our heart into heaven. Let us offer daily worship in the abode of our beloved deity.

28
indriya-nāthan āṇ-indran – svargam
indrann-adhīnam ākumbōḷ
svargam kotikkuvōr arttha-antarattilūṭ-
indriya-ārāmanmār allo

Indra, the Lord of heaven, is the Lord of our sense organs. Those who aspire to heaven are, in fact, seeking to gratify their senses.

29
indriya-ārādhana nīkki – antaraṅgam pavitrī-karikkū
indriyaṅgaḷkk-indhanam ākkukil jīvitam
andhakārattil patikkum

Let us stop indulging our senses and, instead, purify our heart. If our life is just fuel for the senses, we will fall into deep darkness.

30
indriya-atītar ākāte – mṛtyu
bandhanam nīṅgilla nūnam
indriya-ārāmanmār ārum svatantrar all-
andhakārattinde bandhu

When we do not conquer our senses, mortality binds us. Those who seek only sense pleasures are not free; they are bound in darkness!

31

svārttham tyajicc-ātma-lakṣyam – mēlil
sādhippatin udyamikkām
nērum viśuddhiyum uḷḷavarkk-uḷḷattil
uṇma kaṇḍettān eḷuppam

Let us renounce selfishness and strive to attain the *atman*. The truthful and pure ones easily find the Truth within.

32

pāramparyam kai-veṭiññu – viśva
sāhōdaryam kāmb-eriññu
viśvatte āryam ākkān vratam nōṭṭorā
śrēṣṭha-samskāram maṙaññu

We have discarded traditions, and the ideal of universal brotherhood has withered. The great culture of the land that pined for a noble world has disappeared.

33

gōḷāntaraṅgaḷe mēnmēl – svantam
kālkkīzhil ākkum manuṣyā
pōrunna nēram maṙakkāt-orittiri
mānuṣyakam koṇḍu varāmō?

Again and again you conquer outer space and planets, placing them under your feet. Upon returning, please remember to bring a drop of human goodness with you.

34

vēṇēl samāśvāsa-pūrvam – anya
gōḷaṅgaḷil tambaṭikkū

klēśa-bhūyiṣṭam ī bhūmiye kāṇēṇḍa
dūre dūre pōy oḷikkū

Go ahead and settle down comfortably on other planets if that's what you want. Go hide far away and don't look back at this wretched earth!

35
mānuṣika-prēma-vittin – micca-
mūlyam svarūpiccu ñaṅgaḷ
ceyyām kṛṣi atil nīḷe katirkkula
vīśiyāl niṅgaḷum pōrū

We shall sow the seeds of human love, and when it is ready for harvest, we shall invite everyone to join us.

36
mūlyam ellām anyamāyi – tammil
ātma-bandham vēr-aṙuttum
āghōṣam okkeyum ātmāv-ezhāttatāy
tāyvēril ninn-etra māṙi

We are no longer true to values, and mutual trust and friendship have been cut asunder. We have strayed so far from the roots of our culture that our celebrations ring hollow!

37
tānum kuṭumbavum mātram – anya-
kāryattil ārkk-entu kāryam
ārum tanikk-ārum allennu cinticcu
tān tannil oṭṭappeṭunnu

Only me and my family — why should I deal with others? Thinking thus, we become estranged and lonely.

38

daivattin svantam enn-ōtum – nāṭu
pāṭē piśācinn-adhīnam
ātma-praśamsayāl vāstavam mūṭunnu
pāzh-vākkil ellām subhikṣam

Kerala is known as 'God's own country,' but now it has fallen under the influence of the evil of intoxicants. We sing our own praises and are satisfied with empty words.

39

anyāyamāy uḷḷat-entum – nammaḷ
anyūnam ācariccīṭum
anyāyam āyatu nyūnamaṫṫ-ācaricc-
anyarkku drōham vitaykkum

We act unjustly and feel no pangs of conscience. Our unjust actions always sow the seeds of harm for others.

40

martya-snēhattil allēlum – daiva
satya-bōdhattil allēlum
madyōtsavattil āṇ-advaita-siddhi maṫṫ-
eṅkilum sparddhakaḷ mātram

Now people seek bliss in liquor. They have no love for their fellow beings, and no longing to know the divine Truth. But, inebriation only leads to drunken brawls.

41
māṫṫam manassil varāte – lōkam
māṫṫi maṙikkān śramiccāl
klāvuṫṫa pātravum pālum kaṇakk-atu
pāṭē duṣiccu nāṙīṭum

Trying to transform the world without first transforming our own mind is like pouring milk into a dirty vessel. Both mind and action become corrupt.

42
durjjana-ādēśam tyajikkū – makkaḷ
sajjana-ādēśam śravikkū
vigrahicc-arttham grahikkū manassine
nigrahicc-ātmāv uṇarttū

Children, ignore the words of sly people. Listen only to the virtuous ones, and contemplate and imbibe their meaning. Subdue your mind and awaken to your true Self.

43
nī atāṇ-enn-otiṭumbōḷ – aham
brahmam enn-arttham grahikkām
vākku koṇḍ-ārum atākilla tanmanō-
vṛtti-nāśam tanne mukhyam

Through the teaching 'you are That,' we can understand that 'I am Brahman.' But this Truth is not realized by mere words. The Truth only shines forth in a mind in which all thoughts have been subdued.

44
dēhamāy kāṇāte namme – śuddha
bōdhamāy kāṇunnuv-eṅkil
kāzhcayil dēham uṇḍeṅkilum pinne nām
bōdha-svarūpi āṇ-ennum

When we realize our true nature is pure consciousness, we stop identifying ourselves with our body. Though we still function within the body, we remain in the realm of pure awareness.

45
illāttat-uṇmayāy tōnnām – tōnnal
allāte illatinn-uṇma
ātmāvu satyam anātmāvu mithya enn-
ōrān vivēkam sahāyam

We mistake untruth to be the Truth. Untruth is a delusion created by the mind. Through discrimination, we understand that the Self alone is true and non-Self is illusion.

46
tōnnalil taṅgunnat-entum – tōnnal
māṙiyāl śūnyamāy māṙum
ākāśa-puṣpam maṇakkān kazhiyilla
peril sugandham ūṙilla

Thoughts and feelings come and go; they are transient. It is impossible to smell a 'space flower' because an imaginary flower has no scent.

47
allu-pakalukaḷ tammil – baddha
vairikaḷ ennapōl tōnnum

taṅgaḷil kāṇāt-irikkān divāniśam
nallōr-akalam pularttum

Light and darkness appear to be enemies. They distance themselves every day to avoid seeing each other.

48
ajñāna-jñānaṅgaḷ tammil – nitya
śatruta āṇ-ennu tōnnum
onnicc-orēṭattu taṅgilla taṅgaḷil
kaṇḍu muṭṭāṙilla nēril

Knowledge and ignorance are like eternal enemies. They can never stay together in one place, nor do they ever meet each other.

49
ajñānam ennoru vastu – mūnnu-
kālattum illenn-aṙiyū
jñāna-prakāśam parannāl iruṭṭilla
śuddha-bōdham satyam atre

Know that ultimately there is no such thing as ignorance in the three periods (past, present, future). The light of Knowledge casts out darkness, and then we know that pure awareness alone is True.

50
citta-cāñcalyam veṭiññu – karma
yajñam tuṭarnn-ācarikkām
āzhipparappil calikkunnu kallōlam
āzhattil eppozhum maunam

Discard the vacillations of the mind and serve the world selflessly. Ripples appear only on the ocean surface; deep down the ocean is always still.

51

cittavum buddhiyum pinne – manam
maṫṫ-indriyaṅgaḷum ellām
ātma-caitanya-sphuraṇaṅgaḷ mātram
āṇ-ātmāvu mauna-samudram

Mind, intellect and all faculties are a pulsation of consciousness. The Self is the silent ocean!

52

vākkaṫṫ-ezhikkum ā maunam – bōdha
vyākhyānam āṇ-ennaṙiyū
vākkum manassum layicca sākṣāt-kāra
vāṅmayam ākunnu maunam

Silence remains when speech ends. Silence is the commentary of awareness. Silence is the eloquence of Self-realization that remains when speech and mind dissolve.

53

kāmana kai-viṭṭ-uṇarū – ātma
jñānam prakāśicciṭaṭṭe
āśa naśikkāte klēśam naśikkilla
klēśa-nāśam tanne mōkṣam

Let us abandon desires and wake up. Let Self-knowledge shine! Liberation is the end of sorrow. Without renouncing desire there can be no destruction of sorrow.

54
āśakaḷ bāṣpanīr-ēkum – atē
āśakaḷ rōṣāgni ākum
āśaye vennavarkk-āśvāsamē varū
āśa āśvāsam keṭuttum

Desires can cause tears and flaming anger, without any hope of solace. Relief comes only when we renounce all desires.

55
āśaykk-adhīnar ākāte – īśvar
ājñaykk-adhīnar āyeṅkil
ātmāvil niṣpandam ākum manassu pinn-
āzhill-azhal āzhi tannil

When we renounce all desires and surrender to God's will, our mind becomes still in the *atman*. Then there is no sorrow, even in an ocean of troubles.

56
kāṇilla kaṇṇināl ellām – satyam
kāṇunna kaṇṇ-onnu vēṙe
kaṇṇīr pozhikkunna kaṇṇalla ātmāvām
kaṇṇināl kāṇmatē satyam

Our eyes do not see everything; they only shed tears. The eye of the *atman* beholds the Truth.

57
nanma tan vāgdānam ākū makkaḷ
tinma tan tāyvēr aṙukkū

uḷḷaliv-uḷḷavar ākū samanvaya
sandēśa-vāhakar ākū

Children, promise to do only good. Cut asunder the root of evil. Be compassionate and be messengers of unity and integrity.

ōmkāra divya porūḷe 58 (Malayalam)

Disclaimer: The translations of certain verses are not literal; they aim at bringing out the essential meaning from the Malayalam verses in a way that is easily understandable.

ōmkāra divya porūḷe varū
ōmana-makkaḷē vēgam
ōmanayāy vaḷarnn-āmayaṅgaḷ nīkki
ōmkāra-vastuvāy tīrū

Come quickly darling children, you who are the divine essence of Om. Remove all sorrows, grow dear and adorable, and merge with the Absolute.

1
satyam pala-tuḷḷi alla – orē
satyam palat-ennu tōnnum
tōnnalinn-ādhāram ajñānam āṇatu
māṙiyāl māññu pōm śōkam

The Truth is one and indivisible, though it appears as many. Ignorance causes us to see the one Truth as many. When the feeling of duality disappears, all sorrow ceases.

2

aśrunīr-āṫṫi kuṙukki – ēka
kaṇṇir-kaṇam ākki māṫṫi
nirmala-ātmāvinkal arppiccu kanmaṣa
hīnarāy tīruvin makkaḷ

Children, offer all your tears to the pure indwelling Self, and thus become free of all blemish.

3

munn-orukkaṅgaḷ illāte – ārkkum
unnati nēṭāvatalla
abhyāsa-vairāgyam illāte sādhanaykk-
ētum balam kaivarilla

Without adequate preparation, we cannot make progress in life. Without dispassion and discipline, our *sadhana* lacks strength.

4

pāṭān aṙiyātta vidvān – vēdi
māṙiyiṭṭ-entāṇu nēṭṭam?
sādhakam ceyyāte nēre pravēśiccu
vēdiyil pāṭṭ-āru pāṭum?

If you don’t know how to sing, what is the use of going from stage to stage? How is it possible to sing before an audience without adequate practice?

5

ātmaikya-bōdham illāte – brahma
vādam muzhakkunna vidvān

tānē parihāsa-pātramāy māṙiṭum
ātma-sandhānam pradhānam

When a scholar proclaims, 'I am Brahman' without knowing the Oneness of all beings, he is ridiculed by all. Ultimately, knowledge of the Self is all that matters.

6
sādhanā-mandiram ākkām – ātma
dēvālayam-āṇu dēham
kṣētrattil ettiyāl gātram maṙakkaṇam
kṣētrajñane smarikkēṇam

The *atman* is enshrined in the temple of the body. Let us make it a holy place for our *sadhana*. Upon entering the temple, let us forget our identification with the body and contemplate only on the Lord.

7
kōvilil kai-kūppi nilkkē – śraddha
tan 'pādarakṣa'yil taṅgum!
pādarakṣaykk-oru kāvalāḷ – ennapōl
ōrkkunnu daivatte nammaḷ!

When we stand in the temple with folded hands, we forget God and think only of the shoes we left outside. Thus, we make God into a footwear keeper.

8
kṣētrattil ettiyāl pōlum – daiva
cintaykku nēram ill-ārkkum
anya-kāryaṅgaḷe cinticcu cinticcu
vanna kāryam vismarikkum!

Even within the temple precincts we have no time to remember God. Forgetting why we came, we think about other things.

9

gātratte kṣētramāy kāṇām – bāhya
kṣētratte gātramāy kāṇām
ātma-svarūpatte kṣētrajñan enn-aṙiññ-
īśvara-ārādhana ceyyām

Let us see the world as our body and our body as a temple. Remembering that the Self is the temple deity, let us worship the Lord.

10

namme maṙakkunnu nammaḷ – anyam
ellām smarikkunnu nammaḷ
śāstra-tattvaṅgaḷ uruviṭum eṅkilum
āviṣkarikk-illat-uḷḷil

We forget our true nature and remember everything else. We talk about scriptural principles but fail to realize them within.

11

astitva-bōdham uṇarnnāl – pinne
vyaktitvam ennat-onnilla
vyaktitvam uḷḷappozh astitvamill-aham
śuddha-caitanyam onn-atrē

When true awareness awakens, the sense of individuality disappears. When we identify ourselves as the individual, we forget we are pure consciousness. The true 'I' is pure consciousness.

12

adhyātma-jñānam atatre – āru
ñān ennat-ōrunna jñānam
bāhya-vijñānaṅgaḷ ellām avidya enn-
ōtunnu vēda-vēdāntam

Spiritual wisdom is knowing who 'I' am. Worldly knowledge equips us for a living. *Vedas* and *Vedanta* teach us that spiritual knowledge alone is the eternal, everlasting Truth.

13

śāntāntaraṅgattil eṅgum - nitya
śānti santōṣam niṙayum
ākasmikam alla karma-anubaddham āṇ-
ātanka-hētu enn-ōrkkū

Eternal peace and bliss fill a quiet mind. Our mind becomes quiet as a result of pure actions. Know that selfish actions are the cause of sorrow.

14

muṫṫum dhanārtti āṇ-eṅgum – svārttha
lakṣyattin entum upāyam
aṣṭikku nanne paṇippeṭṭu kiṭṭunna
tuṭṭukaḷkk-illoṭṭu mūlyam

Greed for wealth is everywhere. We go to any extreme for our selfish gains. Only money earned honestly, through hard work, has value.

15

madya-anurāgikaḷkk-ellām – nallor-udyānam ākum ī nāṭṭil

cuṫṫi tiriyum piśācine daivamāy
teṫṫi dharikkunnu nammaḷ

When alcohol enslaves you, any place that serves you becomes your pleasure garden. And you mistake the devil to be divine.

16
nālāḷu kūṭunn-iṭattu – madya
śāla onnāy-eṅkil ennāy
āreyum madya-anurāgikaḷ ākkuvān
āyenkil ennāṇu mōham

When a few people gather together, they only desire an inexhaustible supply of alcohol, and want to invite everyone to the party.

17
entu tān ceyt-ennatalla – nēṭṭam
entennu mātramāy nōṭṭam
lābha-koti mūtt-orākrāntam ī daiva
nāṭinde nāṇam keṭuttum

We are not bothered about the right and wrong of our actions. We are only interested in our gains. Greed has taken over our dignity and pride in our land.

18
kānanam kayyaṭakkunnu – martya
kāmanakaḷ kāṭu kēṙi
sasya-latādi tan, pakṣimṛgādi tan
vamśa-vicchēdattin unnam

Rapacious greed has decimated the forests and exploited plants and animals to extinction.

19

lābha-koti mūttu bhrāntam – svanta
kāryattil āṇāsthayārkkum
sasya-jālatteyum jantu-jālatteyum
mātramall-ellām hanikkum

Everyone pursues only their selfish interests. Insane greed is destroying not only plants and animals but the whole earth.

20

ārtti-vināśam varāte – lōka
nāśam taṭukkāvat-alla
āśvāsam anyarkku nalkātta śāstravum
āśāsyam-alla tell-ētum

Until we conquer greed, we will continue to destroy the world. What good is a scripture that does not relieve suffering?

21

maṇkaṭṭayāy kāṇmu bhūmi – jaiva
bandham illāt-ākkiṭunnu
pulkkoṭi pōlum muḷaykkātta maṭṭiliṅg-
ūṣaram ākkiṭunn-ūzhi

Without realizing that the earth is a living being on which our existence depends, we treat it like a ball of mud. We make the earth into a barren wasteland where not even a blade of grass can grow.

22
mātāvu tan maṭittaṭṭāy – kaṇḍāl
vēṇḍat-ellām urvvi ēkum
vāzhvine mānippōr-ūzhiye mānikkum
ūzhi illēl illa vāzhvum

If we treat the earth as our mother's lap, she will meet all our needs. If we value life we should respect the earth because without the earth there is no life.

23
pāristhitika-vijñānam – ārum
ōti paṭhippicciṭēṇḍa
tān tān nayikkunna jīvita-śuddhiyāl
māṙum paristhiti tānē

We have an instinctive knowledge of the environment that sustains us. The purity of our actions positively influences the world around us.

24
peṫṫa-mātāvine pōle – pari
rakṣaṇam ceyt-ūzhi kākkū
vidrōha-vṛttiyil ninnum vimuktarāy
svacchata bhūmikku nalkū

The earth protects us like our own mother. Let us stop harming her and give peace to the earth.

25
mōṭi piṭippicciṭēṇḍa – sṛṣṭi
saundaryam māññu pōkilla

daiva-sṛṣṭikkilla nyūnata – nām atu
pāṭē duṣippicciṭunnu

We do not have to beautify creation; it is beautiful by nature. God's creation lacks nothing; it is we who spoil it.

26
kāṭum malayum kaṭalum – nadī
nāṭum nagaravum ellām
ētinum uṇḍu tanatāya saundaryam
vaikṛtam sṛṣṭippu nammaḷ

Forests, mountains, oceans, rivers, land, cities—everything has its own beauty. It is we who create ugliness.

27
nāṫṫam sahikkāte vannāl – svanta
mūkkinde dōṣamāy kāṇmū
nāṭāya nāṭokke mālinyam ēṫṫi nām
vīṭāke mōṭi kūṭṭunnu

We think that keeping the environment clean is not our personal responsibility. We throw garbage everywhere and pollute the land, but still keep cleaning and decorating our own home.

28
maṇṇum manassum orupōl – śuddhi
ceytāke lōkam teḷikkū
cittam duṣikkāte svārttham kotikkāte
satyam jayikkān uṙaykkū

Let us purify both the earth and our mind and thus brighten the world. Without spoiling our heart, without greed for selfish ends, let us be strong to make Truth victorious.

29

lōkam curuṅgunnu, pakṣē – ēṙe
dūram hṛdayaṅgaḷ tammil
garvv-ezhum mānava-ceytikaḷ lōkattin
āpattu tirkkunnu mēnmēl

Distances are reducing, but our hearts are farther apart. Egoistic actions increasingly endanger the world.

30

anyan illātt-iṭam tēṭi - eṅgum
anyanāy tīrunnit-ārum
ārkkum sahāyakam allātta jīvitam
pāṙappuṙam pōle śūnyam

Searching for a place far from others, we become strangers to our own selves. A life that does not help others is as barren and lonely as a rocky mountain top.

31

nalla vākk-onn-uraceyyū – naṙum
puñciri-tēn-kaṇam tūkū
kāruṇyam ōlunna nōṭṭattoṭ-ālamba
hīnarkk-orāśvāsam ēkū

Let us speak kind words and smile sweetly. Let us console the helpless with our compassionate glance.

32
tānum samūhavum onnāy – kaṇḍu
vēnam dhanārjjanam ceyyān
kiṭṭunnatil ninn-oramśam bhujicciṭām
śiṣṭam anyarkkāyi nalkām

Let us see ourselves as one with society. When we earn wealth, let us take only what we need and give away the rest in charity.

33
jīvippatin etra vēṇam – atra
mātramē svīkarikkāvū
'kūṭutal nēṭuvōr cōrar' enn-ōtumī
nāṭinde samskāram ōrkkū

Let us take only what we need to live. This is the tradition of this land. Those who hoard wealth only for themselves are thieves.

34
onnum koṭukkāte ellām – svantam
ākkuvōr pāpaniṣṭhanmār
onnum eṭukkāte ellām koṭukkuvōr
santatam tyāga-niṣṭhanmār

Selfish people keep everything for themselves and never give or share. We are established in renunciation if we give away everything except what we need.

35
lābham matikkunnu nammaḷ – karma
mūlyam maṙakkunnu nammaḷ

bhautika-lābhaṅgaḷ āgrahicc-unnata
daivika-dautyam mar̊akkum

Counting only worldly profits, we forget the value of good actions. Chasing worldly gains, we forget our divine mission.

36
āśaykku nāśam illētum – onnu
māyumbōḷ mar̊r̊onnu pontum
āzhattira pōle pinneyum pinneyum
antam illāt-āśa pontum

Desires never end. When one vanishes, another replaces it. Desires arise like mighty waves, endlessly, again and again.

37
koccu kocc-ōḷaṅgaḷ tiṅgi – cīrtta
kūr̊r̊an-tiramāla pōle
cer̊r̊u cer̊r̊-āgraham varddhiccu varddhiccu
ter̊r̊ennu mukkunnu tōṇi

Just as small waves merge and form a huge wave, small desires grow until they sink the boat of our life.

38
vṛkṣa-latādikaḷ-āyum – pinne
pakṣi-mṛgādikaḷ-āyum
etrayō janmam vṛthāvilāy, martyata
etrayum durllabham ōrkkū

Earlier, as trees and vines, then later, as birds and animals, we have taken so many births. Let us remember that a human birth is a precious gift.

39

illanya janmam ninaccāl – martya
janmattinum mēle onnum
ennittum ārum śarīra-dāsyattil ninn-
unnidrar ākāttat-entē

No birth is higher than a human birth. Then, why does no one break free of identification with the body, and attain the ultimate goal of life?

40

nēronnatār-ōtiyālum – dōṣa
hīnar ellām ādarikkum
kēvalam bālanāṇ-ōtiyat-eṅkilum
svīkāryam ā satya-vākyam

Everyone recognizes the Truth, no matter who proclaims it. The Truth remains the Truth even if uttered by a child.

41

kāmavum krōdhavum nīkki – dōṣa
hīnarāy varttikka makkaḷ
ellā vipattinum hētuvum mūlavum
kāmavum krōdhavum mātram

Children, give up desire and anger and lead pure lives. The cause and root of all danger is desire and anger.

42

satyam kṣama arjjavam snēham – cittam
ārddavam ārjjikka makkaḷ
āśā-vināśam varāte varillātma
kaivalyam ennōrkka makkaḷ

Children, be straight forward in your actions. Soften your hearts with truth, patience, and love. Know that, without destroying desire, your soul will never be pure.

43

ēkāgra-cittar-āyīṭū – makkaḷ
ēkātma-niṣṭhar-āyīṭū
ātmīyam ākum anubhavam tanmanō-
nāśattil āṇ-enn-aṙiyū

Children, contemplate on the Self with one-pointed focus. Know that spiritual experiences come when your mind is still and one-pointed.

44

duḥkhaṅgaḷ sūkṣmam ninaccāl – dṛḍham
mujjanma-karma-anuniṣṭham
prajñā-balam koṇḍu duḥkham nivarttikka
saccidānandam nukarām

Let us see all sorrow as karma from previous births. When knowledge of the Truth ends our sorrow, we will enjoy truth, consciousness and bliss forever.

45

ajñāna-mānasarkk-uḷḷam – prēma
bhaktiyāl śuddhī-karikkām

īśvarōdbhāsitam ennu kaṇḍ-okkeyum
saprēmam ādariccīṭām

Love and devotion will cleanse our ignorant mind. We will come to see that all of creation is full of God's radiance, and offer our worship with true love.

46

nanmakaḷ kaṇḍāl namikkām – svanta
tinmakaḷ dūrī-karikkām
nalla vākk-ōtām, prasāda-buddhyā svayam
sankīrttanam pōle vāzhām

Let us bow down before goodness and relinquish our bad habits. Let us speak good words, see everything as a gift from the divine, and live our life as a sweet melody.

47

mānava-nanma kāmkṣikkū – atil
ātmīyataykk-ūnnal ēkū
mānava-rāśikku vēṇḍi samarppiccu
jīvitam mūlyavatt-ākkū

Let us long for the betterment of humankind, and emphasize the spiritual path. Let us fulfill our life by offering it for the good of the world.

48

kāzhcakaḷ kāṇunna kaṇṇum – satya
darśanam tēṭunna kaṇṇum
raṇḍum onnall-orāḷ andhan āṇeṅkilum
satyam nidarśikkum uḷḷil

Our physical eyes see the external world and our inner eye searches for the Truth. The two are not the same. A blind person can realize the inner Truth.

49

sanmanō-bhāvam uṇartti - lōka
nanma tan nērkkāzhca nēṭām
uḷkkaṇ teḷicc-atil uṇma kaṇḍ-ettiṭām
nanmayāṇ-ā mārga-dṛṣṭi

When goodness awakens within, we can see the goodness of the world. Let us purify our mind, and seek the Truth within. Our goodness is our guiding light.

50

svarṇṇattil ābharaṇaṅgaḷ – onnu
māṙi vēr-onnu vannīṭām
māṙi vannīṭunnōr-ābharaṇaṅgaḷkku
sākṣiyāy varttippu svarṇṇam

Gold remains the substratum of the different ornaments made from it. The ornament may change, but the gold is always the same. Gold is the constant that witnesses all the changes.

51

dēhaṅgaḷ vannu pōyālum – ātma
sākṣikku māṫṫam illētum
bōdhapūrvam svayam sākṣi-bhāvattōṭe
ācarikkām-lōka dharmam

We may take many births, but the witness Self remains changeless. Acting with awareness and witnessing the mind, let us perform our *dharma* in the world.

52

ennile ñān enna tattvam - tanne
anyanil taṅgunna ñānum
ennōṭ-enikkuḷḷa snēhādaram vēṇam
anyanōṭ-ennatum nyāyam

The sense of 'I' exists in everyone. Justice is giving the same love and respect to others that we give to ourselves.

53

veṇṇayum neyyum abhēdam - maññu
khaṇḍavum nīrum abhēdam
sākāram ennum nirākāram ennum vi-
bhāgī-karikkēṇḍa satyam

Butter and *ghee* are not different from each other; neither are snow and water. Truth is one indivisible whole, with or without name and form.

54

nānātvamāy kāṇmat-ellām - veṙum
nāmavum rūpavum mātram
sattāvadhānamām buddhi-sthiratayāl
satya-anubhūti nukarām

Multiplicity is only in names and forms. With a steady and focused intellect, we can revel in the experience of Truth.

55

jīviccu pōkān orāḷkkum - matam
vēṇam ennilla; ninaccāl

martyan-illē matam-illa, matāśayam
satya-dīkṣā-balam ēkum

We don't need religion to live. Religion is a system of faith developed by man. The purpose of religion is to strengthen our everlasting quest for Truth.

56
jñānam uṇḍ-ennu vannālum – atin
prāyōgikataykku vēṇḍi
abhyāsa-siddhi kayyāḷaṇam, jñānatte
karmamāy vinyasikkēṇam

We may have knowledge, but, to apply it, we must practice and train our mind. Knowledge must be expressed through our actions.

57
mūlyaṅgaḷ śōṣiccu pōyāl – jana
jīvitam kīzhmēl maṙiyum
āsurōnmādam tezhikkum manassoru
matta-mātangamāy māṙum

If values are weak, human life has no foundation. A mind, acting under evil impulses, becomes a force of destruction.

58
veṇam matātīta-lakṣyam – atil
vēṇam atīva prayatnam
ellām atinnāy samarppaṇam ceyyaṇam
ellām atāy māṙiṭēṇam!

We must go beyond religion and tirelessly seek the spiritual Truth. Let us dedicate our life to this quest for the ultimate Truth.

ōmkāra divya porūḷe 59 (Malayalam)

Disclaimer: The translations of certain verses are not literal; they aim at bringing out the essential meaning from the Malayalam verses in a way that is easily understandable.

ōmkāra divya porūḷe varū
ōmana-makkaḷē vēgam
ōmanayāy vaḷarnn-āmayaṅgaḷ nīkki
ōmkāra-vastuvāy tīrū

Come quickly darling children, you who are the divine essence of Om. Remove all sorrows, grow dear and adorable, and merge with the Absolute.

1
eṅgoṭṭu ñān gamiccālum – atu
ninnil ettānuḷḷa mārgam
entu ñān ceykilum ellām aviṭutte
tṛppāda-pūja ākēṇam

"Whichever path I take, may that path lead me to you. Let all that I do be a worship of your holy feet."

2
ninnilēkk-ettum vazhiyil – nī en
munnil viḷakkāyiṭēṇam
'endeyum, ñānum' enn-illātt-or-ēkātma

cintaykku tāṅgāyiṭēṇam

"Be a lamp lighting my path unto you. Strengthen my thought that, in Oneness, there is no 'I and mine.'"

3

prārtthana ī vidham āyāl – antar
ātmāv-udāttamāy tīrum
bhavyamām ī vidha bhāvanayāl sarvam
avidhamāy bhaviccīṭum

These ardent prayers make our inner self pure and noble. Such auspicious thoughts manifest as Truth in our life.

4

kallu kaṇḍīṭilum śilpi – śilpa
bhangi kaṇḍīṭunna pōle
ātmāvabōdham-uḷḷāḷukaḷ ārilum
ātma-caitanyamē kāṇū

The sculptor sees only the beautiful idol in the stone. Those who are established in the Self see only Supreme Consciousness.

5

tyāgam āṇ-amma tan śakti – divya
snēham āṇ-amma tan śuddhi
vātsalya-dugdham nukaruvin makkaḷē
vāykkill-aham dēhabuddhi

Amma's renunciation is her power. Amma's love is her purity. Children, drink the milk of Amma's love and break free of the delusion that 'I am only the body and the mind.'

6

vēdaṅgaḷ nālum kaṭaññāl – kiṭṭum
tūvamṛt-ākunnu snēham
jāti-mata-atītam ākum ā lōkattu
vāzhān kotikkuvin makkaḷ

By churning the four *Vedas*, we get the pure nectar of Love. Children, yearn to live in a world that has risen above the divisions of religion and caste.

7

janmam nirartthakam alla – daivam
tanna varadānam atre
svantam sukhattinum sambattinum vēṇḍi
janmam vṛthāvil ākkollē

Life is not meaningless; it is the gift of God. Let us not waste our life chasing selfish pleasures and wealth.

8

lōka-hitaiṣikaḷ ākū – makkaḷ
jīvitam āghōṣam ākkū
pāti vazhiyil taḷarnnu vīṇīṭāte
karmam parārttham ākkīṭū

Children, make your life a celebration by working for the welfare of world. To avoid being discouraged and falling down, let your actions be for a higher principle.

9

karmaṅgaḷ martyarkk-adhīnam – pāpa
puṇyaṅgaḷ karmāśritaṅgaḷ

māyaykk-adhīnam prapañcam, mahēśvara
prēmam vimōcanōpāyam

Our actions are in our control. Our actions produce merit and sin. Pure love for God liberates us from the *maya* that controls the world.

10
lōkam camaccat-ārennum – pinne
vēdam raciccat-ārennum
cinticcu vādiccu kālam kaḷayēṇḍa
raṇḍilum nanma kaṇḍettām

Who made the world? Who wrote the *Veda*? Why waste time thinking and arguing about such questions. Rather, let us find the good in both.

11
śāstram paṭhiccatin garvil – 'aham
brahmāsmi' ennorāḷ connāl
janmam vinaṣṭam āṇ-ātmaikya-bōdhamaṫṫ-
ennum cidātmāv-uṙaṅgum

If we are ignorant of the Oneness of life, yet flaunt our scriptural learning and proclaim 'I am Brahman,' we will never realize the divine energy within.

12
kattum viḷakkinde citram – kōṙi
bhittiyil tūkkiyāl pōrā
veṭṭam labhikkuvān rātri-kālaṅgaḷil
kattum viḷakk-onnu vēṇam

It is not enough if a picture of a lamp hangs on the wall. To get light when darkness falls, we must light a lamp.

13

śāstra-naipuṇyatte makkaḷ – svayam
prāyōgikam ākkiṭēṇam
abhyāsa-siddhi uṇḍākaṇam, jñānatte
karmamāy vinyasikkēṇam

Children, apply your scriptural knowledge in daily life. Your austerities lead you to perfection, and your actions will reveal your knowledge.

14

vaidyan kuṙicca kuṙippāl – vyādhi
māṙillat-ārum ōrkkēṇam
aṅgāṭiyil pōyi vāṅgaṇam, pinnatu
pākattil sēviccitēṇam

A doctor's prescription alone does not cure illness. We must buy the prescribed medicine and take it as per the instructions.

15

śāstrabōdham koṇḍu mātram – vidvān
āyennu cinticciṭēṇḍa
ācaraṇattinn-utakāykil ārilum
bhāramāy tīrum atōrkkū

Scriptural knowledge alone does not make us a Knower. Knowledge becomes a burden if it doesn't shine through our actions.

16

naṭṭucca nērattu pōlum – veṭṭam

kiṭṭāt-alayunnit-uḷḷam
bāhya-sūryan namukk-uḷḷam teḷikkilla
ātmasūryan sarva-sākṣi

Our mind remains dark even under the midday sun. Only the effulgent sun of the Self, the eternal witness, can illumine our mind.

17
daivikam āyāl etirkkum – martya
vaibhavam vāzhtti stutikkum
mānuṣa-śakti tan ātma-prabhāvatte
āḷdaivam ennum śaṭhikkum

We refute divinity and praise humanity. But when the infinite eternal Self manifests through a human being, we reject the truth.

18
kayyāl kanal-kaṭṭa toṭṭāl – toṭṭa
kaiviral poḷḷi kuṭirum
kayyāl karikkaṭṭa toṭṭālum ōrkkaṇam
kayyil kari puraṇḍīṭum

When we touch an ember, our burnt finger swells. When we touch charcoal, our finger gets blackened.

19
śatruta kāṭṭi ennālum – nammaḷ
mitrata kāṭṭi ennālum
duṣṭarōṭ-ottuḷḷa samsargam eppozhum
kaṣṭata mātram āṇārkkum

Likewise, whether we show enmity or friendliness, bad company invariably brings us sorrow.

20

tīkkaṭṭa āzhiyil iṭṭāl – āzhi
cūṭākukill-atu pōle
ātmāv-uṇarnnōre ārkkum prakōpitar
ākkān kazhiyilla, tellum

If we throw a cinder into the sea, the sea does not heat up. Likewise, the one in whom the Self has awakened is unprovoked under all conditions.

21

nāṭṭil manuṣyar apūrvam – innu
kāṭṭil mṛgaṅgaḷ apūrvam
āvāsa-sthānaṅgaḷ anyōnyam ī vidham
kaimāṟiyō ennu tōnnum

Our minds have lost their nobility and taken on the characteristics of wild animals. It is as if true human beings are scarce in the cities, and animal minds have taken over.

22

peṫṫa-mātāvine pōlum – innu
kuppayil taḷḷunnu makkaḷ
peṫṫu vaḷartti paṭhippiccu eṅkilum
vṛddha-sadanattil antyam

Today, the human mind has degenerated so much that we reject even our own parents once they have outlived their strength and wealth. They live out their lives, sorrowful and neglected, in old-age homes.

23

tan ceyti kāṇunna makkaḷ – nāḷe
tannōṭum avidham ceyyum
vārddhakyam innatte śāpam, manuṣyatvam
ētō śmaśāna-kuzhiyil

Let us remember that our children take after us. They will also neglect us when we are old. Today old-age has become a curse for mankind. No consideration is shown to the old ones.

24

āgraha-tyāgam onnatre – ātma
saukhyattin ennum nidānam
āgraham muṫṫi atyāgraham varddhikkil
āyur-ārōgyam naśikkum

Freedom from desire is the only way to eternal bliss. When desire and greed grow, they destroy health and long life.

25

daivam niyōgicc-ayaccu – namme
daivika-āviṣkāra-dautyam
kayyāl eṭukkunna karmavum cintayum
ammahā-lakṣyattil ūnnām

God has sent us to this world for the divine purpose of Self-realization. All our deeds and thoughts should lead us towards that goal.

26

martya-janmam tannu daivam – lōka
dautyattin āḷ-ākki namme

vākkil kṛtārtthata, nōkkil dayārdrata
vēṇam enn-orkkuvin makkaḷ

God has given you a human birth and made you his messengers. So, children, cultivate gratitude in your words and compassion in your eyes.

27
śaiśava-nairmalyam ārnnāl – hṛttin
ēṙe tiḷakkam ārnnīṭum
arkkēndu-tāraka-vṛndamatin munnil
minnā-minuṅgukaḷ pōle

If our heart is as innocent as a child, we will shine so bright that the sun, moon and stars will look like fireflies.

28
īśvaran tān orāḷ mātram – namukk
āśrayam enn-ōrttiṭāvū
ārilum mēvunnat-ā mahāśakti
onnāṇ-anyam allenn-aṙiyū

God and God alone is our protector and refuge. The great power that dwells within everyone is our own true Self.

29
sankīrttanattinnu nāvum, tannu
satkatha kēḷkkuvān kātum
saundaryam kāṇuvān kaṇṇ-ēki īśvaran
satkarma-pūjaykku kayyum

Our tongue is for singing His praises. Our ears are for hearing His glories. Our eyes are for seeing the beauty of His creation. And He has given us hands to do good deeds in the world.

30

anyūna-bhakti uṇḍāyāl – pinne
anyata kāṇilla eṅgum
daivika-cētana āviṣkarikkukil
daivikamāy kāṇum ellām

When pure devotion arises, we do not see anything as separate from us. When we become established in supreme Consciousness, we see everything as divine.

31

vāg-atīta-poruḷ ākum – ātma
cetana ākunnit-ārum
āviṣkarikkaṇam ā-mahāsatyatte
jīvita-dautyam atallo

Supreme Consciousness is our essential nature and transcends all description. The goal of our life is to realize this great Truth.

32

dēhatte ñān ennu kaṇḍāl – ātma
bōdhattil allatu pōle
bōdhatte ñān enn-uṇarnnāl anātmāvil
tōnnum aham-buddhi māyum

When we identify with our body, we remain estranged from our true Self. When we awaken to the knowledge that we are pure Consciousness, the delusion that 'I am the body' disappears.

33

karmattāl bandhicciṭunnu - jantu
jālam ennār-ōrttiṭunnu
jñānattāl ārum vimōcitar ākunnu
karma-nāśam tanne mōkṣam

All beings in this world are bound by the fruits of their actions. Knowledge liberates us from such bondage.

34

karmaṅgaḷ daivikam āyāl – ellā
bandhavum tānē azhiyum
kartṛtva-bhāvam upēkṣikkukil karmam
okkeyum daivikam ākum

When we discard our sense of doership, all our actions become holy. When our actions become divine, all our bondage is loosened.

35

mānābimānam veṭiññum – dhana
lōbhikaḷ ākunnu martyan
jīvitam koṇḍu nām nēṭēṇḍat-entenna
pāṭhavum pāṭē maṙannu

We have become so greedy that we have discarded our self-esteem and self-respect. We have also forgotten the goal that is the purpose of this life.

36

āśakaḷ klēśatte ēkum – sukham
āgraha-tyāgattil atre

āśaye tārāṭṭi pāl ūṭṭiyāl atu
pāmbin-svabhāvam pularttum

Desire breeds sorrow. Happiness comes when we renounce desire. When we indulge our desires, they come back, like a snake, to bite us.

37
ātmārttham allātta karmam – veṙum
yāntrikam ennōrttiṭēṇam
prēmātmakam alla karmam ennākilō
svāntavum yāntrikam ākum

Insincere actions become mechanical. Actions devoid of love are like those performed by a robot.

38
dharma-anubandham alleṅkil – ellā
karmavum tānē pizhaykkum
ātma-svātantryam manuṣya-avakāśam āṇ-
ā varam pāzh-ākkiṭollē

All actions that are heedless of *dharma* fail of themselves. Eternal freedom is our right. Don't squander that precious boon!

39
āgrahiccīṭunnu saukhyam – pakṣē
ācariccīṭilla – dharmam
abhyunnatiyatum niḥśrēyass-ennatum
dharma-āśrayattilūṭ-atre

We want happiness, but we fail to observe *dharma*. Only through *dharma* can we become prosperous and free.

40
nirvighnam ācariccīṭām – ātma
nirvṛti-dāyaka-yajñam
āgraha-tyāgam enn-ā mahā-yajñattil
vēdi ākkām antaraṅgam

Sacrifice gives fulfillment in life. Let us make our mind the sacrificial altar for the final renunciation of all desire.

41
dēvatvam ennatu pōlum – ātma
lābhatte ōrttāl nissāram
pāpavum puṇyavum karma-āśrayam eṅkil
jñāna-āśrayam āṇu mōkṣam

Compared to Self-realization, even heaven is trivial. Just as our actions determine merit and sin, knowledge brings liberation.

42
tāpa-trayattinnu hētu – svārttha
lābha-pratīkṣa onnatrē
āśā nirāsattāl ātmāv-uṇarumbōl
klēśattin-ill-āśrayatvam

Selfish desire is the source of all grief. Discard desire and all grief dries up. The Self awakens when we renounce desire. Then, there is no more sorrow.

43
ālasyam ēlāte mēnmēl – ātma
sādhana ācariccīṭām

āgama-tēnkuzhamb-ātanka-nāśattin
ādarāl āsvadiccīṭām

Let us remain steadfast and enthusiastic in our spiritual practices. Let us celebrate the end of sorrow by imbibing the message of the sacred scriptures.

44
āsaktiyāl ācariccāl – svayam
pāpa-bhukk-ākunnu nammaḷ
ātmā-avabōdhattāl ātmārtthamāy ceyyum
satkarmam ākunnu yōgam

We have to suffer the consequences of greedy action performed with desire. When our action is established in awareness of the Self, our action becomes auspicious union with the divine.

45
uḷḷ-uṇarnn-uṇma darśikkām – uḷḷil
veṇmayāl nanma darśikkām
anyarall-ārum enn-ēkātma-bōdhattil
uḷḷ-uṇarnn-ādariccīṭām

Let us awaken and witness the true Self. In the light of the Self, let us witness the goodness within. With knowledge, 'otherness' disappears, and Oneness, love and respect flow towards one and all.

46
vāṇī-guṇam vēṇam ārkkum – hīna
vākk-ōtiṭāyka nām ārum
mitram ākkunnatum śatru ākkunnatum
vākkinde svādum kavarppum

Let us speak good words that do not hurt others. The sweetness or bitterness of our speech makes a friend or an enemy.

47

arttham grahiyātt-avarkkum – vākkil
hṛdyata tōnnām taniye
bhāṣā-paricayam vēṇam ennilla, nal
śābda-bōdham hṛttil ūṙum

Even if they can't grasp the meaning in our words, they feel their sweetness. Even without knowing the language, their hearts respond to our good will.

48

vāgvaibhavam mātramāyāl – pōra
vācālata atum pōrā
vāgdēvata tann-anugraham uṇḍeṅkil
vākkinde svād-onnu vēṙe

It is not enough to have an excellent vocabulary, or even to speak brilliant words. If the Goddess of speech is gracious towards us, our words will spread a lingering sweetness.

49

vākkum vicāravum tammil – nalla
pārasparyam pularttēṇam
cintayum vākkum parasparam yōjiccu
karmaṅgaḷ ācarikkēṇam

Let our words be true to our thoughts. And let our thoughts and words reflect in our actions.

50

kiṭṭunnatil tṛpti pōra – svanta
kartavyam ōrttīṭukilla
iṅgoṭṭu vēṇam enn-allāte yātonnum
aṅgoṭṭu nalkīṭukilla

Forever discontent, forever forgetting our duty, we always want to receive and never think of giving.

51

ōrōnnum anyūnam atrē – sarvam
ōtavum prōtavum pōle
vaividdhyam eṅkilum sṛṣṭi-vidhānaṅgaḷ
ētonnum ēkātma-nūlil

Everything in creation is mutually dependent, like the warp and woof of the woven cloth. Though creation appears diverse, the one Self is the thread that connects all.

52

nanmakaḷ kaṇḍ-eṭuttīṭū – makkaḷ
tinmakaḷ santyajiccīṭu
kanmaṣa-hīnarāy tīrū, parasparam
sanmanō-bhāvam pularttū

Children, find the good within yourselves and discard your negative tendencies. Rid your mind of all impurity and nurture a heart that is friendly to all.

53

manda-hāsānvitar ākū – sarva
sandēha-hīnarāy tīrū

samphulla-mānasar ākuvin, santatam
santōṣa-nirbharar ākū

Let us always smile and be rid of doubt. Let our hearts blossom fully and let happiness fill us always.

54
saumya-vākkonn-uriyāṭām – nar̄um
puñciri-tēn kaṇam tūkām
pāzh-allatin phalam nīr̄um manassukaḷkk-
ēt̄t̄am samāśvāsam-ākum

Let us speak gentle words and let our love blossom in our smile. May that love give solace and comfort to the burning hearts of the distressed.

55
ēkān dhanam kayyil illēl – snēham
ākum dhanam namukk-ēkām
vīzhān tuṭaṅguvōrkk-ēkān dhanam vēṇḍa
vīzhāte kaikaḷāl tāṅgām

Even if we have no money to help someone, we can give them the wealth of our affection. Helping hands that lift up the fallen are often more needed than the gift of money.

56
mēgha-taṇal enna pōle – kṣaṇam
māññu pōm bhōga-sukhatte
sthāyi ennōrttatil mōhitar-ākukil
māzhki taḷarnnu pōm ārum

Sense pleasures pass like the shadow of a cloud. Thinking them permanent, the deluded one seeks fulfillment in them and soon becomes exhausted.

57

jātam ākumbōzhē nammaḷ – daiva-
nēril samarppitar allō
śaiśavam māṙiyāl māyāpaṭam mūṭi
pāṭē maṙayunnu satyam

At the moment of our birth, we are very close to the divine. But as we grow up, *maya* veils the Truth entirely.

58

vīṇḍ-eṭuttīṭuvin makkaḷ – hṛttil
śaiśava-sāraḷya-śuddhi
sākṣāt-karikkaṇam ōrō manuṣyanum
śaiśava-ramya-svabhāvam

Children, reclaim the pure innocence of your childhood. We should all have the simple and loving nature of a child.

59

cāndra-pol imayil nīḷe – mulla
pūvalli ennapōl-ennum
prēmōllasat-kānti pūrattāl cētassum
tānē kuḷirtt-āṭiṭaṭṭe

Like jasmine flowers spreading their fragrance on a moonlit night, let our heart delight in the cool brilliance of love's light.

ōmkāra divya porūḷe 60 (Malayalam)

Disclaimer: The translations of certain verses are not literal; they aim at bringing out the essential meaning from the Malayalam verses in a way that is easily understandable.

ōmkāra divya porūḷe varū
ōmana-makkaḷē vēgam
ōmanayāy vaḷarnn-āmayaṅgaḷ nīkki
ōmkāra-vastuvāy tīrū

Come quickly darling children, you who are the divine essence of Om. Remove all sorrows, grow dear and adorable, and merge with the Absolute.

1
cōṭukaḷ nīṭṭi caviṭṭām – neṭum
pātayil kāzhca kāṇāte
jīvitam pūrva-pitākkaḷ teḷiccor-
appātayil bhavyam nayikkām

Children, let us stride along the path of life without getting distracted by roadside scenes. Let us humbly tread the bright path cleared by our ancestors.

2
veḷḷattil vaḷḷam kiṭannāl – vēṇḍa
tellum bhayam vēṇḍa – pakṣē
vaḷḷattil veḷḷam kaṭakkāte nōkkaṇam
allēl anartthamāy tīrum

When the boat of our life floats in the waters of the world, we have nothing to worry about. To avoid danger, we should be careful that the waters of the world do not leak in.

3

lōka-anuvarttikaḷ ākām – svārttha
lōbha-anuśīlar ākāte
lōkatte neññ-ēṫṫum bhōgattil āsakti
lōpikkum āyussum ōrkkū

Let us be in the world without letting its selfishness and greed enter into us. Let us remember that over-indulgence in worldly pleasures shortens and wastes our life.

4

paṫṫezhāt-i prapañcattil – makkaḷ
śraddha-avadhānam vasikkū
karmattil naiṣkarmyam kāṇmavarkk-eppozhum
hṛttil atyānandam atre

Children, with poise and alertness, live in the world without attachment. When you act without a sense of doership, your heart will remain blissfully happy.

5

kēḷkkān paṭhikkuvin makkaḷ – ellām
keḷviyil ninnē paṭhikkū
ādeśavum nall-upadēśavum mātram
āyāl svayam paṭhikkilla

Children, learn to listen. Only through listening can you learn. If you only instruct and advise, you will never learn anything.

6

anyarkku kāt-ōrttiṭāte – ellām
anyarōṭ-ōtiyāl pōra
āvaśyam eṅkil nalla-ādēśam iṅgōṭṭum
ādānavum ceytiṭēṇam

Talking to others without listening to them is not enough. We must learn to hear their good words also.

7

pūrita-pānayil vīṇḍum – kṣīra
dhāra kōrīṭunna pōle
kēḷkkān iṭam koṭāt-ōtunn-avarkk-onnum
ārjjippatinn-āvukilla

If we talk without listening, we learn nothing. It is like pouring milk into an already full vessel.

8

ellām kṣamayōṭe kēḷkkām – kēṭṭāt-
ellām nirūpicc-uṙaykkām
saprēmam anyōnyam āśaya-sallāpam
uḷḷatte utphullam ākkum

Let us listen patiently, and think and contemplate on what we hear. Mutual and loving exchange of ideas broadens our mind.

9

vēdam aṙiññavar atre – nēril
lōkam aṙiññavar ākū
ōti paṭhippikkum vēda-vēdāntam all-

āru ñāṇ enn-ātma-bōdham

Those who truly know the *Vedas* have realized the nature of the world. The *Vedas* and *Vedanta* can only teach us the way. The awareness of 'who am I' is the realization of the Self.

10
lōkam namikkunnu namme – ātma
lōkam teḷiccatin mūlam
sarva-carācara-samrakṣaṇam enna
bhavya-samskārattin mūlam

The world bows before this land for revealing the Self and for our noble tradition of protecting all beings, moving and unmoving.

11
jñāna-dānattin caritram – nammaḷ
āracicc-ādara-pūrvam
mānava-lōkattin ākeyum śāśvata
śāntidamāya caritram

With respect and humility, let us give the gift of the Knowledge that offers eternal peace to the whole world.

12
śvāsa-niśvāsatte pōlum – nammaḷ
ātmīyata ākki māṫṫi
kaṇḍatum kēṭṭatum koṇḍalla, toṭṭ-aṙiññ-
antar-ātmāvil ramiccu

Our very breath, every inhalation and exhalation, can be a path to Self-awareness. The bliss of the Self is a direct experience, not something merely to hear or read about.

13

jñānavum jñāniyum tammil – bhēdam
kāṇmat-ajñānam enn-ōti
jñānavum ñānum abhēdamāy kāṇunna
kāzhcaye darśanam ennum

Ignorance is the thought that the knower and knowledge are different from each other. The Truth is to see that 'I', the knower, am the very essence of knowledge.

14

uḷḷatent-āṇenn-aṙiyān – makkaḷ
uḷḷatte nannāy aṙiyū
uḷḷatonnē onnu, tān atāṇ-ennu tān
uḷḷāl aṙiññāl aṙiññu

Children, to know the eternal Truth, know well your inner world. Existence is One and you are That. When you know this Truth, Knowledge dawns.

15

jīvitam sandēśam ākkum puṇya
pūruṣanmār, samūhattil
ēṫṫam mahattāya mātṛka sṛṣṭiccu
lōka-vyavasthiti māṫṫum

Holy men make their lives their message. Their noble actions inspire positive transformation in the world.

16

mannin vyavasthiti ellām – pāṭē
onnāyi māṫṫāvatalla

tāḷa-kramam viṭum mānava-jīvitam
chinni teṙiccu takarum

We should take care not to disturb the harmonious balance that sustains the earth. Doing so disrupts the rhythm of nature and destroys the future of mankind.

17
rōgattin auṣadham pōle – kṛtyam
āyōr anupātam vēṇam
onnāyi sēvikkil annōṭe rōgavum
rōgiyum onniccu tīrum

Like taking medicine, progress happens in measured doses. If a patient takes all the medicine at once, both the disease and the patient end together.

18
māṫṫaṅgaḷ nannu tann-ennāl – onnāy
māṫṫi maṙikkarut-onnum
mellennu mellennu māṫṫam varuttuvān
innum mahātmākkaḷ ennum

Change is good, indeed, but sudden change upends the world. The great ones have always transformed the world in a gradual way.

19
bandham uṇḍ-ellāṫṫinōṭum – pakṣē
bandhitam all-onninōṭum
snēhikkum ennāl kaṭappāṭu kāṇilla
lōka-hitaiṣikaḷkk-ētum

They bond with all through their love, yet are not attached to anyone. Their love is devoid of expectation.

20

cāturyam-ōlunna śilpam – śilpi
kāṇunnu vṛkṣattil ādyam
cēlil teḷiyicc-eṭukkumbōḷ mātramē
kāṇmavarkk-āsvādyam ākū

A sculptor sees the beautiful idol within the tree. Only when it is carved and polished can the onlooker appreciate its beauty.

21

vigraham kalliluṇḍennāl – kallu
kāṇumbōḷ kāṇīllat-ārum
kallalla kāṇmatu śilpi atil cāru
vigraham darśicciṭunnu

Although the idol is concealed within the stone, people see only the stone. The sculptor sees the stone, but he also beholds the idol within it.

22

kāṇum prapañcattil ētum –daiva
sānniddhyam ōrilla ārum
kāṇmū mahātmākkaḷ ētilum daivika
cāruta – sāmōdam eṅgum

Mahatmas blissfully behold divine beauty everywhere; but, most people don't see God anywhere in the world.

23
sattukkaḷ ācariccīṭum – karmam
okkeyum vāsanā-muktam
lōkōpakāram, atin phala-vyāptikku
sīmayill-ākāśa-sāmyam

The actions of the great ones are pure. They act only for the good of the world. The impact of their actions is limitless like the sky.

24
ātmīya-śakti uṇartti – ādyam
yōgasthiti kaivarikkū
ātma-yāthārtthyam aṙiññu nivēdikka
sāmūhya-nanmaykku nammaḷ

Awakening our spiritual power, let us attain the state of yoga (union with Supreme). Let us know the Truth of the Self, and dedicate our life for the good of society.

25
āśrayamaṫṫ-avarkkāyi – tellor-
āśvāsam ēkāte nammaḷ
īśvara-niścayam enn-ōrtt-ozhiyukil
āśrayamaṫṫu pōm tānum

If we feel that the suffering of others is the will of God, and fail to offer them help, no one will help us in our time of need.

26
daivahitam entum ākām – svanta
kartavyam entenn-aṙiyū

īśvara-niścayam ennōrttu duḥkhitarkk-
āśvāsa-hastaṅgaḷ nīṭṭū

Let us accept the will of God and know well what our duties and responsibilities are. Our duty is to help those in distress, considering that also to be the will of God.

27

karma-phalam ennuṙaccu – anya
duḥkhattil ill-aliveṅkil
niścayam, tānum ā duṣkarma-dōṣattin
duṣphala-bhukkāyi māṙum

If we do not sympathize with another's sorrow, but see it as the deserved fruit of their actions, we will certainly experience the bitter fruits of our indifference.

28

ceytat-ōrttādhi vēṇḍārkkum – bhāvi
kāryam-ōrtt-utkaṇṭha vēṇḍā
varttamānam tannil nikṣiptam ākayāl
entum tirutti kuṙikkām

Let us not worry about the past or the future. Our actions in the present moment can cancel the bad effects of past actions and build a brighter future.

29

āśicc-aśikkarut-ārum –allēl
āśa aśicciṭum namme
āśaye vennavarkk-ātma-lābham varum
āśa vellum namme allēl

Let us not befriend desire because desire will finally devour us. When we conquer desire, we gain the Self. Otherwise, desire conquers us.

30
koḷḷal koṭukkal illāykil – tān tān
tannil taniye curuṅgum
anyathā bōdhavum nairāśyavum svārttha
cinta tan santānar atrē

If we don't give and receive, we shrivel within ourselves. Selfish thoughts breed estrangement and discontent.

31
cāritārtthyam tōnniṭēṇam – karmam
ācariccīṭuvōrkk-uḷḷil
nēṭṭam samūhattin-ākukil ātmāvil
cāritārtthyam varum ārkkum

Let us feel fulfilled in our actions. When our actions benefit society, we will feel joyful and content.

32
kātal illāte ezhikkum – perum
pādapam ennapōl, makkaḷ
samskāra-hīnamām śuṣka-vyaktitvaṅgaḷ
ākarut-unnidrar ākū

Children, don't be like a huge tree with a hollow trunk, parched and devoid of the noble culture that is your essential nature. Awaken to the higher Truth!

33
bālyattil ninnum vaḷarnnu - nēre
vārddhakyam pūkunnu martyan
kaṣṭam! yuvatvam nirarttham ākkīṭunnu
svatvam tamaskaricc-ēvam

We go straight from childhood to old-age. Alas! Our youth is meaningless and our life wasted if we ignore our true Self.

34
tējassum ōjassum cōrnnu - karma
vīryavum śauryavum cōrnnu
nāṭin yuvata tan vaibhavam kāntikeṭṭ-
ā hanta! ālasyam ārnnu

Valor and vigor slip away, and we lose vitality and prowess. Alas! The youth of Bharat have lost their radiance and become indolent.

35
kaipiṭicc-amma nayikkām - jñāna
cakṣuss-unmīlitam ākkām
nirmāyam āreyum snēhicciṭumbozhum
nirmamar-āyi varttikkū

Mother will lead you, holding your hand. Open the eye of awareness. Love all sincerely but remain unattached.

36
snēham uḷḷēṭattu karmam - tellum
āyāsamāy varill-ārkkum
ceytennu tōnnāte ceyyunna karmattāl

nirllēpa-cittarāy tīrum

Where there is love, action is effortless. Actions performed without a sense of doership purify our heart.

37

svārtthamaṫṫ-ācariccīṭum – karmam
ātmaharṣam tiṅgi viṅgum
lōkōpakāramāy ācarikkum karmam
āyāsa-hīnamāy tīrum

Selfless action gives inner happiness. Action dedicated to the welfare of the world becomes easy and effortless.

38

ceyyēṇḍat-ennaṙiññāl – pinne
ceyyān amānticciṭolle
annannu ceyyēṇḍat-annannu ceyyāykil
pinnatu ceyyān prayāsam

Once we become aware of what needs to be done, let us not delay. If we keep aside today's work, it will be more difficult to finish it later.

39

karmatte naiṣkarmyam ākkām – ellām
ceykilum ceyyātirikkām
lābha-naṣṭam ninaykkāte nissvārtthamāy
ceyyumbōḷ naiṣkarmya-siddhi

Let us perform our actions without the sense of doership so that action simply flows through us. Selfless action done without thought of gain or loss is not binding. Such actions become perfect.

40

āreyum śikṣicciṭilla – daivam
ārilum rakṣakan mātram
duṣkarma-duṣphalam duḥkham enn-ōrkkaṇam
satkarma satphalam saukhyam

God never punishes anyone; God only protects. Sorrow is the negative outcome of our bad actions, and happiness is the positive outcome of our good actions.

41

ceytennu tōnnunna karmam – tanne
tannil nibandhicciṭunnu
ceyyāte ceyyunna karmattāl tān svayam
tanne svatantran ākkunnu

Action done with doership binds us to its fruits. Action done without sense of doership liberates us.

42

svanta-kāryam ninacc-andham – sadā
santapiccīṭarut-ārum
anya-kāryārtthamāy paryākulappeṭum
sadguṇavānmār aniśam

Let us not be depressed and blinded by selfishness. The great ones think day and night only of the welfare of others.

43

āśa vacc-ācariccīṭum – karmam
klēśa-sankīrṇṇamāy tīrum

āśayaṫṫ-ācariccīṭum svadharmattāl
klēśa-nāśam sambhavikkum

Action done from desire leads to misery and grief. When we do our duty without desire, misery and grief end.

44
dēha-naṣṭattil tapikkum – ārum
ātma-naṣṭam smarikkilla
āyussum dēhavum ātma-sākṣātkāra-
lābhōdyamattinnat-atre

We mourn the loss of our body, but we don't bother about the loss of the Self. Life and body are only tools for Self-realization.

45
janmāntaraṅgaḷilūṭe – martyan
karmāntaraṅgaḷilūṭe
mṛtyuve niṣkramicc-addhyātma-vidya tan
siddhiyāl ārjjippu mōkṣam

We have taken countless births and performed countless actions. Finally, let us put an end to death and be liberated through Self-knowledge.

46
ellām iruṇḍatāy tōnnām – namukk-
ellām nirartthamāy tōnnām
kaiyāl eṭuttatum ceyyān uṙaccatum
kai ettā-dūrattāy tōnnām

We may find everything to be dark and meaningless, and we may feel that our goal is beyond our reach.

47

nairāśya-grastar ākāte – makkaḷ
naivēdyam ākkuvin karmam
ellām saphalamāy tīrum, kṣamā-pūrvam
uḷḷam samarppiccu ceyyām

Children, never give in to despair. Make your actions an offering to the Divine. Success will be yours when you offer your heart and wait with patience.

48

cintakaḷ chidricciṭāte – dautyam
entennu vismarikkāte
vidvēṣa-buddhikk-adhīnarāy tīrāte
sargātmakam pravarttikkū

Let us act creatively, with total concentration. Let us not be distracted, but always remember our mission and never succumb to hate and anger.

49

dhyānōnnatam hṛttil ninnē – divya
snēha-sugandham parakkū
dhyēya-avadhānata vannāl varum jīva
kāruṇyam, ā mahān dhanyan

The fragrance of love spreads only from a deeply meditative mind. Compassion springs from within when we gain alertness. Then we become exalted and blessed.

50

mōha-mālinyam ozhiññāl – buddhi

sūryōpamaṃ tējassōlum
kāma-sankalpa-vivarjjita cētassāl
kāṇām cidātma-svarūpam

When impurities caused by desire leave us, our intellect gains the brilliance of the sun. In a mind devoid of desire, we behold pure consciousness as our own true Self.

51
kautukattāl alla ārkkum – bhakṣya
pēyaṅgaḷ āpēkṣyam ōrkkū
jīva-sandhāraṇa-kāraṇam enna pōl
dhyānavum jīvitāpēkṣyam

Food and drink are essential for life; they are not just for amusement. Meditation is also essential for life.

52
dēhapuṣṭikk-annam eṅkil – dhyānam
ātmōnnatikk-atē bhēdam
āyur-ārōgyavum ātma-vikāsavum
jīvitōtkarṣa-pradhānam

We need to eat good food for a healthy body; and we need to meditate for a healthy mind and for spiritual upliftment. A healthy body and an expansive mind are both essential for the fulfillment of life.

53
rāmāyaṇam katha pāṭām – pāṭi
rāmanōḷam dhīrar ākām
kṛṣṇa-gītāmṛtam āsvadicc-ārjjavam
kṛṣṇanōḷām hṛttil āḷām

Sing the story of Rama and become as brave as Rama. Enjoy the nectar of Krishna's Gita, and become as courageous and straightforward as Krishna.

54

sītā-padānaṅgaḷ pāṭām – pāṭi
sītayōḷam kṣama nēṭām
ādariccīṭēṇḍat-ādariccīṭumbōḷ
ātmānandābdhiyil nīntām

Sing the glory of Sita, and achieve her patience. When we admire what is worthy of admiration, we swim in the ocean of the blissful Self.

55

ātmāmśamāy kāṇumeṅkil – ārum
ātmārttha-snēham curattum
pāzhalla janmam parārttham ākkīṭuvōr
pārinde ātmārttha-mitram

True love springs forth when we see everyone as our own Self. The lives of those who serve others is never wasted. They are the true friends of the world.

56

snēhamuḷḷ-ēṭattu bhēdam – illa
bhēdam-uṇḍēl illa snēham
sūryan jvalikkunn-atin prakāśam sarva
bhūta-jālattinum tulyam

Where there is love, there is no division. Where there is division, there is no love. The sun shines equally on all that exists on earth.

57
vēdaniccīṭuvōrkkāyi – uḷḷam
vēdanikkātta vēdānti
ātmāvu tān itinokke atītan enn-
ōtum ā vākk-etra śuṣkam

How hollow are the words of the *vedantin* who proclaims he is the Self and beyond all suffering, then fails to feel the pain of others!

58
tēn enn-ezhuti ruciccāl – atin
mādhuryam ār-āsvadikkum?
jīvitam koṇḍu nām āviṣkarikkāykil
vēda-vēdāntavum vyarttham

If we write honey and lick the paper, do we taste the sweetness of honey? If our life fails to express the Self, *veda* and *vedanta* (scriptures) are useless.

59
advaitam atyanta-satyam – atu
buddhikk-uṇarttu pāṭṭalla
anya-duḥkham svanta-duḥkham enn-ōrkkāykil
advaitam-atyantam vyarttham

Advaita (non-duality) is the ultimate Truth. It is not a wake-up call for the intellect. We have failed to imbibe the truth of *advaita* if we fail to feel others' pain as our own.

60
sattayil ninn-udbhavikkum – ellām
sattayil cenn-astamikkum

nityam allāttatu satyam all-ātmāvu
nityam at-advaita-satyam

In the beginning is *sat* (existence), and existence is also in the end. The non-eternal is not the Truth. The eternal Self alone is the Truth of *advaita*.

ōmkāra divya porūḷe 61 (Malayalam)

Disclaimer: The translations of certain verses are not literal; they aim at bringing out the essential meaning from the Malayalam verses in a way that is easily understandable.

ōmkāra divya porūḷe varū
ōmana-makkaḷē vēgam
ōmanayāy vaḷarnn-āmayaṅgaḷ nīkki
ōmkāra-vastuvāy tīrū

Come quickly darling children, you who are the divine essence of Om. Remove all sorrows, grow dear and adorable, and merge with the Absolute.

1
cella kiṭāṅgaḷe niṅgaḷ – amma
collum ādēśam śravikkū
uḷḷam malarkke tuṙakkum vaccassukaḷkk-
uḷḷattil kātōrtt-irikkū

My little ones, listen to Amma's words. Listening intently to those words opens wide the doors of your heart.

2
kṣīra-nīraṅgaḷkku tammil – nitya
līnata sāddhyam āṇ-ennāl
kṣīram kaṭañña naṙu-veṇṇa raṇḍilum
līnam ākill-oṭṭu pōlum

Water and milk can always merge into one; but, the butter made from churning milk can merge into neither.

3
avidham karmattil oṭṭum – makkaḷ
oṭṭal-illāte varttikkū
karma-vaimukhyatte karma-vimuktiyāy
teṫṫi dharikkāt-irikkū

Similarly, children, like butter floating in water, remain detached from the fruits of your actions. Merely refraining from external action does not liberate you from bondage.

4
karmam niṣēdhiccu mātram – ārkkum
karma-nivṛtti varilla
viśramam vēṇēl śramam vēṇam alleṅkil
viśramam nidrayāy māṙum

Rejecting all action does not free you from karma. You must work hard to gain equipoise. Otherwise, your reluctance to act only makes you indolent.

5
karma-rāhityattil alla – śānti
karmam akarmamāy māṫṫū

karttavya-rāhityam ārkkum guṇappeṭill-
arttha kāmaṅgaḷkku pōlum

Performing action without the sense of doership gives peace. Refraining from our duties and responsibilities does not. Even to gain wealth and fulfill our desires, we must behave responsibly.

6
ñānum enikk-ennum ēvam – svārttha
cintayil bandhicciṭāte
nām namukk-enna vicāram vaḷarttiyāl
āyāsam ākilla karmam

Let us not be ensnared by selfish thoughts of 'me' and 'mine'. Our actions become effortless when we start thinking of 'us' and 'ours'.

7
āsaktar-ākāte ellām – ceytu
nirlipta-cētassāy tīrū
ajñāna-nāśam bhavikkān at-uttamam
karma-vimukti atatre

Let us act with detachment and thus purify our heart. The light of knowledge shines within a pure heart.

8
ceyyēṇam enna 'vidhikaḷ' – ārum
ceyyān orukkam allennāl
ceyyarut-enna 'vidhakaḷ' ellāyppōzhum
ceyyuvān utsāham ēṟum

Very few are prepared to act according to the *Vedic* teachings. Many people enthusiastically perform the actions prohibited by the *Vedas*.

9

kayyum kaṇakkum illāte – tān tān
koyyunna jīvita-anarttham
ceyyunna karmattin kaippizha ennōrttu
ceyyuvin niṣkāma-karmam

We reap our misfortunes by acting without discrimination. Remember that this is due to our karma. Learn to act without desire.

10

'anyathā cintippu kāryam – daivam
anyatra cinticciṭunnu'
śiṣṭarkku duḥkhavum duṣṭarkku saukhyavum
nirvacikkāvat-allonnum

Our thoughts may not be in tune with the ways of God. Often, we do not understand why sorrow befalls the good and the wicked prosper.

11

bhāgya-daurbhāgyaṅgaḷ ellām – tande
pūrva-janmārjjita-rūpam
bhāviye rūpappēṭuttēṇḍat-innatte
jīvitattāl vēṇam ārkkum

Our karma from previous births brings us good and bad fortune. Today's actions determine tomorrow's fortunes.

12

jīvitam karmam ennōrkkū – karma

rāhityam mṛtyu ennōrkkū
tān tān niyantriccu ceyyunna karmamē
svātantrya-lōkam teḷikkū

Life is full of actions that cease only at death. Only actions performed with self-control bring freedom.

13
kāmana kai-ozhiyumbōḷ – ātma
svātantryam vīṇḍ-eṭuttīṭum
tān tān svayam tīrtta-bandhanam āṇatu
tān tān azhikkēṇḍat-allō

When desire ceases, the freedom of the Self dawns. We have created our bondage, and we alone can undo it.

14
kāmana kai-viṭṭiṭumbōḷ – bhāvi
kālavum kai-viṭṭiṭunnu
ōrmmayil ninn-uṇarnnāl bhūta-kālavum
kai-viṭṭu varttikkum innil

When desire ceases, thoughts of the future cease. When memories cease, the past also ceases. Then we can live in the present.

15
ōrmmakaḷ tikki tirakkum – cittam
bhūta-kālattil āṇ-ōrkkū
āgraham muṭṭi paṭarnn-ezhikkum cittam
bhāvi-kālattil āṇōrkkū

A mind full of memories lives in the past, and a mind full of desire lives in the future.

16
vāzhvaṭṭu nilkkunnu nammaḷ – bhūta
bhāvi-kālaṅgaḷil taṅgi
jīvitam varttamānattil enn-ōrkkāykil
bhāviyum vyartthamāy tīrum

Trapped in the past or the future, we do not really live. If we fail to live in the present, the future is lost to us.

17
ōrmmayil jīvikke nammaḷ – bhūta
kālatte pulkunnu tānē
āśayil jīvikke bhāviye pulkunnu
cōrnnu pōkum varttamānam

Living in our memories, we embrace the past. Living in dreams of the future, the present slips through our fingers.

18
varttamānam cōrnnu pōkē – svayam
jīvitavum cōrnnu pōkum
kaivanna saubhāgyam āṇ-ennu cinticcu
varttamānattil carikkū

As the present slips away, our life slips away with it. Let us always remember that the present is a gift and live in it.

19
lōkam samādariccīṭum – puṇya

pūruṣa śrēṣṭhare ōrttāl
karmattāl mārgam teḷiccu munn-ēṟiyōr
jñānattāl mōkṣam bhaviccōr

The great ones, who are revered by the world, cleared the path for us through their selfless actions and gained liberation through knowledge.

20
sarvātma-bhāvam viṭāte – sarva
karmavum ācariccīṭām
nirmala cittarāy tīrumbozh-ātmāvil
ātmāv-uṇarnnu śōbhikkum

We should perform all our actions remembering that everything is a manifestation of the *atman*. When our mind is pure, the *atman* shines radiantly within.

21
paidāha-śāntikk-upāyam – tēṭi
ceyyunna karmaṅgaḷ pōlum
bhāva-viśuddhiyāl yōgamāy tīrnniṭām
bhāvātmakam ākkū karmam

Even the actions that earn our daily bread can be a union with God if we perform them with purity.

22
uḷḷil taniccu tān nilpū – kūṭṭin-
uḷḷil kiḷi enna pōle
uḷḷil upasthitam ākum ā sattayil
uḷḷam samarppikka makkaḷ

You are alone within yourself like a bird in its nest. Children, surrender to your true essence.

23
anyan illātt-iṭam tēṭi – sarvam
tandētu mātram ākkīṭān
vembunna svārtthande kūmbicca hṛttinde
niśvāsam ēlkkilum nīṙum

The very breath of one who aspires to possess everything and leave nothing for the others is harmful. Their heart is closed with selfishness.

24
arppaṇa-bhāvam uḷḷappōḷ – ellā
mārgavum svīkāryam ennāl
ellām niṣēdhiccu taḷḷiyāl tanneyum
taḷḷēṇḍatāy vannu kūṭum

With surrender, every path is possible. If we reject every path to the Truth, we end up rejecting our very Self.

25
illennu nammaḷ uraccāl – uḷḷat-
illāte āvilla nūnam
nāvill-enikk-ennu nāvāl uraykkunna
rōga-āturanmār iteṅgum

What exists does not cease to exist just because we say it does not exist. We are like the deluded ones who use their tongue to say they have no tongue.

26
jīvitam vyartthamāy kāṇum - cilar
sārtthakamā ṇennu kāṇum
gaurava-pūrvamāy kāṇum cilarkk-atu
yādṛccikam ennu tōnnum

Some see no point to life; others find life has meaning. Some take life seriously; for others, it is mere coincidence.

27
hāsyātmakam ennu kāṇum - cilar
svārttha-lābhattin āṇ-ennum
bhōgattin-āṇennu tōnnum cilarkk-atu
lōkōpakārattin-ennum

Some find life to be a joke; others waste it chasing selfish desires. For others, life is only for enjoying sense pleasures. The wise ones live for the welfare of the world.

28
dēhātma-buddhikk-itellām - svanta
bhōgattin-āṇennu tōnnum
buddhikku tāṅgāy vivēkam illēl atu
vidrōha-śaktiyāy māṙum

When we think we are the body and intellect, the world is only for enjoying sense pleasures. Unsupported by wisdom, intellect becomes a destructive power.

29
āsura-vṛttikaḷkk-entum - svantam
ākkuvān vyagrata ēṙum

ātma-niṣedham niśācarar-ākkiṭum
ārtti tann-ākrāntam eṅgum

When we reject the Self, we dwell in darkness. Our wicked actions and greed drive us to possess everything.

30
nōkkilum vākkilum krauryam – kṣudra
vṛttikaḷkk-utsavāghōṣam
kāṭu kai-ēṙiyum nāṭu kāṭ-ākkiyum
ārkkunn-orākrāntam eṅgum

Cruelty colors the look and words of those who gloat over their wicked deeds. They encroach upon forests and destroy them. The rule of the jungle becomes the law of the cities.

31
agniyāl-uṣṇam keṭilla – taṇu
nīrāl śamikkilla śaityam
ellām atātinde dharmam pularttumbōḷ
martyan svadharmam maṙakkum

The intrinsic quality of fire is heat; that of water is coolness. Fire and water always stay true to their *dharma*. Only humans betray their *dharma*.

32
matsara-grastamām buddhi – svayam
pakṣam piṭicc-aṭarāṭum
bāhya-śatrukkaḷ illeṅkil svayam raṇḍu
cēriyāy matsariccīṭum

A mind intent on competition always takes sides. If no external enemies are available, the mind divides itself in two and fights with itself.

33

dvēṣattil kḷēśam sphurikkum – divya
snēhattil śānti curattum
dvēṣam aniścitam snēham anaśvaram
snēhattil jīvikka makkaḷ

Anger is unpredictable and creates hardship and sorrow. Divine love is eternal and brings peace. Children, live in love.

34

mitraṅgaḷ śatrukkaḷ ākām – nēril
śatrukkaḷ mitraṅgaḷ ākām
astitva-bōdhattil aikyappeṭumbhozhē
vaiparītyam nivarttikkū

Friends can become enemies, and enemies can become friends. When we realize our true Essence, all enmity ends.

35

satyam kṣama-arjjavam uṇḍēl – uḷḷil
vidvēṣam āḷilla tellum
śuddha-antaraṅgam kṛpārdram āṇ-eppozhum
buddhi-bhēdam durbalatvam

When we have true patience and straightforwardness, we do not hate anyone. A pure heart is always compassionate. Intolerance reveals weakness.

36

svantam mahattvaṅgaḷ vāzhtti – svayam
vandanīyan-enna bhāvam
alpatvam ennē paṙayāvū tan ceyti
nindyam svayam hatya ākum

Glorifying ourselves and feeling worthy of worship is pitiable and despicable. This attitude destroys us.

37

ātma-praśamsa tan bījam – makkaḷ
ōrkkuvin – mithyābhimānam
nindanam ceyvatin prērakam ōrkkukil
himsa-anuvṛtti onnatre

Children, pride is the seed of arrogance. The desire to degrade others comes from the desire to hurt.

38

satya-abhilāṣam janiccāl – ellā
mithya-abhimānavum māyum
satya-abhilāṣattil nitya-anuvarttikaḷ
satya-anuvarttikaḷ mātram

Desire to know the Truth destroys pride. Our actions in search of the Truth come only from Truth.

39

mithya-abhimānam veṭiyū – makkaḷ
satya-abhimukhyam pularttū
citta-samśuddhi kaivannāl śarīrattil

satyatva-buddhi nīṅgīṭum

Children abandon pride, and cling to the Truth. When your heart becomes pure you will no longer identify yourselves with the body.

40
vandicciṭēṇḍum janatte – hīnam
nindiccāl konnatin pāpam
ārāre ennatall-ārum ārum tammil
ādarikkēṇḍ-avar eṅgum

Insulting and abusing those worthy of reverence is a sin akin to murder. Everyone, without exception, is worthy of our respect.

41
nindyam paraninda atre – atu
ceyyuvōr himsānuvartti
kaṇṇinum kātinum nalvirunnāy avarkk-
anyande dūṣyam onnatre

Abusing others is a despicable act of violence. Some people enjoy finding fault in others. Their eyes widen when they listen with rapt attention to malicious gossip.

42
vanmala maṇkūna ennum – pinne
maṇkūna vanmala ennum
citrī-karikkuvān sāmartthyam eppozhum
satya-virōdhikaḷkk-ellām

Those who oppose the Truth make mountains out of mole-hills and mole-hills out of mountains.

43
ārkkum viḷi puṙatt-ettum – daivam
ārenn-aṙiññu viḷiccāl
ātmāvil anyamāy kāṇāte vēṇam iṅg-
āhvānam ōtēṇḍat-ōrkkū

When we call out with faith, God comes to us. When we call out to God, let us remember that He is none other than our own self.

44
īśvara-anugraham vēṇēl – ādyam
dēśika-anugraham vēṇam
īśvaran dēśikan āṇ-ennu kāṇukil
dēśika-anugraham mōkṣam

We need the *guru's* blessing to gain God's blessings. When we see the *guru* as God, the *guru's* blessing leads us to liberation.

45
nērine nērāy aṙiyum – nēram
nēril ñān-ār enn-aṙiyum
nērē gurōr-ājña ācariccīṭukil
nērutān enn-ōrum ārum

When we really know the Truth, we come to know our own Truth. When we faithfully obey the commands of the *guru*, we realize ourselves as that Truth.

46
dharmatil ākaṇam śauryam – tyāga
karmatil ākaṇam vīryam

bhōgattil ākaṇam vairāgyam ātmaikya
bōdhatil ākaṇam dārḍhyam

Let us fiercely adhere to our *dharma*, and manifest our courage through acts of renunciation. Having dispassion towards worldly pleasures, let us be firm in the knowledge of our oneness with the Self.

47

mōkṣam āśikkunnu pakṣē – vēṇḍum
mōkṣa-mārgaṅgaḷ ajñātam
mōhitar ākāykil mōcitar āyiṭum
mōhattāl bandhikkum ārum

We long for liberation, but we do not know the path to liberation. We are bound by our delusion. When we break free of delusion, we gain liberation.

48

jñāna-tapass-ācarikkān – ādyam
vēṇam viṣaya-vairāgyam
svātma-anusandhāna-cittarāy arjjikka
svātmāvil ātmā-avabōdham

Only with detachment from worldly objects, can we perform austerities to gain Knowledge. Through Self-inquiry, let us gain the knowledge of the Self.

49

bhakti tan bhāvam utkṛṣṭam – prēma
bhakti tan lōkam viśiṣṭam
bhaktiyāl uḷkkaḷam śuddhamāy tīrukil
bhakti-muktikkilla bhēdam

Loving devotion is exalted and wondrous. When our heart becomes pure through devotion, it is no different from liberation.

50

vēdaṅgaḷ nālum kaṭaññāl – kiṭṭum
tūvamṛt-ākunnu prēmam
prēma-svarūpamāy māṙumbozh-ātmāvil
bhēdamill-anyamall-onnum

When we churn the four *Vedas*, we get the nectar of pure love. When we become embodiments of love, we realize that we are the *atman*, and there is nothing other than us.

51

sattamanmār ākū makkaḷ – nityam
sadguṇa-śālikaḷ ākū
citta-mōdattōṭe arppikkū jīvitam
sadgati ēvarkkum ēkū

Children, be true to your Essence and perform noble actions. Offer your life with a happy heart and uplift everyone.

52

parvata-arōhaṇam pōlum – dhīra
karmam enn-ēvarum vāzhttum
ātma-avarōhaṇam dhīrata mātramall-
ēṫṫam pavitram ā lakṣyam

People praise mountaineering as a courageous act. Realizing the Self is the most courageous act and also the purest goal.

53

ñān ennum nī ennum nammaḷ – namme
vērtiriccīṭunnu, pakṣē
dēhattin allāte cētanaykk-ārilum
vērtirivill-enn-uṇarū

We distinguish between 'you' and 'me'. Let us awaken to the fact that only physical bodies are many; the supreme Consciousness is One.

54

bhaktikku yukti kāṇēṇḍa – yukti
buddhikk-adhīnam-enn-ōrkkū
bhakti tan tāyvēr hṛttil ākunnatu
yuktikk-atītam ennōrkkū

Logic is limited to our intellect. Devotion needs no logic. The root of devotion is our heart, and it transcends logic.

55

buddhi-vijñāna-pradhānam – ātma
hṛtt-anubhūti-pradhānam
nanmayum tinmayum buddhi nalkām hṛttu
nirmala-ātmānanda-kēndram

Knowledge is for the intellect, but we can know the *atman* only through blissful experience. The intellect can discern right from wrong, whereas the heart is the center of the pure blissful Self.

56

buddhiyum yuktiyum pōra – bhāva
śuddhiyāl satyam tiḷakkū

yuktikk-atītamām bhakti koṇḍ-uḷḷattil
satyam tiḷakkuvin makkaḷ

Children, only a pure heart can realize the Truth. Realize the radiant Self through pure devotion that transcends intellect and logic.

57
kānmat-ellām yukti-niṣṭham – buddhi
ettāttatō yukti-atītam
yuktikk-adhiṣṭhitam ākaṇam satyam enn-
oṭṭum śaṭhikkēṇḍa ārum

Logic governs the phenomenal world. What we see is bound by the rules of logic. But logic is transcended where the mind cannot reach. Logic cannot prove the Truth.

58
uḷḷam kṛpārdram ākaṭṭe – dharma
bōdham karutt-ezhikkaṭṭe
anpin prakāśamāy munpil naṭakkuvin
pinpē gamikkaṭṭe lōkam

Let our heart be full of tender compassion, and let us remain strong in the awareness of our *dharma*. Let us go forth as the light of love, and let the world follow us.

59
agni-sphuliṅgaṅgaḷ ākum – vākku
cuṭṭum prakāśam parattum
cūṭum prakāśavum varṣikkum eṅkilum
hṛttinu śītaḷa-sparśam

Words born from the fire of Truth spread warmth everywhere. They soothe the mind, and rain down as radiant light.

60
vākkukaḷ sūkṣicc-uraykkū - vākku
nindyavum vandyavum ākām
naññu vākk ōtiyāl ōtum janattinde
neññum viṣayaccūru vāykkum

Let us be careful with our words because words can abuse as well as adore. Poisonous is the breath of those who speak venomous words.

61
tīyum pukayum vamikkum - vākku
dvēṣavum duḥkhavum ēṭṭum
śāntiyum snēhavum tūkunna vākkukaḷ
vāgdēvata tan prasādam

Angry words of fire and smoke hurt others and cause sorrow. Words full of peace and love are the blessings of the Goddess of speech.

ōmkāra divya porūḷe 62 (Malayalam)

Disclaimer: The translations of certain verses are not literal; they aim at bringing out the essential meaning from the Malayalam verses in a way that is easily understandable.

ōmkāra divya porūḷe varū
ōmana-makkaḷē vēgam
ōmanayāy vaḷarnn-āmayaṅgaḷ nīkki
ōmkāra-vastuvāy tīrū

Come quickly darling children, you who are the divine essence of Om. Remove all sorrows, grow dear and adorable, and merge with the Absolute.

1
kāruṇya-puṇyam vitaṙum – nōkku
vākkum nilāvoḷi ākki
pūrṇata tēṭum sudhanyare sadguru
ādi-mahassil nayikkum

The words and glance of the *sadguru* shower compassion like moonlight, and lead those who seek liberation to the resplendent Self.

2
aśru-tōya-ārṇṇavam tannil – nīnti
āvatatṫ-āzhunn-avarkkāy
kaittalam nīṭṭi paricil parirakṣa
ceyyum mahātmākkaḷ ennum

When we are exhausted from swimming in the ocean of tears, mahatmas reach out and pull us ashore.

3
śikṣaṇam kūṭāt-orāḷkkum – daiva
darśanam sāddhyam ākilla
sadguru prēmam illeṅkil mahēśvaran
pōlum tuṇaykkilla namme

It is impossible to reach the vision of God without discipline and obedience to the words of the guru. Even God does not befriend us unless we love the *sadguru*.

4

uḷḷil uṇḍ-īśvaran pakṣē – nammaḷ
uḷḷil allenn-ōrttiṭēṇam
uḷḷ-uṇarānuḷḷ-upāyam tirayāykil
uḷḷil uṇḍēl entu puṇyam?

God is within us, but we look outside. If we do not awaken within, of what use is it that God dwells there?

5

advaita-dṛṣṭīyil tānum – pinne
daivavum ēkam enn-ōtām
sadguruvum tānum onnenn-orikkalum
ōtarutā guru-ninda!

From the perspective of *advaita*, we can say, 'God and I are one.' But we can never say, 'The *sadguru* and I are the same.'

6

peṫṫa-mātāvinum mēle – namme
vātsalya-pūrvam nayiccu
ātmaikya-bōdhatin āḷākkum sadguru
sākṣāl mahēśanum vandyan

The *sadguru* guides us tenderly with more love than our own mother, and awakens us to our oneness with the *atman*. Let us worship the *sadguru* as higher than God.

7

uḷḷam uṇarān sahāyam – nalki
uṇma kaṇḍettān kaniyum

sarvajñar ākum ā sūrya-tējasvikaḷ
sarvādaraṇīyar-ennum

The brilliant and omniscient ones graciously help us to awaken and realize the Truth. They are forever revered.

8
kīzhppōṭṭ-ozhukum puzhapōl – manam
kīzhpeṭṭu pōṇam guruvil
mēlpōṭṭu nōkkikaḷ ākāte makkaḷē
kīzhpeṭṭu vidya ārjjikkū

As the river flows downwards, your mind should yield to the guru. Children, do not raise your head in pride and arrogance. Receive knowledge in all humility.

9
sāvakāśam kāttirikkān – kṣama
sādhakanmārkk-anivāryam
samśuddha-cētass-āyīṭaṇam sādhakan
samyama-śāli ākēṇam

Patience is essential for spiritual aspirants. We must have the patience to wait until our mind becomes pure and equipoised.

10
vēṇam svabhāva-lāḷityam – sadā
vēṇam vicāra-śīlatvam
pōṇam viṣāda-ātmakatvam hṛdayattil
vēṇam kṛpā-lōlupatvam

Our character should be clear and simple. We should learn how to reflect and never be doubtful and depressed. Let us learn to receive the grace of our own heart.

11

sadbhāvanakaḷ niṙaccu – makkaḷ
citta-kāluṣyam akkaṫṫū
nanmaye kōṇḍu nām tinmaye vellaṇam
vellāykil illātma-śānti

Children, fill your mind with positive thoughts and the turbulent thoughts will subside. Through goodness, win over evil or you will never find peace within.

12

muḷḷine muḷḷāl eṭukkām – pinne
muḷḷu raṇḍum santyajikkām
sadvṛttiye koṇḍu duṣvṛtti nīkkaṇam
sadvṛtti nissaṅgam koṇḍum

We use one thorn to remove another, and then throw them both away. Good deeds done with detachment cancel out the effects of bad deeds.

13

arppaṇam ceyt-uṇarumbōḷ – uḷḷam
darppaṇam pōle tiḷaṅgum
satya-prakāśattāl nirbharam ākumbōḷ
vṛtti-samskāraṅgaḷ māyum

When we surrender and awaken within, our heart shines like a mirror. When the light of Truth fills our heart, all our latent tendencies disappear.

14
vēdavum śāstravum ōtum – nammaḷ
daivikata enna satyam
ennāl at-āviṣkarikkān paṭhikkāte
ōtunnu tān atenn-ārum

The *Vedas* and *shastras* proclaim we are divine. But we merely repeat "I am That," without putting it into practice.

15
bāhya-prapañcavum pinne – bāhya
dēhaṅgaḷ okkeyum tulyam
ātma-caitanyavum daivika-sattayum
sārattil onnu tann-ennum

Our physical body and the physical universe are composed of the five elements. Yet the consciousness that resides within us as the Self and the divine essence are one and the same.

16
ādyam vivēcicc-aṙiyū – svantam
mēdhayāl satyānṛtaṅgaḷ
pinnatil cētana tān enn-uṇarumbōḷ
dēhābhimānam poliyum

Let us discern between Truth and untruth. When we awaken to the knowledge that we are the all-pervading Consciousness, we no longer identify with the perishable body.

17
ñān ennum nī ennum nammaḷ – raṇḍu
cēriyil vartticciṭunnū

bōdham immaṭṭil vibhāgī-karikkumbōḷ
jīvitam samsāra-baddham

When we think in terms of 'me' and 'you', we divide ourselves into opposing sides. As long as our understanding remains divisive, we will remain bound to the world.

18
dēhattin ennennum vēṇam – pakṣya
pēyaṅgaḷ pōṣaṇattinnāy
ātma-samrakṣaykku dhyāna-japādiyum
ācariccīṭaṇam ārum

Just like our body needs food for nourishment, we need to practice meditation and prayer to attain clarity and purity.

19
durgati āgamikkumbōḷ – daivam
nirddayan ennu nām ōtum
karma-dōṣatte nirupādhikam viṭṭu
cārttunnu daivattil kuṫṫam

When bad fortune comes, let us not blame God and say He is merciless. Let us admit that misfortune is the consequence of our past actions.

20
ellām vidhi-enn-uṙaccu – onnum
ceyyān tuniyāt-irunnāl
janmam nirarttham prayatnam upēkṣiccāl
daivam tuṇaykk-eṅgan-ettum?

When we say that everything is fate and make no effort, our life has no meaning. If we do not strive, how can God help us?

21
ellām vidhi ennu connāl – pinne
karmattin entāṇu yukti?
innu vitaccat-entākilum nāḷe nām
koyyum vidhi-rūpamāyi

If we say that everything is predestined, what is the role of karma? Our fate is of our own making. We reap tomorrow only what we sow today.

22
kālakkēṭ-ennum paṙayum – pakṣē
kālam anusyūtam allē?
kālattil tānē nizhaliccituṃ ceyta
karmattin-otta phalaṅgaḷ

We say that bad times are the cause of our misfortunes, but time simply flows. The fruits of our actions ripen when the time is right.

23
ellāṫṫinum sākṣi āyāl – pinne
illa, bandhikkilla karmam
ellām orēkātma-cētana ennōrttu
uḷḷam samarppiccu ceyyām

If we remain a witness to everything, our actions cannot bind us. Let us offer our heart, and act knowing that all is the one Consciousness.

24
mūnnu dēhattinum sākṣi – tathā

mūnnu kālattinum sākṣi
viśvanum taijasa, prājñan - ityādiyām
tritvaṅgaḷkk-okkeyum sākṣi!

Let us be the witness of the three bodies — gross, subtle and causal. And to the three times — past, present and future. And to the three states of waking, dreaming and deep sleep.

25
āzhiyil pontum tira-pōl - ellām
ātmāvil ponti māyunnu
tān ākum ādhāra-sattayil addhyāsam
ākunnu nāma-rūpaṅgaḷ

Like waves rising and subsiding in the ocean, everything arises and subsides in the *atman*. All names and forms are superimposed on the *atman*.

26
grāhyamām vastu tānalla - ōrttāl
grāhyam allātt-atum alla
jñānam svarūpamāy uḷḷavan tān ennu
kāṇātt-avan jñāni alla

'I' (*atman*) is not an object to be perceived and understood through the senses. At the same time, it is the intrinsic part of all experience. Only those established in Knowledge really know the inner Self.

27
addhyātma-sādhana ennāl - veṙum
sadyaykk-upadamśam alla
alpam japa-dhyāna prārtthanayum kṣētra

darśanavum mātram alla

Spiritual practice is not like a side-dish at a feast. Just a little bit of meditation, prayer and temple worship do not suffice.

28
cittam samāhitam ākki – nitya
jīvitam prārtthana ākkū
ceyyunnat-okkeyum bhāvātmakam, karma
yōgam ākkiṭuvin makkaḷ!

Children, introspect and make your life a prayer. Perform your actions with utmost love, sincerity and awareness, and then they become karma yoga.

29
uḷḷam viḷakkum ā karmam – appōḷ
uḷḷil viśrānti niṙayum
dīnare uddhariccīṭum svadharmattāl
ātmāvum uddharikkunnu!

Such sincere actions purify our mind and bring us tranquility. When we help the distressed we uplift ourselves.

30
indriyaṅgaḷ uḷvalikkū – atu
tan manassil layippikkū
mānasam buddhiyil līnam ākkīṭukil
buddhi ātmāvil layikkum!

Let us withdraw our senses and merge them in the mind. Let us merge the mind in the intellect. Let the intellect then merge in the *atman*.

31
bhakti-bhāvōnnatam āyāl – atum
advaita-satya-anurūpam
bhakti tan unmatta cittattil addhyātma
satya-pīyūṣam curattum

Supreme devotion is the Truth of *advaita*. The nectar of immortality fills our heart. Then our heart exults in the divine intoxication of devotion.

32
uḷḷinn-akakkāmb-uṇarnnu – satyam
uḷḷapōl darśicc-aṙiññāl
pinne prapañcam niṙaññu varttippatum
uṇma tann-āṇenn-aṙiyum

When we awaken and realize the Truth, we know that the same Truth pervades and acts throughout the universe.

33
svarga-nivāsi all-ōrkkū - daivam
kṣētra-nivāsiyum alla
namme pratīkṣiccu santatam vāzhunnu
svantam hṛdantam tuṙakkū!

God does not reside in the heavens or in temples. He waits for us with great expectation. Let us open wide the doors of our heart.

34
uḷḷat-onnuṇma ennōrkkū – uṇma
allāttat-illāttat-ennum
eḷḷiluḷḷ-eṇṇa pōl uḷḷil uṇḍ-īśvaran

uḷḷ-uṇarnn-uṇma darśikkū!

Truth is the changeless reality; whatever changes is not the Truth. God is within us, like oil within the sesame seed. Let us awaken and see the Lord within.

35

bhōgārtti-yōgam hanikkum – manam
māyā-bhramattil madikkum
bhrāntam manass-abhimānam veṭiññ-ārtti-
pūṇḍ-akkare pacca tēṭum

An insatiable desire to experience the world blocks our realization of the Self. In our delusion, our mad mind loses self-respect as it ever seeks new pastures.

36

ōrō cuvaṭum pizhaykkē – martyan
mṛtyu-lōkattōṭ-aṭukkum
etra mātram bāhya-dṛṣṭi ākunnu; tān
atra mātram yamādhīnan!

Every wrong step takes us closer to death. The more we are attracted to the outer world, the stronger the hold that death has over us.

37

uṇḍ-abhaya-sthānam uḷḷil – pakṣē
uḷḷōṭṭu nōkkān bhayakkum
saccidānandam veṭiññ-indriya-dvārā
bhikṣa yāciccu naṭakkum

Fearlessness is inside us but we are afraid to look within. We abandon the experience of pure *satchitananda* (truth, consciousness, bliss) and go begging at the doors of our senses.

38
satya-anubhūtikku vēṇḍi – makkaḷ
mithyā-abhimānam veṭiyū
dēhatte cūṇḍi 'ñān' 'nī' enn-uraykkavē
mithyā-abhimānam-atatre

Children, let go of your false pride and experience the blissful Truth. When we point to the body and say 'me' and 'you', we are deluded by the ego.

39
tīkkal-āyirunnālum – koccu
paitaṅgaḷ vāri puṇarum
satya-anṛtaṅgaḷ vivēcicc-aṟiyāte
mṛtyuve pulkunnu martyan!

Small children gather even hot embers. We embrace the relentless cycle of life and death because we cannot discern Truth from untruth.

40
ñān enna bhāvam veṭiññu – ellām
nī ennu bhāviccitēṇam
nām alla namme nayikkunnat-īśvaran
āṇennu bōdhiccitēṇam

Let go of the notion of "I" and consider everything as "You." Know that our lives unfold according to God's plan and not ours.

41
dē, varunn-ennu tān collum – tānum
kūṭe varunn-ennu collum
kāl-tenni raṇḍām cuvaṭu veykkum mumbe
prāṇan piṭaññu vīṇīṭām

We may say, “Wait, I am coming too.” But before we take two steps, we may tumble down and lose our life.

42
daivika-sattaye melle – makkaḷ
dhyānattilūṭ-ānayikkū
bāhya-lōkattilum svarga-lōkattilum
tēṭēṇḍat-uḷḷattil tēṭū!

Children, gradually realize God within through meditation. Do not search for God in the external world or up in the heavens; search for the divine essence within.

43
jīviccirikkavē vēṇam – mukti
ārjjicciṭēṇḍat-iṅgārum
mṛtyuvum muktiyum tammil vyatiriktam
mṛtyuvil mukti tēṭēṇḍa

Let us not expect death to grant us liberation. We must gain liberation while living.

44
sṛṣṭiyil peṭṭatil ellām – daivam
nitya-anuvartti āṇēlum

brahmāvalōka dhiṣaṇā-balam koṇḍu
martyan sadā anugṛhītan

God pervades the entire creation. We are blessed with an intellect that allows us to realize this supreme Truth.

45
satya-avabōdhatināyi – eṅgum
tēṭi tiraññ-alayēṇḍa
satyatte ārāyum addhyātma-yātra tan
hṛttilēykkāṇ-anyam-alla

We need not wander the world seeking the Truth. The search for Truth is a spiritual journey that happens only within our own heart.

46
cintayil kāluṣyam ēlān – iṭam
samjātam ākarut-ētum
sadbhāvanakaḷum satkarma-śraddhayum
satsaṅga-śuddhiyum vēṇam

Let us not allow any circumstances to trouble our mind. Let us think good thoughts, perform good actions, have faith, and seek the purity of good company.

47
śuddham allātta manassu – lōkam
okke aśuddham ākkunnu
sṛṣṭiyil dūṣyam illeṅkilum durbuddhi
toṭṭat-ellām duṣippikkum

An impure mind sees the world as impure. Creation is perfect, but a wicked intellect sullies everything it touches.

48

vṛtti-rāhityam varāte – ārkkum
citta-viśuddhi varilla
cittam viśuddham-āyāl satya-darśanam
siddhamāy enn-uṙaccīṭām

Our mind becomes pure only when our thoughts subside. When our mind is pure, we will certainly experience the Truth.

49

samharikkēṇam ahanta – cinta
samskarikkēṇam ēkāntam
svārtthamaṫṫ-ātmārttha bhaktiyōṭ-īśvara
sēvayāy māṫṫuvin karmam

Let us destroy our ego and purify our thoughts in solitude. Let devotion transform our selfishness and make each action a service to God.

50

nānātvam kāṇunna kaṇṇāl – satyam
kāṇillat-andham āṇ-ennum
ēkatva-bōdhattil kāṇunn-avan vēṙe
āṇenn-uṇarnn-aṙiññīṭum

The outer eye that sees diversity is blind to the real Truth. It is the inner eye that realizes the Oneness of pure Consciousness that pervades the universe.

51
vṛttikaḷ chidricc-ozhukum - iruḷ
grastam hṛdantam teḷiyān
sadguru-prēmavum niṣkāma-sēvayum
śraddhayum jīval-pradhānam

Faith, selfless actions and love for the *sadguru* bring light, while fragmented thoughts and emotions darken our heart.

52
jīvēśvaranmārkku bhēdam - varum
jīvatva-bhāvam uḷḷappōḷ
bhēdam allaikyam āṇātma brahmaṅgaḷkk-
at-addhyāsa-kālattu pōlum

When we are established in the knowledge of the supreme Self, we see Oneness in all names and forms.

53
raṇḍ-uṇḍu mārgam namukku - onnil
jīvitam maṫtonnil mṛtyu
jīvitam ennāl nivṛtti ennākunnu
anyam pravṛtti-panthāvum

There are two paths before us. The path of renunciation leads to liberation, and that of selfish actions entangles us in the cycle of birth and death.

54
raṇḍil ētum svīkarikkām - atil
pūrṇa-svātantryam uṇḍ-ārkkum

buddhimānmār atil mṛtyuve kaiviṭṭu
nityata pulkum sayuktam

Everyone has total freedom to choose one of the paths. The discerning ones drop death's hand and embrace eternity.

55
tān onnumall-ennu tōnnum - buddhi
tan sahayātrikan ākum
tān mahān-āṇennu tōnnum aham-buddhi
tan gati durghaṭam ākkum

An intellect endowed with humility is a companion on our path. An intellect that deludes us into assumptions of greatness only creates difficulties on the path.

56
buddhi vivēkattoṭ-ottāl - atu
satya-sākṣātkāra yōgyam
buddhi avivēkam ennāl at-eppozhum
ātma-naṣṭattinnu hētu

When the intellect unites with discernment, it becomes fit to realize the Truth. An intellect that lacks discernment becomes the cause of self destruction.

57
munnil teḷiyunnu pāta - śiṣyan
munnōṭṭ-aṭi vacciṭumbōḷ
vighnaṅgaḷ nīkkiṭum sadguru, tan kṛpā
veṭṭam teḷiyikkum satyam

When the disciple moves forward along the path before him, the *Sadguru* removes the obstacles and lights the lamp of grace.

58

agni onnuṇḍ-uḷḷil ārkkum – sadā
ujjvalattām satya-jyōti
tellum pukayillat-uḷḷil nirantaram
ninnu tiḷaṅgum ā jyōti

The fire within everyone is the ever-blazing flame of Truth. It shines forever bright and clear in our heart.

59

ārum koḷuttiyatalla – munnē
hṛttil svayabhū āṇōrkkū
arkkēndu tāraka-vṛndam atin visphu-
liṅgaṅgaḷ mātram enn-ōrkkū

This fire was never lit by anyone. It blazes by itself within the heart. The sun, moon and stars are only sparks of this glorious fire.

60

akkeṭā dīpatte śāstram – ōtum
pratyag-ātmāv-enn-ajasram
satya-sākṣātkāram ennāl atum brahma
satyavum onnenna bōdham

The scriptures call this flame the indwelling Self. To realize the Truth is to know that this indwelling Self is one with the absolute reality.

61

yātonnum āśrayicc-alla – atin

vāzhv-ennu kāṇaṇam makkaḷ
cittatte ūti teḷiccāl cidānanda
vastu-svarūpam teḷiyum

Children, know that it stays lit within, independent of everything else. When you clear away the dirt and darkness from your heart, the radiant and eternally blissful Self is uncovered.

62
satyam veḷippeṭunnilla – ennāl
sārvatrikam āṇat-ennum
ārat-āviṣkarikkunnu svantam hṛttil
ā mahān ōrunnu satyam

Truth is not revealed, yet it is everywhere. The great ones, who realize the truth within their hearts, express it through their words.

ōmkāra divya porūḷe 63 (Malayalam)

Disclaimer: The translations of certain verses are not literal; they aim at bringing out the essential meaning from the Malayalam verses in a way that is easily understandable.

ōmkāra divya porūḷe varū
ōmana-makkaḷē vēgam
ōmanayāy vaḷarnn-āmayaṅgaḷ nīkki
ōmkāra-vastuvāy tīrū

Come quickly darling children, you who are the divine essence of Om. Remove all sorrows, grow dear and adorable, and merge with the Absolute.

1
ārtt-ullasiccu rasikkām – ennum
āghōṣa jīvitam ākkām
ārbhāṭam all-antarātmāvil saundaryam
āsvadicc-uṇmattar ākām

We can live joyfully, celebrating each new day. Real beauty is not in external luxuries. Let us exult in the radiance of the inner Self.

2
kaṇṇ-onnu teṫtiyāl vēgam – uṇṇi
maṇṇu tinnān kuticc-ōṭum
śraddha onnalpam pizhaccāl uṭan manam
tenni ōṭum viṣayattil

If we look away, even for a moment, our child runs off and eats clay. When our awareness lapses, even for a moment, our mind runs to external objects.

3
ōmana makkaḷē kālam – ārkkum
kāttu nilkkill-ēṙe nēram
audāryam ārilum kālattin-illa tan
bhāvi tān tanne sṛṣṭikkū

My darling children, time will not wait for you; it makes no exceptions for anyone. Your future is in your own hands.

4
kālam kuṙiccu sūkṣikkum – ōrō
karmavum cintayum sūkṣmam

akarma sākṣi tan kai-kaṇakkil tellu
kai-pizha pōlum varilla

Time notes each subtle thought and act. Time, the witness of all actions, makes no mistake in its record.

5
ōrōnnum tūkki kuṙikkum – kṛtyam
ōrō phalam nirṇṇayikkum
satphalam ākilum duṣphalam ākilum
teṫṫāt-aḷann-ēkum ārkkum

Our every act will be weighed and judged, and its fruits determined. We will receive the fruits of our actions whether they bring sorrow or joy.

6
vēṇḍatu mātram śravikkū – makkaḷ
vēṇḍatu mātram ninakkyū
vēṇḍat-entenuḷḷ-uṇarnnu kaṇḍ-ettuvin
vēṇḍatu svāmśī-karikkū

Children, hear only what is auspicious, and think only worthy thoughts. Awaken within, realize what you need to imbibe, and make it your own.

7
anya-dūṣyam cikaññīṭum – ennāl
svanta-dūṣyam maṙannīṭum
nanma onnum nambukilla nām anyande
tinmakaḷ cikki cikayum

We search for the faults of others and forget our own faults. We have no faith in the goodness of others, and see only their faults.

8
azhakku vidya kai-vannāl – kūṭe
kūṭunn-ahantayum pakṣe
tān ahaṅkāriyāy enn-aṙiyāte – tān
pōkunn-anarthattilekkāy

We become arrogant when we gain even a tiny measure of knowledge. If we do not realize our own arrogance, we are doomed to misfortune.

9
uḷḷam curuṅgi curuṇḍāl – lōkam
uḷḷam kaviyum nissīmam
uḷḷam vikāsam bhaviccāl prapañcam or-
eḷḷōḷamāyi curuṅgum

When our mind shrivels up, the world overwhelms us. When our mind becomes expansive, the world will become like a tiny sesame seed within.

10
cuṫṫum prakāśam paratti – katti
nilkkum viḷakk-uṇḍu pakṣe
cōṭṭil iruṭṭ-enna pōle tan hṛttilum
ātma-prakāśam ill-oṭṭum

A lamp sheds light all around, but there is darkness beneath it. We see the entire world with the light of consciousness, yet we are unable to realize it within us.

11
antaraṅgattil uṇḍ-īśan – ennāl
santṛpti illoṭṭu pōlum

mandasmita-amṛtam tūki ninnīṭilum
antaraṅgam kūriruṭṭil

God resides in our heart, yet we are not content. Even though God smiles at us blissfully, our heart stays steeped in darkness.

12
ānanda-sindhuvil nīntān – bhayam
nīntām bhavārṇṇavam tannil
ātmāvu tān enn-uṇarān bhayam; dēham
tān ennu kāṇān utsāham

We are afraid to swim in the ocean of bliss, but how willingly we swim in the ocean of *samsara* (life and death)! We are afraid to awaken to the knowledge that 'I am the *atman*', but we enthusiastically identify ourselves as our body.

13
utpanna-vastukkaḷ ellām – alpa
kālam nila ninnu māyum
utpanna-dēhavum astamikkum munpē
nityata sākṣāt-karikkū

All that is created exists only for a while and then ceases to be. Our created body also comes to an end. Let us realize the Truth before our death.

14
kaṇṇum karaḷum kavarum – kāzhca
kaṇḍu kaṇḍ-āyuss-oṭuṅgum
kaṇṇāyat-onn-uṇḍ-atuḷḷil āṇennu nām
kaṇḍāl atin bhaṅgi vēṟe

We have to leave this world even before having our fill of its sights and sounds. We do not realize the beauty of the Truth that we can behold with our inner eye.

15

nīyatāṇ-enn-ōtiṭumbōḷ – svayam
tān atāṇ-enn-aṙiññeṅkil
śāstraṅgaḷ ellām aviṭ-astamicciṭum
sāddhyamāy sādhana ellām

If we realize 'I am That' we will no longer need the scriptures to guide us. All our austerities will have borne fruit.

16

ennile enne maṙaykkum – 'ende
ende' ennuḷḷava ellām
ennil ninn-endēt-akaṫtiyāl śēṣikkum
ennile 'ñān' enna bōdham

The selfish 'my' thought obscures the real Self within 'me'. When we discard 'mine' from the 'me', only the awareness of 'I' as pure consciousness remains.

17

tān enn-aham tattva-sāram – cittu
mātram enn-uṇma grahikkām
allāttat-ellām jaḍam; tan śarīratte
citt-ennu kāṇarut-ārum

The essence of the 'I' principle is pure Consciousness. Everything else is unreal. Let us not be deluded by the thought that our physical body is our true essence.

18
vēda-vēdāntaṅgaḷ ellām – ōtum
tān atāṇ-ennuḷḷa satyam
satyatte mithyayāy kāṇmavar ōtiṭum
tan dēham tān ennu mūḍham

All the *Vedas* proclaim, 'I am That'. Only the ignorant ones who mistake the unreal as Truth proclaim, 'I am the body'.

19
uṇḍ-ennu tōnnum itellām – ennō
uṇḍāyat-āṇennu kāṇām
uṇḍāyat-āṇēlat-illāte āyiṭām
uṇḍāyat-all-ūṇma nityam

All that we see here now was made sometime in the past, and all that was made will one day cease to be. Truth was never made. The Truth has always existed.

20
kuriruḷ māyum prakāśam – varum
sūryan svayam prōjjvalikkē
santāpa māṙum sukham varum śāntiyum
antarātmā ujjvalikkē

Light dawns when the sun shines of itself and dispels darkness. When the inner Self shines effulgent, all our sorrows cease and we become peaceful and content.

21
dēham janikkum dahikkum – pakṣe
dēhi vēṙonnil vasikkum

dēhi dēham veṭiññīṭilum tān enna
dēhi ādyanta vihīnam

The body is born, dies and is cremated. Then the *atman* takes on another body. The *atman* has no beginning or end, though the body ceases to be.

22
kṣētrattil dēvata pōle – gātra
kṣētrattil uṇḍ-ātma-dēvan
kai-kuppi nammaḷ tozhumbozhum ullil ā
dēvane vēṇam smarikkān

Like God residing in a temple, the divine resides within us. When we fold our hands in prayer, let us pray to the God dwelling within.

23
gātra-kṣētrattil viḷaṅgum – mahā
kṣētrajñan ārenn-aṙiyū
āroṭum ñān ñān enn-ātmāvil cūṇḍunna
ñān ārenn-āräññ-aṙiyū

Let us come to know the Deity that shines within the temple of our body. By self-inquiry, let us know the real nature of 'I', which is pure consciousness.

24
ōrttāl śarikkuḷḷa kṣētram – gātra
kṣētram āṇenn-ōrttiṭēṇam
kṣētram pavitramāy kāṇum kaṇakkil nām
gātram pavitramāy kāṇām

Know that the real temple is our body. We should consider our body to be as pure and sacred as the temple.

25

tān ār-ennār-orāḷ ōrum – ayāḷ
tān aṙiv-āṇenn-aṙiyum
tān aṙivāṇ-enn-aṙiññāl anātmāvil
tōnnum aham-buddhi māyum

If we ask, 'Who am I'? we come to know that our true nature is knowledge. When we know that knowledge is our essence, our sense of 'I' disappears.

26

nēravum nāḷum kuṙiccu – ātma
bōdhōdayam varill-ārkkum
ōrō nimiṣavum vēṇam pratīkṣa nām
svīkārya-cittarāy tīrū

We will not realize the Self on a particular date and time of our choosing. We must wait expectantly, moment to moment, with hope and an open heart.

27

nāḷekkyu māṫṫi vaykkumbōḷ – nīḷe
nīḷunnu nāḷekaḷ vīṇḍum
nāḷe entākum ennāruṇḍ-aṙiyunnu
nīḷumbozh-āyussu naṣṭam

When we procrastinate, we see only a long line of tomorrows. Who knows what will happen tomorrow? As we procrastinate, the days go by and our life passes in vain.

28
innil viśvāsam illeṅkil – āru
nāḷeye viśvasiccīṭum?
inn-eppozh-eṅkilum ennalla; nēṭēṇḍat-
inn-ippozh-enn-uṙaccīṭām

If we have no faith in today, how will we believe in tomorrow? Let's not expect to gain at some future time; let us realize the Truth here and now.

29
anya-lōkattalla daivam – ennāl
tan arikattum all-ōrkkū
tan uḷḷin uḷḷil tanicc-irikkunn-avar
tanne aṙiññāl aṙiññu

God is not in another world, nor is God nearby. Those who are established in the oneness of the Self realize their divine essence.

30
svantam suhṛttukkaḷ pōlum – ōrttāl
tannil ninn-anyamāy nilpū
svanta-mātāvum pitāvum puṙatt-eṅkil
antaraṅgatt-āṇu daivam

When we reflect, we realize that even our closest friends are separate from us. Even our father and mother are outside us. Only God resides within.

31
apparamārttham grahiccāl – pinne
ippāril ent-aṙiyēṇḍū?

ippozhē tān atāṇenna vēdōktikaḷ
eppozhum cinticc-uṙaykkū

If we know this great Truth, then what else is there to know? Let us reflect on the *Vedic* teaching 'You are That' and be established in Knowledge.

32
anya-matam svīkariccāl – svargam
annu tan enn-ōrttu kaṣṭam
cintā-vihīnarāy pāññu cellum cilarkk-
annatte annam labhikkām

What a pity that people believe they can reach heaven on the same day that they convert to another religion. Some people rush to convert without thinking. They only want food for the day.

33
onnilum tellum viśvāsam – avarkk-
illennu tanne uṙaykkām
tannil viśvāsam illātt-avarkk-eṅgane
anya-viśvāsam uṙaykkum?

They say they have no belief in anything. How will they firmly believe in another faith when they have no faith in themselves?

34
tṛṣṇā parityāgam atre – ātma
niṣṭhaykk-upayukta mārgam
tṛṣṇaye venn-avarkk-ātma-sākṣātkāram
puṣpitamāy enn-uṙaykkām

Renunciation of desire is the path to realization of the *atman*. When you have conquered desire, realization of the *atman* is as natural as the blooming of a flower.

35

bāhya-sukha lōlupanmār – tyāga
bāliśam ennē ninaykkū
tyāga-dhananmār ī nāṭin veḷiccavum
bhōga-dhananmār iruṭṭum

Those who indulge in external pleasures say sacrifice is for the weak-minded. Those who have renounced desire are the light of this land. Those who are immersed in fulfilling their selfish desires are its darkness.

36

āke iruṇḍor ī lōkam – vīṇḍum
kūriruḷ ākkunnu martyan
dēhēndriyaṅgaḷkk-aṭimayāy tīrukil
ātmāv-aṭaññu mūṭīṭum

Selfishness makes an already dark world even darker. When we are enslaved by our body and sense organs, the *atman* remains veiled.

37

vastuvil vismayam pūṇḍāl – vastu
sattayil śraddha taṅgilla
sattayil taṅgātta śraddha orēṭattum
svasthamāy taṅgilla tanne

When objects of the world carry us away, our mind doesn't focus on its essence. A mind not focussed on the all-pervading divine essence never attains tranquility.

38
adbhutam kuṙunna kaṇṇil – kāzhca
hrasvam enn-ōrkkuvin makkaḷ
lōkam ennadbhuta sṛṣṭī ōrttāl vastu
kāzhca ellām aprasaktam

Children, all the wonders of the world are short lived. When you realize the divine essence of this wondrous creation, external sights become irrelevant.

39
vismayiccīṭēṇḍa ārum – sṛṣṭi
saundaryam anyūnam atre
ellām vilakṣaṇam ākkum manassinde
vibhrāntam ākum ākrāntam

We can only be wonder-struck at the beauty of creation. Our greed deludes us into seeing ugliness everywhere.

40
martya-janmam kai-variccu – pakṣē
martya-dharmam vismariccu
vāṭi kozhiyum ila pōle jīvitam
nēṭiyiṭṭ-entāṇu puṇyam?

If we have gained a human birth but have forgotten human *dharma*, what is the use of living? Finally, we will fall away like a dry leaf without having gained any merit.

41
illāttat-uḷḷatāy tōnnum – uḷḷil
uḷḷat-illāttatāy tōnnum

uḷḷ-uṇarnn-ōrukil uḷḷat-illāttat-enn-
uḷla tōnnal tēññu māyum

We think that the transient is the eternal, and we are not aware of the *atman* within. When our inner Self awakens, only oneness remains.

42
āzhiyil kāl tenni vīzhum – sūryan
āzhnnatil līnam ākāte
nīnti kara ēṙunnu pūrvādri-sānuvil
vīṇḍum navōnmēṣamōṭe

The sun that sets into the ocean does not sink and merge in its waters. It swims across to the other shore and rises with renewed enthusiasm.

43
mṛtyu-samudrattil vīzhum – jīvan
āzhnnatil līnam ākāte
pontunnu maṫṫoru dēhattil pinneyum
antyam uṭalinnu mātram

The *jivan* that falls into the ocean of death does not sink and merge in its waters. It surfaces in another body. Only the body comes to an end.

44
ceyyunnu tān enna bhāvam – viṭṭu
ceyyumbōzhē ceytat-ākū
ceyyunnu tān ennu cinticcu ceyyukil
neyyunnu bandhanam tānē

Actions performed without the 'I' notion lead to freedom. Actions performed with the doership notion further entangle us.

45

cintakaḷ kṛtticcu nōkku – atil
minnunnat-ētennu kāṇū
tan gatikk-āśrayam ākunnat-ārjjikka
anyam ellām santyajikkū

Let us examine our thoughts and choose the good ones. Let us keep what helps us to move forward on our path and abandon the rest.

46

kḷavu-pātrattil niṙaykkum – kṣīram
pāṭē duṣikkunna pōle
cittam duṣiccatāyāl atil pontunna
cintayum pāṭē duṣikkum

Like milk that sours in a dirty vessel, when our mind turns bad, only wicked thoughts arise in it.

47

dēham veḷuttat-āyālum – manam
kḷāvicc-iruṇḍat-āyīṭām
dēham kuṙattat-āyālum manam veṇma
tēri tiḷaṅgunnat-āvām

The color of the skin does not reveal the quality of the mind.

48

dēhatte munnirtti mātram – vyakti
vaiśiṣṭyam kāṇarut-ārum
vākkum svabhāvavum karmavum mātramē
vyaktitva-mānam ākāvū

Physical appearance alone does not make us noble. Only good words, actions and character make us noble.

49

mitramāy aṅgīkarikkum – nammaḷ
indriya-vṛndatte ādyam
pinnava śatruvāy māṙum, manuṣyande
nanmakaḷ ellām keṭuttum

Initially we believe the sense organs are our friends. Later on, they turn out to be enemies and destroy all the good within us.

50

meyyum manassum orupōl – daiva
kāryārttham-āy calikkumbōḷ
payyavē tan mey maṙannu mahēśvara
tanmaya-bhāvam bhavikkum

When our body and mind act together for good, slowly we stop thinking that we are the body. Then we realize we are one with God.

51

bhaktikk-orūnam varāte – jñāna
vijñānam ārjjicciṭēṇam
bhakti ennāl satya-niṣṭhaykku nalkunna
śraddha ennarttham grahikkām

Spiritual knowledge does not lessen our devotion. Devotion is perfect awareness of the Truth.

52

ānandam ātma-svabhāvam – eṅgum
ākulam dēha-svabhāvam
mōha-nirmuktiyum bhōga-nivṛttiyum
śōka-nivṛttikk-upāyam

Anxiety is the nature of the mind. The nature of the *atman* is bliss. The only way to put an end to sorrow is to break free from desire and delusion.

53

indriyam ōrōnnāy melle – nammaḷkk-
uḷḷ-aṭakkān kazhiyumbōḷ
kāzhcayum kēzhviyum sparśam maṇam ghrāṇam
okke atātil layikkum

When we slowly subdue the *indriyas* (senses organs), one by one sight, sound, touch, smell and taste return to their source.

54

śēṣikkum indriyam mātram – eṅkil
indriya-nāśam bhavikkum
indriya-abhāvattil kūriruḷ varttikkill-
ātma-sūryan prōjjvalikkē

Then only the sense organs remain, and desire for sense objects is totally destroyed. Then, the sun of Self-knowledge shines forth and dispels all darkness.

55

mārddavam hṛttinnu vēṇam – sadā
mādhuryam vākinnu vēṇam

mārga-nirddēśaṅgaḷ kāt-ōrkkaṇam, manam
mōha nirmuktam ākēṇam

Let our heart remain tender and our words sweet. Let us listen attentively to the directions on how to move forward on the path. Let our mind become free of all delusion.

56
nallatē cinticciṭāvū – makkaḷ
nallatē anyarkk-ēkāvū
uḷḷile cintayum bāhya-karmaṅgaḷum
nallat-āyāl uḷḷ-uṇarum

Children, think only good thoughts, and offer only good to others. When your thoughts and actions are pure, the Self awakens.

57
vāsanta rāmaṇikatvam – cittam
bāhyamāy cañcalippikkum
tyāgam tapam dīrgha-vairāgya sadguṇam
cētass-acañcalam ākkum

Objects of the senses turn our mind outwards. Renunciation, austerities, dispassion and goodness bring a firm resolve in our mind.

58
uḷḷil vivēkam udiccāl – ṛtu
bhēdattāl uḷḷ-ulayilla
ellām bhagavat-prasādamāy kāṇkilum
uḷḷam ulaññ-āṭukilla

When discernment dawns within, objects of the senses can no longer shake our resolve. Then we perceive everything as the gift of God.

59

ceytāl namukk-entu kiṭṭum – enna
cinta āṇentilum munnil
ceyyunnatil śraddha taṅgilla; kiṭṭunna
dravyattil āṇinnu kaṇṇu!

As we perform each action, our foremost thought is about the benefit we will receive. Our mind is inattentive to the action and is focused on the gains.

60

uṇṇān uṭukkān illāte – cuṭu
kaṇṇīru vīzhunna maṇṇil
tiṇṇam taṭukkuvān ākātta śāpatte
uṇṇān vidhikkappeṭum nām

Some people are starving and have no clothes to wear. Their tears fall on this earth, and we will have to face the consequences of our selfish actions.

61

nēṭunnatil alla mēnma – anyarkk-
ēkunnatil āṇu nanma
nalkkunnat-ēṫtavum nallat-āyīṭaṇam
nēṭunnatil tṛpti vēṇam

Nobility lies in giving to others, not in gaining for ourselves. Let us give our best and be content with what we have.

62
sārtthakam ākkuvin janmam – śatru
svārtthata mātram ennōrkkū
vēdiyil kattum viḷakku pōl jīvitam
dīpti parattunnat-ākū

Let us make our life meaningful. Our only real enemy is selfishness. May we spread light all around on the stage of our life.

63
tēn kadamba-pūkkaḷ pōle – cāru
tū mandahāsam pozhikkū
onnicc-uṇarnn-ezhīcc-onnicc-ānandiccu
eṅgum sugandham pozhikkū!

Let us smile with the nectarine beauty of kadamba flowers. Let us awaken together, become blissful together, and spread our fragrance all around.

ōmkāra divya porūḷe 64 (Malayalam)

Disclaimer: The translations of certain verses are not literal; they aim at bringing out the essential meaning from the Malayalam verses in a way that is easily understandable.

ōmkāra divya porūḷe varū
ōmana-makkaḷē vēgam
ōmanayāy vaḷarnn-āmayaṅgaḷ nīkki
ōmkāra-vastuvāy tīrū

Come quickly darling children, you who are the divine essence of Om. Remove all sorrows, grow dear and adorable, and merge with the Absolute.

1

santata-ānandam nukarām – tānē
svāntam samarppitam eṅkil
bhāva-ātmakam dhyāna-sādhanā-sauṣṭhavam
bhāsuram ākkaṭṭe uḷḷam

When we surrender ourselves, we savor infinite bliss. May our mind be purified and illumined through meditation and spiritual practice.

2

svantam allonnum ennālum – entum
svantam ākkān entu mōham
svantamāy uḷḷatē santyajicc-īṭāvū
svantamāy entuṇḍu pārttāl?

Nothing can really be our own; still we desire to possess things. In reality, there is nothing in this world we can call our own.

3

svantam ākkān vembum cinta – svantam
antaraṅgam duṣippikkum
svanta-kāryam mātram cinticcu cintayām
tantuvāl bandhippu svāntam

Our longing to own everything pollutes our mind. Caring only for our own affairs binds us.

4
svānta-antarīkṣam teḷiccu – svayam
tān tannil ettān paṭhikkū
svantam manassinde samsāra-nirmukti
santāpa-śāntikk-upāyam

Let us illumine our inner world and realize our true Self. Let us liberate our mind from this world and become free of sorrow.

5
san-manass-āṇu tan bandhu – veṙum
dur-manass-āṇu tan śatru
śatru-mitraṅgaḷe sṛṣṭiccat-eppozhum
san-manassum dur-manassum

Our mind becomes our true friend when it is suffused with goodness. Our mind becomes our enemy when it turns towards evil. We create friends and enemies depending on the quality of our mind.

6
ātma-samarppaṇam uṇḍēl – hṛttil
ātmaikya-bōdham uṇarum
cintayil nañcu-kalarātta-neñcakam
nandanōdyāna-samānam

Through self-surrender our heart awakens to its oneness with the Self. A heart free of poisonous thoughts is like the garden of heaven.

7
arppaṇam ceyyēṇḍat-alla – tānē
arppitam ākēṇam uḷḷam

ñān bhāva-hīnam samarppitam ennāl
samarppaṇam ñan bhāva-niṣṭham

Our mind should surrender spontaneously. In reality, all that we have to surrender is our sense of 'I'.

8
ceyyunna bhavam uḷḷappōḷ – phalam
ceytatin-otta pōl atre
ceyyunna bhāvam illate nām ceyyukil
ceyyāte ceyyunnu sarvam

When we act with a sense of doership, we have to experience the fruits of our actions, both good and bad. If we act without doership, divine energy acts through us.

9
svāśrayar ākēṇam eṅkil – īśvarar-
āśrayar ākēṇam ādyam
īśvara-anugraha-hīnar ārākilum
āśraya-hīnar āṇ-ennum

If we want independence, first we must depend on God. The blessings of God are all the support we ever need.

10
bhāvanā-pūrṇam ākēṇam – martya
jīvitam sōllāsa-pūrṇam
nīhāra-nirmala-nīla-nilāvu pōl
nīntaṭṭe sad-bhāvanakaḷ

When spiritual contemplation fills our mind, our life becomes joyful. Let good thoughts flood our mind like pure, radiant moonlight.

11
bhāvana illēl prakāśam – keṭṭa
jīvitam entinnu koḷḷum
pūviṭāṙillātta pāzh-ceṭikaḷkk-entu
jīvitam? janmam nirarttham

A life not rooted in goodness is dark. Such a life is as futile as plants that do not flower.

12
pūjaykk-eṭukkātta puṣpam – pōle
pāṭātta vīṇakaḷ pōle
jīvitam enna vara-prasādam vṛthā
pāzh-vastu ākkarut-ārum

Like flowers not offered in worship of the Lord, like a *veena* that never sings, the gift of life is in vain.

13
nāma-rūpaṅgaḷ illēlum – martya
bhāvanā-śaktikku munnil
nānā-prakāram bhavikkum parātparan
sattu-citt-ānanda-sāram

Though devoid of name and form, the supreme Self (existence, consciousness, bliss) shines within as our spiritual strength.

14
kāṇmatinn-āvēśam uṇḍēl – daivam
kaṇ-munnil nṛttam caviṭṭum
ētētu bhāvattil kāṇān kotikkilum
kāṇām vibhāvanā-yuktam

When we are eager to see God, His blissful form manifests before our eyes. We behold His glory in the form we desire.

15
dūratt-enn-ōrkkunnu daivam – toṭṭu
cāratt-ennōr-ārill-ārum
āzhattil ātmāvil ātmāv-uṇarumbōḷ
ātmāvu brahmam enn-ōrum

God seems far away, but God is nearer than the nearest, residing within as our true Self. When we awaken, we realize we are one with the absolute, all-pervading Self.

16
pāti-mayakkattil eṅkil – martyan
pāti-mauḍhyattilum allo
nidra-viṭṭ-unnidram ākum hṛdayattil
nityam pularkālam allo

We are half asleep and steeped in the folly of *maya*. When we awaken within, our hearts are ever fresh and joyful.

17
jīvarāśikk-utakāykil – svanta
jīvitam niṣprabhamallo

tellum koṭukkāte ellām eṭukkunna
vallabham pullilum tāzhe

A life that is of no use to the world is devoid of light and joy. If we take without giving even a little, we are lower than a blade of grass!

18

ōrttāl śūbhāpti-viśvāsam – nammil
vyartthatā-bōdham akaṫṫum
nalla nāḷ vann-ettum enn-ōrttu, māzhkāte
melle mell-ennu munn-ēṙum

Trust in a bright tomorrow removes the sense of futility. Believing in a good future, let us steadily move forward.

19

onnum tyajikkān illārkkum – uṇḍēl
tann-aham-bhāvam onn-atre
dēhōha-cintaye lāḷikkāt-etrayum
vēgam tyajippatē tyāgam

All we have to renounce is our ego, our sense of 'I'. Let us not pamper our body any further, but realize that it is not our true Self.

20

raṇḍu vibhāgam āṇ-eṅgum – onnum
illāttōr uḷḷavar ennum
mūnnāmatāy ellām uṇḍeṅkilum onnum
vēṇḍāttor ī maṇṇil mātram

There will always be 'haves' and 'have-nots' in this world. The great ones also live on this earth. They are content in the Self and need nothing from the world.

21
ā puṇya śālikaḷ mēnmēl – vannu
pōkunna maṇṇ-āṇ-it-ennum
samsāra-vāridhikk-akkarekk-ettikkān
tōṇiyumāy kāttu-nilkkum

Those realized ones manifest again and again in this land. They are the boats that ferry us across the ocean of *samsara*.

22
himsaye himsiccu nammaḷ – sarva
lōkādarav-ārnnu munnam
jīvitam prēma-naivēdyamāy arppiccu
nirvṛtarāy annu nammaḷ

In times past, the wise ones conquered cruelty and earned the reverence of the world. When our lives become an offering of love to the divine, we gain liberation.

23
kattum purayil ninnārō – cuṭṭu
poḷḷi veḷḷam tēṭum pōle
poḷḷunnor uḷḷattōṭ-uḷḷinde uḷḷil uṇma
kaṇḍettān śramikkū

Just as someone in a burning house desperately seeks water, seek the Truth in the depths of your burning heart.

24

satyattil jīviccāl ennum – namme
sajjanam ādariccīṭum
sad-bhāvanakaḷāl cittam prasādiccāl
sattayil jīvikkum ennum

The noble ones respect us if we live in Truth. Sincere intentions and good thoughts will give us the grace of our own mind and allow us to live in Truth.

25

ajñāna-lōkavum tannil – tanne
vijñāna-lōkavum tannil
tann-uḷḷil illāttat-onnum puṙattilla
uṇḍenna tōnnal allāte

Both knowledge and ignorance are within. In reality everything is within, though it seems to be outside.

26

jīvitam tīrill-orāḷkkum – mṛtyu
jīvita-śatru allārkkum
jīviccu jīvitam tīrilla – tīrunnat
āvilla jīvitam nityam

Life never ends and death is not the enemy of life. Life is eternal; death does not put an end to it.

27

tēn kiniyātuḷḷa pūvum – kāṫṫil
tūṫṫi kaḷañña patirum

kātal illātta pāzh-pādapavum pōle
pāzh-janmam ākkarut-ārum

Let not our life be futile like the flower with no nectar, or like chaff blowing in the wind, or like weak wood.

28
ponnōmal pūvukaḷ makkaḷ – ennum
ammaykk-ārōmal kiṭāṅgaḷ
tāṇu taṇutt-izhaññ-ettum pūn-tennal pōl
saumya-svabhāvikaḷ ākū

Children, you are my darling flowers, you are my cherished children. Be of humble and calm nature, like the gentle soothing breeze.

29
bāhya-snēhattinn-upari – daiva
snēham kotikkuvin makkaḷ
dāham śamippikkān kānal-jalam pōrā
bhōgam viśrānti ēkilla

Let us yearn for God's love, not for love from the world. Dirty water cannot quench thirst, and worldly experiences never give peace and repose.

30
vannu pōkunnatu mithya – satyam
vannu pōkillatu nityam
mithyaye pulkāte satyatte pulkkuvān
śraddha uḷḷōrkkilla duḥkham

Illusory objects come and go. Truth is eternal. Those who renounce the illusory world and embrace Truth become free of sorrow.

31
dēha-kāryārttham allallo – janmam
dēva-kāryārttham allallo
lōka-kāryārttham āṇ-ī dhanya-jīvitam
pūjita-anugraham allo

We are born to realize our divinity, not to merrily fulfill our material desires. Our life is a blessing from the One we worship. It is for serving the world.

32
duḥkhaṅgaḷil vaccu duḥkham – eṅgum
dāridrya-duḥkham onnallo
dāridryam entenn-aṙiyātt-avarkkum
uṇḍ-ātma-dāridryam enn-ōrkkū

Poverty is the greatest sorrow. Even those who have never experienced material poverty still suffer from the inner poverty of selfishness.

33
śōkattin okkeyum hētu – svanta
dēhāspadam enn-aṙiyū
bōdhattil ninnum śarīratte nīkkiyāl
śōkattin ādhāram illa

Identification with the body is the basis of all sorrow. When we stop identifying with our body and realize we are pure awareness, sorrow has no foundation.

34
pēril pratāpattil onnum – ārum
ēṙe pratīkṣa-vaykkēṇḍa
ārjjiccat-entum naśicciṭum samyōgam
ellām viyōgattil ākum

Name and fame do not last. Whatever we gain is soon destroyed. Everything we hold dear will soon leave us.

35
mōha-manass-or-āraṇyam – atil
mēyunna himsra-jantukkaḷ
mānuṣa-bhāvavum daivika-bhāvavum
ellām caviṭṭi metippū

The deluded mind is like a forest overrun by cruel animals. It tramples down all our humane and divine qualities.

36
śiṣṭarkk-iruvarkkum munnil – mūnnu
mārgam enn-ōtum budhanmār
śiṣṭa-duṣṭanmārkku rāṇḍāṇu pātakaḷ
duṣṭarkk-iruvarkkum ēkam

The wise ones say there are three paths for the noble, two for those who are both good and bad, and only one for the cruel.

37
pin-vāṅgiṭāṙilla ārum – tammil
neñcōṭu neñc-iṭayunnu

tān āṇu kēman enn-ēvarum cintikkē
jīvitam niścala-citram

No one is ready to make peace. They only stand chest to chest, ready to fight. When no one is willing to compromise, life freezes.

38
anyan-illātt-iṭam tēṭi – svanta
dēhattil oṭṭi piṭikkum
tēraṭṭa pōl curuṇḍīṭum tanikk-anyan
ārum allennu kāṇumbōḷ

We cling to our body and search for a spot where no one else is. We curl up within ourselves, unable to accept the truth that no one is a stranger.

39
rakta-asthi-māmsa-nibaddham – dēham
etra nāḷ kāttu sūkṣikkum?
tānum tanikk-ennum cinticcu cinticcu
tānē vazhi muṭṭi nilpū

How long can we protect this body made of blood, bones and flesh? Thinking only of ‘I’ and ‘mine,’ we reach a dead end.

40
dēhavum dēhiyum tammil – bhēdam
vērtiricc-ōrum vivēki
nīravum kṣīravum cērttu vaccīṭukil
kṣīramē hamsam nukarū

The wise know the body is not the Self. They are like the swan that can separate milk from water and drink only the milk.

41

ñān ennum nī ennum collum – collān
āvātta ñān āṇu satyam
'ñān'enna samjñakk-ādhāram ātmāv-eṅkil
'nī' ennat-ikkāṇmat-ellām

We say 'you' and 'I', but the real 'I' is the supreme Self. If the Self is the substratum for 'I', 'you' is the Self manifesting in the universe before us.

42

arttha-kāmaṅgaḷ puṇarnnu – martyan
mōkṣa-dharmaṅgaḷ veṭiññu
dharmārttha-kāmaṅgaḷ mōkṣattil āṇ-antya
viśramam koḷḷunnat-ennum

We embrace wealth and desire and abandon the path of righteousness and liberation. Liberation is the final goal and the end of the pursuit of *dharma*, wealth and desire.

43

puttan pularikku vēṇḍi – hṛttil
nityam pratīkṣa pularttū
satya-avabōdham sphuriccāl hṛdantattil
puttan pulari āṇ-ennum

Let us always hope for a new dawn in our mind. When awareness of the eternal Truth enlightens our heart, it is ever a new dawn!

44

karmaṅgaḷ sādhana ākkū – allēl
pūjā vidhāyakam ākkū
ātma-anusandhāna-rūpamām bhaktiyāl
aiśvarya-ānandam svadikkū

Let us transform our actions into spiritual practice and make them an act of worship. Let us know the Self through devotion, and experience bliss.

45

vīṇā ninādam kaṇakke – hṛdyam
ākaṭṭe sallāpam ellām
dhyāna-anurūpamāy māraṭṭe jīvitam
śālīnam ākaṭṭe śīlam

Let our conversation be melodious like the music of the *veena*. Let us make life a meditation, and gentleness our character.

46

sampattu sambhariccīṭām – mūlya
sampattu sañcayiccīṭām
santāpa-śāntikku sandēham illātma
sampatt-allāte illonnum

We can amass wealth and valuables, but only the wealth of the *atman* can remove our sorrows.

47

svantam ākkān ent-utsāham – ennāl
santyajikkān nirutsāham

ēkān paṭhikkāte nēṭān kotikkuvōr
cōraril cōrar enn-ōtum

We are eager to possess everything and reluctant to relinquish anything. If we are greedy to gain without giving back anything, we are a thief among thieves.

48

ōrkkunn-uṭal saundaryatte – ārum
ōrkkārilla ātma-sāraḷyam
saundaryam bāhyam all-uḷḷile nanma
āṇ-ā veḷiccattil jīvikkū

We care about physical beauty without caring about our inner purity. Real beauty is the goodness within. Let us live in the light of that goodness.

49

tīrtthaṅgaḷ āṭunnu nīḷe – ātma
tīrtthattil āṙāṭiṭāte
ātmāv-azhukkil puraṇḍu kiṭakkilum
dēham minukki naṭappū

We travel to bathe in holy waters, yet fail to bathe in the sacred waters of our true Self. We clean and burnish our body and leave our mind coated in dirt.

50

kartavyam ācarikāññāl – ṛṇa
bāddhyataykk-all-azhiv-ārkkum
dēham dhariccittu dharmam maṙakkuvōr
mūḍharkku munpar-āṇ-ennum

If we fail to perform our responsibilities, we will be unable to repay our debts. If we take a human birth and forget our *dharma*, we are foremost among the foolish.

51

āvatuḷḷappōḷ yathēṣṭam – bhōgam
āsvaddikkām ārttiyōṭe
vārddhakya kālattu vēṇēl śramicciṭām
ātma kāryārttham enn-ōrkkum

When our body is fit and strong, we greedily indulge in worldly pleasures. We plan to engage in the spiritual quest in our old age, if we feel like it.

52

oṭṭu nēram kazhiññilla – mṛtyu
peṭṭennu vātukkal etti
muṭṭi viḷikkavē keṭṭum pramāṇavum
iṭṭ-eṙiññ-ettaṇam kūṭe

But, suddenly Death appears and knocks at our door. We have to leave everything and go with him.

53

pinnāle nīṅgunnu jīvan – eṅgum
tiṅgunna kūriruḷ mātram
neñc-uraññ-aṅgan-izhaññ-izhaññ-etti nām
taṅgunnat-eṅgenn-aṙiññu

We follow Death and see only pitch dark all around. We do not know where Death leads us.

54
karma-āśrayam āṇ-ī lōkam – karmam
yōgattil etti nilkkēṇam
karmatte aśrayikkunn-avarkk-ākunnu
bhōgavum puṇyavum pōlum

This world depends on action, and our action should lead us to union with the divine. Without that, our action brings only merit and worldly experiences.

55
kārya-kṣamata illeṅkil – dēha
kārāgṛhattil kiṭakkām
śāntiyum kṣāntiyum illāte kḷāviccu
kānti keṭṭīṭunnu janmam

If we are unskilled in our action and do not hold the highest goal in our mind, we remain imprisoned in our body. We have no peace and calm, and our life loses its brightness and beauty.

56
ātaṅkam illātta lōkam – svantam
antaraṅgam mātram ōrkkū
ānanda-dhāmavum śānti-nikētavum
antaraṅgam tanne ōrkkū

The only world free of all distress lies deep within us. In reality, the abode of peace and bliss is our true Self.

57
uḷḷam vikasitam-āyāl – pinne
ellāṭavum kāṇmat-uṇma

dēha-gēhattile kārāgṛha-vāsam
dēhikk-atōṭe azhiyum

When our heart has blossomed, we see Truth everywhere. Then, we are freed from the delusion that we are our body!

58
illennu colluvorkk-illa – daivam
uṇḍennu kāṇmavarkk-uṇma
illennum uṇḍ-ennum all-antarātmāv-
uṇarnnāl uṇarv-āṇu daivam

Those who deny the existence of God cannot realize their divine essence. God exists as the ultimate Truth. God awakens within us as our true Self, and we cannot deny the existence of our own Self.

59
ālayam tōṙum naṭannu – veṇṇa
pāl tayir viṫ-azhiccīṭum
gōpāṅganamār svayam rādhika ennu
bhāviccu rādhayāy māṙi

The *gopis* of Vrindavan went from house to house selling milk, curd and butter. Imagining themselves to be Radha, the beloved of Krishna, they finally attained her state of supreme Love.

60
ā kaṇakk-ārkkum bhajikkām – daiva
saṅkalpam entāyāl entu?
kāṭhinyam ēṙunna sādhanaykk-appuṙam
prādhānyam bhāvanaykk-ēṙum

We can worship God in whichever form we cherish. More important than the practice of severe penance is the depth of our love for God.

61

āṭal ozhiññ-illa nēram – ennāl
āśakk-azhivilla ētum
āśā-nirāsam āṇ-āśvāsam ēvarkkum
āśa āṇ-ādyanta śatru

Desire is our greatest enemy and the cause of our grief. Only when we renounce desire will we find true relief.

62

kāmiccu nēṭēṇḍat-alla – hṛttil
dhyānicc-uṇarēṇam satyam
dēham patikku mumb-ātma-anusandhānam
pāṭham manaḥ pāṭham ākkām

Worldly desire can never lead us to the Truth. Through our meditation, the Truth dawns in our heart. Let us realize the Self before our body fails!

63

vēdam viḷaññor-ī maṇṇil – tellum
bhēda-bhāvattil illarttham
vastuvum vyaktiyum satyam allenn-ōrttu
sattaye pulkkuvin makkaḷ

In the land of the *Vedas* (which proclaim the oneness of all beings), there is no meaning in fostering differences. Children, know that objects and individuals are not the Truth, and embrace your real essence!

64
snēhiccāl tīrilla snēham – vīṇḍum
snēha-tēn-ūṙunnu hṛttil
snēha-dāridryattāl ātmāv-eriyāte
snēhiccu saurabham tūkū!

The heart is a wellspring of love that never runs dry. The nectar of that love ever brims over. Children, do not let your heart shrivel in the poverty of love, but spread the fragrance love all around!

ōmkāra divya porūḷe 65 (Malayalam)

Disclaimer: The translations of certain verses are not literal; they aim at bringing out the essential meaning from the Malayalam verses in a way that is easily understandable.

ōmkāra divya porūḷe varū
ōmana-makkaḷē vēgam
ōmanayāy vaḷarnn-āmayaṅgaḷ nīkki
ōmkāra-vastuvāy tīrū

Come quickly darling children, you who are the divine essence of Om. Remove all sorrows, grow dear and adorable, and merge with the Absolute.

1
ōrō hṛdaya-tuṭippum – bhāva
lāvaṇya-dīptam ākaṭṭe
ōrō vicāra-taraṅgavum lōkōpa-
kāra-pradam āyiṭaṭṭe

Let the radiance of good thoughts fills each heartbeat. May the vibration of each thought benefit the world!

2

satyam-kṣama-ārjjavam uṇḍēl – hṛttil
vidvēṣam tī paṭarilla
śuddha-antaraṅgam kṛpārdram āṇeppozhum
buddhi-bhēdam durbalatvam

The flames of hatred do not spread in a truthful heart that is forgiving and straightforward. A pure heart is always tenderly compassionate; a weak mind sees only differences.

3

tañcaṇam añc-indriyavum – pinne
tañcaṇam prāṇaṅgaḷ añcum
tañcaṇam pañca-mahābhūta-sañcayam
tañcaṇam tan manam neñcil

The five sense organs must turn inward and the five *pranas* must be controlled. Let us control our body (made of the five elements), and turn our mind inward.

4

kalpa-drumattinde cōṭṭil – taṇal
paṫti nām bhikṣa yācippū
pānthar āreṅkilum nīṭṭi eṙiyunna
nāṇaya-tuṭṭil santṛpti

We stand like beggars in the shade of the wish-fulfilling tree. Yet, we are content with the coins thrown by passers-by.

5

enne enikk-aṙiyilla – ende
aunnatyam ñān aṙiyilla
enniṭṭum ñān enne poykkāl vaṭi tumbil
ponticcu pokkam naṭippū

We do not know ourselves, nor are we aware of our own divinity. Instead of knowing our greatness, we balance on stilts and boast about the heights that we have reached.

6

ammaykk-atirukaḷ illa – pakṣe
makkaḷkk-atirukaḷ vēṇam
amma collum paṭi ācariccīṭukil
makkaḷkk-atirukaḷ tāṇḍām

Amma is beyond all boundaries, but my children must follow a discipline. If you obey Amma's words you will be able to transcend all boundaries.

7

ceyyaṇam ceyyarut-ennum – ādyam
vēṇam vidhi-niṣēdhaṅgaḷ
innatu ceyyaṇam, innatu ceyyarut-
enna niyantraṇam vēṇam

Initially, we need clarity on what to do and what not to do. We must be able to control our mind and our actions.

8

ñānum en dēhavum pōle – pinne
ñānum en jīvanum pōle

ñān ende ī vaka-cinta ākunn-ende
ajanma-śatrukkaḷ ōrttāl

Thoughts such as 'me' and 'my body,' and 'me' and 'my life' are our life-long enemies.

9
ñān ennum nī ennum bhēdam – kāṇmat-
ākāra-bhēdattāl mātram
bhēdaṅgaḷ dēhatte āśrayicc-ākunnu
dēhikku bhēdam illētum

The distinction between 'you' and 'me' depends on seeing differences between bodies. Difference is only at the physical level. The indwelling life force is one.

10
snēha-vākk-onn-uriyāṭān – pōlum
nāv-anaṅgātt-avar-āyi
jīvitam pārasparyattil ninn-etrayō
dūram vazhi-māṯṯi nammaḷ

We are not able to speak even one loving word. Our lives have changed direction, and we have strayed far from the ways of mutual love and cooperation.

11
illinn-ayal bandham ārkkum – ārkkum
illinn-upakāra-cinta
ill-anyarōṭ-oṭṭu pōlum kṛtajñata
ill-ārilum tell-aṭuppam

We have no bond with our neighbors and no thought of helping others. We are not close with one another, nor do we have even the least bit of gratitude.

12
ellām svakārya-vicāram – tellum
ill-uṇṇikaḷkk-uḷḷiṇakkam
tallum talōṭalum illeṅkil uṇṇikaḷkk-
uḷḷil vaḷarcca kallikkum

Our lives now revolve only around ourselves. Even small children are unable to open up their hearts. If children are not loved and shown the right path, their hearts become hard.

13
gauravam buddhikku vēṇam – sadā
saumyata hṛttinnu vēṇam
vākkinnu mādhuryam nōkkinnu kāruṇyam
vēṇam prasāda-ātmakatvam

Our intellect should be noble and our heart calm and composed. Our words should be sweet, our eyes kind, and our heart full of cheer.

14
kār-irumb-uṇḍa nīrttuḷḷi – vīṇḍum
vīṇḍ-eṭukkāvat-all-ārkkum
cāruta ōlunna bālyavum avidham
vīṇḍ-eṭuttīṭāvat-alla

You can never recall a bullet or save a fallen water drop. Once lost, the innocent beauty of childhood can never be reclaimed.

15
āṭi timarkkum ahatte – vīṇḍum
āḷi paṭarttāt-irikkū
āśa-varddhicc-aham cīrtt-ezhiccīṭumbōḷ
ātmā-iruṭṭil āzhnnīṭum

Let us not stoke the wild flames of our dancing ego. When desires increase and our ego swells, the *atman* is hidden in darkness.

16
āśiccu nēṭunna nēṭṭam – tīre
āśvāsa-nēṭṭam ākilla
āśā-nirāsam āṇātma śānti-pradam
āśa āṇāmaya hētu

Gains prompted by selfish desire never give real peace. Inner peace and calm dawn when we renounce desire, the cause our misery.

17
tēṭunnat-entum nissāram – svayam
bōdhippat-ākunnu sāram
nēṭēṇḍat-allātma-sāram svayam tānat-
āṇennat-ākunnu sāram

We can never find our true essence by searching outside. Truth reveals itself within. The Self is not gained; it is to be realized as one's own nature.

18
tēṭi piṭikkuvān ōṭum – ennāl
tēṭunnat-ōṭunnor enne

tān tande pinnāle ōṭi kitakkunnu
tān tanne bōdhikkuvōḷam

We run to catch ourselves. We keep on running and exhausting ourselves in the chase until we realize who we really are.

19
kāṇunna kāzhcaykku pinnil – ninnu
kāṇum orāḷ ārenn-ōrām
anya-nirīkṣaṇam tannil ninn-eppozhum
tanne akaṫṫunnat-ākām

Let us turn our gaze inward and realize the witness of all is our very Self. When we turn our gaze outward, we turn away from the knowledge of our true Self.

20
innallēl ennāṇ-iniyum - tannil
tānāyi varttippu nammaḷ?
inninu mātram āṇinn-ākān yōgyata
innallēl ennāṇu mukti?

When will we become true to our own Self, if not today? When will we realize the Self, if not in the present moment?

21
tāzhōṭṭu pōya puzhaye – keṭṭi
mēlēkk-eṭukkāvat-alla
pōya puzhayeyum pōya kālatteyum
ōrttu vilapicciṭēṇḍa

A river flowing downward can never reverse to flow upwards. There's no use in lamenting over water that flowed down or over lost time.

22
bhūta-bhāvikkāyi namme – svayam
bhāgī-karikkāt-irikkām
satyam innallēl pinn-ennāṇu makkaḷē
sattā-svarūpar āṇ-ārum

Let us not fragment our thoughts between the past and future. If not in the present, when will the Truth ever be found? Children, you, yourselves, are the very form of Truth.

23
vembi piṭaykkāt-irikkū – ellām
mumbē vidhicc-irikkunnu
bhāvikku vēṇḍi prayatnikkām allāte
bhūta-kālam kai-varilla!

Let us not cling to the past. Everything was meant to be. Our actions today determine our future, but the past is gone and will never return.

24
innale ceytat-ōrtt-ārum – innu
khinnar āyīṭēṇḍat-illa
innu ceyyunnatu niṣkāmam ākukil
khinnar āyīṭēṇḍa nāḷe

There is no point in crying over the wrongs we committed yesterday. If our actions today are unselfish, we will have no cause for grief tomorrow.

25

sattaye māniccitāttōr – brahma
vidyayum māniccitilla
satya-niṣēdhattin āyāsamill-ētum
illill-enn-ōtēṇḍat-uḷḷū

Those who cannot acknowledge the Self do not accept the existence of the Absolute. We can glibly deny the existence of the Truth. All we need to say is, "The Truth does not exist."

26

illill-ennalla collēṇḍū – kāṇmat-
allall-ennallo collāvū
allall-enn-onnonnāy taḷḷiyāl śēṣippat-
uḷḷat-onnē uḷ-ennōrum

Instead of saying 'it does not exist,' we should say that it is unseen. When we negate all that is not us, what remains is our true Essence.

27

telloru duḥkham varumbōḷ – kuṫṫam
ellām nām daivattil cārum
nallat-uṇḍāyāl atende mikavennu
colli ahaṅkariccīṭum

We blame God for even the slightest misfortune in our life. Then, when something good happens, we take all the credit.

28

uḷḷam malarkke tuṙakkām – namukk
ellām orātmā ennōrkkām

uḷḷum puravum illāt-uḷḷa caitanyam
allāte illaṅgum iṅgum

Let us open our hearts and remember that all is one Self. Pure Consciousness alone pervades all.

29
indriyam namme catikkum – kāṇmat-
indriyattōṭe naśikkum
indriya-lakṣyam bahir-mukham ākayāl
indriya-artthaṅgaḷē kāṇū

Our sense organs betray us by dragging our attention outward. Our senses only perceive the transient external, not the eternal *atman*.

30
mānuṣa-garvvil madippōr – adhō
mārgattil āṇennu vyaktam
mānuṣa-nanma teḷiyuvōr daivika
mārgattil ennum suvyaktam

Pride and ego take us down the wrong path. Those who reveal goodness in their thoughts and actions walk on the path of God.

31
svantam enn-ōrttava entum – nāḷe
antakan bhakṣiccu tīrkkum
kālande kālocca ētu nērattum ī
kōlāyil ettiṭām mandam

Tomorrow death will eat up all that we claim as ours. We may hear the soft footsteps of the God of death at any time.

32

pāpa-karmaṅgaḷ ozhiññāl – tēññu
māyum aham-buddhi tānē
pāpa-karmaṅgaḷkku hētuvām ajñānam
māyukil āmayam māyum

When we stop acting selfishly, our ego fades away naturally. When ignorance, the cause of all selfishness, disappears, all impurities vanish.

33

uḷḷam pariśuddham āyāl – pinne
eḷḷōḷam ill-allal-eṅgum
ellām dhanam koṇḍ-aḷakkukil allal inn-
eḷḷōḷam illa virāmam

When our mind becomes pure, not even a speck of sorrow remains. If wealth alone is our yardstick, our mind will never be at peace.

34

onnu nām cinticc-uṙaykkum – daivam
maṫtonnu kalpicc-uṙaykkum
svanta hitaṅgaḷe daiva-hitam ennu
cinticcāl cinta pizhaykkum

We propose and God disposes. Let us not misrepresent actions prompted by our likes and dislikes as the will of God.

35

āreyum drōhikkayilla – daivam
ēvarkkum samrakṣa nalkum
rakṣa tēṭunnavar eppozhum daivattil

arppitar āyirikkēṇam

God always protects everyone and never harms anyone. Let us have firm faith and surrender to God, and seek protection.

36
nammaḷ vicārikkum pōle – vēṇam
daivam vicārippān ennu
śāṭhyam piṭikkēṇḍa, svantam vicāratte
daivikam ākān paṭhikkū

Let us not demand that God should be on our wavelength. Rather, let us align our thoughts with the divine will.

37
ōrōnnum ōrō vidhattil – daivam
vārttu veccīṭunn-anyūnam
nērē viparītam ākkān śramikkāte
nēr-kāzhca kaṇḍ-āsvadikkām

God's creation is unparalleled. Let us try to imbibe and appreciate its Truth and not make a mockery of it.

38
sṛṣṭiyil dōṣam-darśikke – atu
dṛṣṭi tan darśana-dōṣam
dṛṣṭi-dōṣam koṇḍu sṛṣṭi-dōṣam kaṇḍāl
sraṣṭāvin allatil naṣṭam

When we find fault in creation, it is our vision that is faulty. The creator transcends our faulty vision.

39
kollākkola ceytiṭāte – sṛṣṭi
vaibhavam āsvadiccīṭām
āsvādanam ennāl ātmāvil āvāhicc-
aiśvarya-ānandam ākkīṭām

Let us not destroy. Rather, let us appreciate the glory of creation. The beauty that we perceive in the world leads us to the bliss of the *atman*.

40
cōrum haritābha namme – duṣṭa
cōranmār ākān vidhippū
cōrunna saundaryam bhūmikku nalkkuvān
pōrunnōr alla nām ārum

Earth's green abundance will be lost forever if we do not stop thieving. We are not capable of restoring the bounty that is fast fading away.

41
ākāra-sauṣṭhavam nōkki – nammaḷ
saundaryam āsvadikkunnu
sauśīlam ākunna saundarya-bōdham āṇ-
āsvādanattinnu mānam

We only appreciate the perfection of physical form as beauty. Real beauty is in a good heart and noble character.

42
cēvaṭi-tāriṇa kūppi – tozhum
ācāram āvilla bhakti
satya-saundaryattil līnamām hṛttile

sattenna mutt-āṇu bhakti

Devotion is not just rituals like folding our hands in prayer before the lotus feet of the Lord. Devotion is the luminous pearl of the heart immersed in the eternal beauty of Truth.

43

lōla-hṛdayam āṇ-ārkkum – ennum
daivikam āyor āsthānam
kḷāvicc-iṭāt-atu tānē tiḷaṅgaṇam
snēha-anuśīlattilūṭe

Just as we polish away the green layer that dulls the sheen of copper, let us free our hearts from all impurity. A tender and pure heart filled with love is the seat of God.

44

snēha-vāyp-illātta hṛttil – uḷḷat
āsura-vṛttikaḷ mātram
āsura-vṛtti tiṇarttāl prakṛtikku
nāśam vitaccu kutikkum

The heart devoid of love harbors only wicked thoughts. When such thoughts become action, they cause destruction all around.

45

dēham dharicc-annu toṭṭu – nammaḷ
prāyam kaṇakk-ākkiṭunnu
prāyam śarīrattin allāte ātmāvin
illenn-aṙivāṇ-aṙivu

We start aging from the day we are born. Real knowledge is knowing that only the body ages, not the *atman*.

46
illonnum uṇḍāvukilla – uḷḷat
allāttatil ninnum onnum
uḷḷatil ninnallāt-uḷḷat-uṇḍāvilla
illāyma uḷḷat-all-uṇma

Nothing eternal is born of this transient world. Truth will always be complete and eternal.

47
śuddhī-karikkaṇam ādyam – svanta
hṛttinn-akattaḷam nannāy
citta-viśuddhiyāl allāt-uṇarilla
sattu-cittānanda-rūpam

First, let us purify our heart. Only a pure heart can awaken to the Truth of *satchidananda* (existence, consciousness, bliss).

48
ētoru teṫṫum kṣamikkum – teṫṫu
tān ceytat-āṇeṅkil mātram
avidham anyande teṫṫum kṣamikkuvān
ārjjavam ārjjicciṭēṇam

We forgive ourselves for our every fault. Let us gain the strength of mind to forgive the mistakes of others also.

49
vīṭu nannākuvān ādyam – svanta
nāvu nannākaṇam ārkkum
vīṭu nannāy illēl nāṭu nannāvill-enn-

ādya-pāṭhattil tuṭaṅgām

Speaking honest and good words is a way to build a good home. A good home is the first step in building a good country.

50

nannāy kuḷicc-oruṅgīṭum – pakṣe
svantam manass-andhakāram
bāhya-dēham mōṭi eṫṫi veccītīlum
antar-manass-andhakāram

We bathe and dress well, but darkness bathes our heart. We dress our body beautifully, but our heart is covered in darkness.

51

kaṇḍ-eṭukkān uḷḷ-upāyam – onnum
kaṇḍ-ettiṭāt-andharāyi
candanam pūśi naṭann-ambalam tōṙum
cennāl tuṇakkilla daivam

Wearing sandal paste and going from temple to temple is not the way to find Truth. God will not help us unless we turn inward.

52

kaṇṇu koṇḍalla nām kāṇmū – kaṇṇil
pinnil uṇḍ-uṇmayām kaṇṇu
kāṇunna kāzhcaykku pinnil ār-ennatu
munnē nirīkṣikkum kaṇṇu

The external eyes see by the light of the inner Eye. That eternal witness perceives the 'I' that sees all sights.

53
ī lōkam svantam allārkkum – svantam
āṇēl ellāvarkkum svantam
daivavum svantam allārkkum atalleṅkil
daivam ellāvarkkum svantam

If one person owns this world then everyone owns this world. No one person owns God; or, if so, everyone owns God.

54
ñān ende ī vaka raṇḍum – viṭṭu
kāṇumā kāzhca uṇḍāyāl
tēn uṇḍu ceṇḍil mayaṅgunna vaṇḍinde
mauna nirvēda sthititvam

When we can see everything without the feeling of 'I and mine', we become like the bee full of nectar that sits in silent rapture within the flower.

55
nēṭēṇdatall-īśvaratvam – hṛttil
mēvunnatām ātma-satyam
tānē śvasikkum param-jyōtiss āṇatu
tān ennorā mahā-satyam

Divinity is not something to be attained. It is the Truth that ever resides within. Our very nature is the supreme Truth.

56
mēyān viṭātirikkēṇam – manam
māyā jagattil yathēṣṭam

māyā viṣayattil vyāmoham ēṟiṭām
māyikamāya manassil

Let us not allow our mind to wander freely in this illusory world. The world of illusory objects creates strong cravings in our mind.

57
yātonnu kāṇunnu nammaḷ – kāṇmat-
ētonnum ennil ninn-anyam
kāṇmat-ētonnum tān alleṅkil pinne ī
kāṇmatin entāṇ-or-arttham?

If we do not know who we really are, everything will appear separate from us. When we realize our true Self, we realize that nothing is separate from us.

58
dēhavum dṛśyam ākunnu – dṛśyam
ētum anityam ākunnu
draṣṭāvām enne ñān dēham enn-ōrkkumbōḷ
kaṣṭam! ñān dṛśyam ākunnu

Everything we perceive is perishable, even our own body. Let us not identify ourselves with our perishable body. We are, in truth, the eternal Self.

59
daivam allāttava ellām – uḷḷil
ninnum upēkṣikku makkaḷ
illa pinnilla allal uḷḷil sadā daiva
sallāpa sānniddhyam mātram

Children, abandon all that is not God. Then the presence of God will fill your heart and all grief will disappear. You will always be conversing with God!

60

ellām upēkṣikka ennāl – uḷḷam
melle samarppikka allo
uḷḷam samarppiccāl ellām upēkṣiccu
taḷḷuvān illa pinn-onnum

To abandon everything means to offer ourselves entirely to God. Once we offer our heart to God, there is nothing for us to reject.

61

sthāpikkān vādikkum nammaḷ – daivam
uṇḍ-ennum illennum ellām
kāṇum ī kāzhcakaḷ nērennu kāṇkil ī
kāzhcakaḷ etra nāḷ nīḷum?

We hold many debates to establish the existence or non-existence of God. We delude ourselves when we think that the Truth is only what we can see.

62

anya-hastaṅgaḷilūṭe – daivam
namme sahāyikkān ettām
rūpam illātt-avan ētu rūpatteyum
pulkān prayāsam ill-oṭṭum

God comes to help us through the hands of others. The formless God easily assumes any form.

63
nīrccālu tāzhēykku pōkum – agni
jvālakaḷ mēlēykk-uyarum
ēkātmam eṅkilum vyatyastha rūpattil
jīvan pravarttikkum eṅgum

Water always flows downwards, and fire always burns upwards. All is the one Self appearing as different forms.

64
akṣara-lakṣam japiccāl – japa
lakṣyam ārum prāpikkilla
lakṣōpalakṣam all-unnam japattinde
lakṣyam manassinn-aṭakkam

We will not attain the goal just by chanting our mantra a million times. The purpose of chanting is to subdue the mind.

65
tī-kkanal ūti perukki – mahā
jvālayāy māṫṫunnu kāṫṫu
āḷi paṭarttān parayēṇḍatu pōle
ūti teḷikkuvin satyam!

Like fanning embers to stoke a mighty blaze, fan the embers of Truth and let it shine forth.

ōmkāra divya porūḷe 66 (Malayalam)

Disclaimer: The translations of certain verses are not literal; they aim at bringing out the essential meaning from the Malayalam verses in a way that is easily understandable.

ōmkāra divya porūḷe varū
ōmana-makkaḷē vēgam
ōmanayāy vaḷarnn-āmayaṅgaḷ nīkki
ōmkāra-vastuvāy tīrū

Come quickly darling children, you who are the divine essence of Om. Remove all sorrows, grow dear and adorable, and merge with the Absolute.

1
satyamē nityam jayikkū – nitya
satta tān addhyātma-satyam
nityam allātt-ava satyam enn-ōrtt-ōrttu
satya-niṣēdhi ākallē

The Truth of existence, our pure Essence, always wins. Let us not refute the Truth by mistaking the transient world to be eternal.

2
uḷḷatin illāyma illa – eṅgum
illāttat-uḷḷat-ākilla
uṇḍennum illennum vāṙaṫta vādaṅgaḷ
raṇḍinum mēle āṇ-uṇma

The all-pervading Truth is eternal. That which is limited by time and space will cease to be. The Truth transcends both.

3
jvālayil ninnum anēkam – jvāla
vyāpṛtam ākkān kazhiyum
ātmīyatayil ninn-ātmīyata nēṭām
ātmīya satyam gurutvam

A single flame can light many fires. To gain spiritual knowledge we need the *guru's* grace.

4
vēda-adhikārikaḷ ārum – jñāna
vairāgya-śīlam uṇḍeṅkil
tī-kanal pōle tiḷaṅgunna buddhikku
jñāna-vairāgyam susādhyam

When knowledge and dispassion set our intellect ablaze, we are able to imbibe the essence of the *Vedas*.

5
tannil niyantraṇam illa – tellum
tanne tanikk-aṙiyilla
tanneyum tan jīvitatteyum tān allit-
onnum niyantrippat-ōrttāl

We have no control over ourselves, nor do we really know who we are. If we ponder on this, we realize we are not in control of our own life.

6
entum niyantrikkān mōham – pakṣē
svantam manass-onn-ozhike

āṭal ozhiññor-ēṭatt-onnu svasthamāy
kūṭān manassin ill-āśa

We desire to control everything except our own mind. Our mind has no desire to remain silent and still its frenzied dance.

7
entu ceyyumbōzhum nammaḷ – nannē
cinticc-uṙaccu ceyyēṇam
ceytiṭṭu cinticciṭṭ-entu kāryam? phalam
ceytatin otta pōl ettum

Let us reflect and be clear about our intentions before we act. What is the use of thinking after we act? Even if we regret our actions, we will have to experience their fruits.

8
bandhanam ākāte karmam – ceyyān
santatam sādhikkum eṅkil
janmāntara andhyam nivarttamāy hṛttaṭam
kanmaṣa-muktam carikkum

Let us perform our actions without being entangled by them. Then our mind will remain pure and we can end the cycle of birth and death.

9
vēṇḍunnat-ācarikkilla – oṭṭum
vēṇḍāttat-ācariccīṭum
kāṇunnatil kaṇṇ-uṭakki nilkkum, satyam
kāṇēṇḍa kaṇṇ-aṭaccīṭum

We fail to practice what should be practiced, and we engage in what is undesirable. Our eyes latch on to external sights, and are closed to the Truth.

10
vāda-kōlāhalam viṭṭu – makkaḷ
vēda-sārāmśam ārāyū
jñāna-bhāram cumakkāte puṇyātmākkaḷ
nēṭiya vēda nēr-ōrū

Children, avoid debates and arguments and contemplate the essence of the *Vedas*. Lay down the burden of vain knowledge and listen to the truth of the *Vedas* taught by the divine ones.

11
dvaita-avasānam varumbōḷ – martyan
martyataykk-appuṙam pōkum
daivika-sattayil svatvam nivēdiccu
nitya-svātantryam svadikkum

When the illusion of duality disappears, we transcend our human nature. When we offer ourselves to the divinity within, we experience eternal liberation.

12
īśvaran ārennat-alla – svanta
sārāmśam ārāññ-aṙiyū
tān ennat-ārennu tān tān aṙiyukil
nāka-lōkam veṙum tuccham

Rather than pondering on the nature of God, let us discover who we really are. The joys of heaven are trifling compared to the bliss of our own true Self.

13
munnamē svargam āṇuḷḷam – martyan
pinnatil nañcu kalarttum
karma-dōṣattāl narakam ākkum svargam
cīrtt-ezhum martyande muṣkku

The real nature of the mind is pure joy, but we poison it with our selfish thoughts. Our wrong actions turn heaven into hell, and arrogance grows unchecked.

14
raṇḍinum appuṙam pōkān – pāta
paṇḍē tuṙanna ṛṣimār
mantra-draṣṭākkaḷāy vāzhttum avaruṭe
darśanam ākaṇam kaṇṇu!

The ancient sages, the seers of sacred mantras, shed light on the path to liberation. Let us realize their vision.

15
akkaṇṇu kaṇṇāy varumbōḷ – pinne
ikkaṇṇu kaṇṇalla ārkkum
kāzhcakaḷ kaṇḍu kaṇḍ-uḷḷam aṭaññavar-
uḷḷinde kāmbu kāṇilla

When their vision becomes ours, we see only Oneness everywhere. Eyes engrossed in the world remain closed to the inner Essence.

16
ayira tāṇḍukaḷ-āyi – namme
anayicc-ādariccīṭān

ā vazhi-tārakaḷ kāttu kiṭakkunnu
kātōrttu pāda-vinyāsam

The path to liberation has waited thousands of years to welcome us and lead us on. It eagerly awaits the sound of our footsteps.

17
arṣam appātayilūṭe – pōyāl
atmaikya-lakṣyattil ettām
mūrtti-bhēdaṅgaḷkkum appuṙam ātmīya
saubhāgya-śālikaḷ ākām

When we travel this ancient path laid down by the sages, we realize our Oneness with the Self. Established in the Self, we will transcend the many forms of the divine.

18
abhram kaṇakkuḷḷam ēṫṫam – bhavyam
śubhram ākunneṅkil mātram
icconna lakṣyatin uttama-pātramāy
saccinmayam minni minnum

When our heart becomes pure and blemish-free, the radiance of eternal Truth will shine within.

19
tṛkkāliṇakaḷ vaṇaṅgi – makkaḷ
saprēmam ātmārpaṇattāl
sadguruviṅkal samāśrayam tēṭiyāl
samśuddha-hṛttinn-udayam

Children, bow down with love before the sacred feet of the *sadguru*. When you seek refuge in the *sadguru*, your heart becomes pure.

20

āśakaḷ aśru nīr ēkum – klēśa-
nāśattin āśā nirāsam
āśayil ninnum nirāśa janikkunnu
āśa aśānti niṙaykkum

Desire brings sorrow. Only by abandoning desire will we become free of all distress. Disappointment and disquiet are born of desire.

21

ārtti tan ājanma-śatru – ārtti
kīrtti nāśattinnu hētu
ārtti viṭṭāl kīrtti mātram all-ātmīya
tīrtthattil nīnti nīrāṭām

Greed is our lifelong enemy. It destroys our sense of honor. Let us be free of greed and live with honor, bathing in the sacred waters of the Self.

22

ceyyāte ceyyunna karmam – nannāy
ceyyukil karma-vimukti
karmattil jñānam kalarilla eṅkilum
karma-viyōgam bhavikkum

Let us perform our actions without doership and thus transcend action. In real knowledge there is no sense of doership.

23

naṭṭu nanaccu vaḷarttām - nanma
peṭṭu pōkāt-ennum kākkām
tinmaye velluvān vāḷ eṭuttīṭēṇḍa
nanmakaḷ nīḷe vitaykkām

Let us sow seeds of goodness everywhere, and cultivate and protect it from withering. Thus, let us conquer evil.

24

vyarttha-svapnaṅgaḷ menaññu – svanta
kartavyam ellām maṙannu
dīrghanāḷ nīṙi pukaññ-eriññīṭāte
ūrjjasvalarāy jvalikkū

Be a bright flame. When we neglect our duties and responsibilities, we dream vain dreams. Thus, we squander life's potential, like embers smothered in ashes.

25

kāṇum divā-svapnam ellām – namme
kāṇākkayaṅgaḷil āzhttum
icchā-prabalata lakṣyattōḷam cennu
muṭṭi viḷippatē svapnam

Our daydreams drive us into a deep chasm. Our real dream should catalyze a strong will that knocks at the door of the goal.

26

dēham variccāl marikkum – vīṇḍum
bhūvil janikkum marikkān

uṇḍum kūṭiccum kaḷiccum rasiccum iṅg-
eṇṇiyāl tīrātta janmam

One who is born will die, and again take birth just to die again. We eat, drink and frolic in vain pleasure through countless lives.

27
karmam niśśēṣam naśiccē – ārkkum
janma-vināśam bhavikkū
puṇya-bhōgam bhujicc-ullasikkān svarga
lōkam gamikkān tiṭukkam!

The cycle of birth and death ends only when our karma is exhausted. Yet we perform actions in order to reach heaven and enjoy the fruits of our meritorious deeds.

28
cāndra-lōkam gamiccīṭum – jīvan
ceyta satkarmam naśiccāl
śēṣicca vṛttiyumāy pōya mārgēṇa
vīṇḍum piṙakkunnu bhūvil

When the merits of our good deeds are over, we come back from the higher worlds to earth to experience the fruits of our remaining karma according to our latent impressions.

29
śēṣicca vṛttikaḷ ellām – nannē
samskaricc-illāte āyāl
jīvan vimuktamāy dēha-nāśam vare
ātma-viśrāntiyil vāzhum

When our mind is free of all blemish, all remaining impressions disappear. The liberated one remains established in tranquility until it departs from the body.

30
kālam uṇḍāyatin munnē – lōka
jālam uṇḍāyatin munnē
uḷḷat-entāyirunn-uṇma connāl dvandvam
ēlātta cētana mātram

Before time, before the creation of this illusory world, only pure Consciousness existed, free of all duality.

31
māṙi maṙiyum ī lōkam – ōrttāl
māyaykk-adhīnam enn-ōtām
ōṭunna vaṇḍikaḷkk-ōṭātta pātapōl
sthāyi āṇ-īśvara-astitvam

Maya is the cause of this ever-changing, illusory world. God, the changeless substratum, is like the motionless road beneath the moving vehicles.

32.
kāḷum viṣayēccha māṙi – manam
lōlamāy nirviṣayattāl
jñānōnmukham dhyāna-līnam carikkukil
māṙum manass-enna mānam

When our flaming desire for worldly objects dies, our mind becomes pure. Let us turn our attention to knowledge and practice meditation. Then, the sky of our mind will be transformed.

33

jñāna-cakṣussināl vēṇam – enne
ñān onnu toṭṭ-aṙiññīṭān
yajñōpavītam upanayanam ennat-
ēṫṫam samīpastha dṛṣṭi

We need the eye knowledge to know ourselves. Knowledge of the essence of the *Vedas* will give us the insight.

34

collām samīpastham ennāl – ātma
samvēdanattinnu yōgyam
kāzhcakaḷ kāṇunna kaṇṇalla kaṇṇinum
kaṇṇāya cinmizhi mātram

This inner eye lets us delve into the true Self. It is the eye of knowledge, not the eye that sees the outer world.

35

vaividhya-pūrṇam ī lōkam – atil
ēkata kāṇēṇam eṅkil
ātmaikya-bōdhattil āṙāṭi vāruṫṫat-
ākaṇam cētassu mēnmēl

To see Oneness in this diverse universe, our heart should bathe in the bliss of the effulgent Self.

36.

kḷāviccu kānti kēṭāte – dīrgha
kālam nilāvu paratti

śōbhāya mānam virājikka āṇ-innum
vēda-samskāram ī maṇṇil

To this day the *Vedas* have survived, without losing their luster and vitality. They inspire us to seek the ultimate Truth.

37
vaividhyam ēṙe uṇḍēlum – tellum
vairūpyam illavakk-ētum
ācāra-bhēdaṅgaḷ ātmīya-lakṣyattil
ēkaśśila pōl baliṣṭham

The diverse traditions and rituals stand firm as a rock in their goal of helping us attain the Self.

38
mārgaṅgaḷ vyatyastam ennāl –lakṣyam
atmaikya-bōdham onnatre
svacchanda-sañcāra mārgattin okkeyum
saccidānandam svalakṣyam

Paths may differ but the realization of the Self is the only goal. We travel steadily along these paths towards *satchidananda* (existence, consciousness, bliss).

39
cattu cenniṭṭalla mukti – mukti
ippōzh iviṭe ārjjikkām
ippōzh iviṭe illāt-uḷḷa mukti pinn-
eppōzh eviṭunnu kiṭṭān?

Let us gain liberation here and now, not after we die. Where and how will we gain liberation if not here and now?

40

mṛtyuvin appuṙam kāṇān – vēṇam
etrayum niścaya-dārḍhyam
hrasva-dṛṣṭikk-entu sādhyam? ślathamaṫṫa
buddhiyil tattvam udikkum

To see beyond death, we need incredible determination. It is impossible for people of narrow vision. The spiritual principle awakens in a one-pointed intellect.

41

hṛttil atāviṣkariccu – svayam
sattayāy tanne varttikkām
śuddhī-karicca tan hṛttil āṇ-advaita
satyam svayam prakāśippū

When the Truth of *advaita* (non-duality) awakens in our heart, we will remain established in the Essence of existence. The Truth naturally dawns in a pure heart.

42

buddhi-sāmartthyam uṇḍēlum – ātma
svatvam niṣēdhicciṭumbōḷ
satyam śarīrattil kalpiccu cittatār
nityam muraṭiccu pōkum

We may be highly intelligent, but if we reject the Truth of the Self and believe that we are only the body, all goodness drains away.

43
asthira-vastuvil taṅgi – cittam
asthiram ākkāt-irikku
citta-sthirata āṇ-adhyātma-lakṣyattin
atyantam āvaśya-siddhi

When our mind gets caught in perishable objects, it will be unsettled. A settled and steady mind is essential to reach the goal of the Self.

44
tēṭum tān ārenn-aṟiññu – vēṇam
tēṭēṇḍat-ārum ennōrū
daivika-sthānam hṛdayam āṇ-ātmā
avabōdhōdayattin viyattu

We are seeking our true Self. Divinity dwells within our heart. That is where true awareness dawns.

45
daiva-sānnidhyam uṇḍ-eṅgum – pakṣe
darśippat-illārum eṅgum
śūnyamāy tīraṇam cētassu svīkārya
bhāvattil vartticciṭēṇam

God is everywhere, but we fail to see Him. For us to feel His presence, our mind should be receptive and open.

46
nanmakaḷ tan samāhāram – ākān
janmam upakarikkumbōḷ

tinmakaḷkk-āyussill-uḷkkaḷam ullasicc-
uṇma darśicc-uṇma ākum

When we use this life to perform good deeds, all negativities fall away. Then we will be joyous and merge in the Truth.

47
nanmayil nañcu kalartti – eṅgum
tinma viṭaykkāt-irikkū
eḷḷil uḷḷeṇṇa pōl uḷḷil uḷḷuṇma nām
taḷḷāte koḷḷān śramikkū

Let us not sow the seeds of evil disguised as goodness. Truth is within us, like oil within the sesame seed. Let us embrace this Truth and strive to experience it.

48
uḷḷāl uṇarnnavar āyāl – svayam
ellā vipattum ozhiyum
uḷḷam duṣippicc-amarttum arādiye
vellāte ill-ātma-lābham

When we awaken to our true Self, danger ceases. We cannot realize the Self without conquering the enemy that subjugates and pollutes our mind.

49
nannē manassilāy ennu – manam
connāl manassil āyilla
onnum manassil ākill-eṅkilum sadā
tenni maṫṫonnilēykk-ōṭum

If our mind says, 'I understand the Truth clearly,' it has not understood it. The mind slips away and runs after worldly objects and experiences.

50

uṇḍō manass-enna cōdyam – vannāl
illenn-oruttaram kiṭṭum
uṇḍenna cintayāl ārāyukil manam
tellum vazhaṅgilla ārkkum

If we inquire into the nature of the mind, we discover that the mind does not exist. If we believe in the existence of the mind, we will never be able to subdue it.

51

illāttat-uṇḍennu tōnnān – manam
vallāte prēraṇa ēkum
taṅgillor-ēṭattu kāṫṫattu paññi pōl
aṅg-iṅgu pāri paṙakkum

Flying around like a wisp of cotton in the wind, our mind tries to make us believe that the transient is the eternal reality.

52

śikṣaṇam kiṭṭiyāl pakṣē – diśa
teṫṫāte pōy enn-irikkām
śikṣaṇattinn-onn-irunneṅkilāy ceṫṫ-
irunnāl atin pēru buddhi

A disciplined mind may travel without losing its direction. When the mind allows itself to be disciplined even for a little while, it becomes the intellect.

53

kaṇṇima cimmiyāl ōṭān – taram
kāttirunnīṭum manassu
kākkunnat-āre āṇāreyum innōḷam
kēvalam vañcicca śīlam

The mind waits to escape in the blink of an eye. It always betrays the one who stands guard over it.

54

dēśāṭana-pakṣikaḷkkum – kṛtya
śīla-guṇaṅgaḷ uṇḍākām
dēśam maṙakkāte āvartticc-ettunna
śīlam avarkk-uṇḍu kṛṭyam

Even migrant birds have set behavior patterns. They return to the same habitats year after year, never forgetting the migratory routes.

55

pōyāl tirike vannīṭān – pakṣe
mōham manassin illētum
santata-sañcāri ennāl diśā-bōdham
entennu toṭṭu tīṇḍilla

Our mind does not desire to return home. It is our constant companion, but it has no sense of direction and no aptitude for the goal.

56

ōṭunnu vēgattil ārum – nērē
ōrkkārill-eṅgōṭṭ-enn-ārum

pōkēṇḍa lakṣyam maṙannavar eṅkilum
vēgata pōr-enna tōnnal

We run without knowing where to go. Though we have forgotten our destination, still we feel we run too slowly.

57
munnōṭṭu pōnnennu tōnnum – dūram
pinnōṭṭu tāṇḍunnu vīṇḍum
ann-annu nām ceyyum nanmayāl allāte
munnōṭṭu nīṅgill-orāḷum

We think we are moving forward, but, in fact, we are moving backwards. Performing good deeds is the only way to move forward.

58
nanmakaḷ kai-varikkānum – pinne
tinmakaḷ kai-ozhiyānum
tanmanam mēnmēl vivēkam ārjjikkaṇam
nanmayē kāṇū nām eṅgum

To free our heart of negativities and attain goodness, our mind should be discerning. Then we will see only goodness everywhere.

59
kāmatte prēmamāy kaṇḍāl – prēmam
kāmamāy kāṇum nirarttham
kāmavum prēmavum tammil dhruva-antaram
kāṇmōrkku prēmam pavitram

If we mistake desire for love, then true love becomes meaningless. Love becomes pure when we realize that love and desire are poles apart.

60
ātmīya-bōdha-prakāśam – lōkam
svātmī-karippatin-āyi
ātmāv-uzhiññavar ākuvin makkaḷē
ātma-avabōdhattilūṭe

Children, inquire into the nature of your own Self. Give your life for the world that the effulgent light of the Self may shine within everyone.

61
duḥkhaṅgaḷ entum sahikkān – balam
hṛttin upalabdham ākum
saprēmam ātmārppaṇam ceytu sadgurōr-
ājñakk-adhīnam carikkū

When we offer ourselves with love to the *sadguru* and walk the path He instructs, we become strong enough to bear any sorrow.

62
nēṭum birudaṅgal ētum – namme
nām ākki māṭṭilla nūnam
ñān enne cūṣaṇōpādhi ākkīṭunnu
ñān enna bhāvattilūṭe

All the certificates we earn do not make us true to ourselves. We use them to strengthen our ego and to deceive ourselves.

63
yātonnu kāṇunnu nammaḷ – kāṇmat-
ētonnum ennil ninn-anyam

kāṇmat-ētonnum tān alleṅkil pinne ī
kāṇmatin entāṇ-orarttham?

If we see everything as separate from us, what is the meaning of our life? Unless we see everything as our own Self, we have not fulfilled this human birth.

64
dēhavum dṛśyam ākunnu – dṛśyam
ētum anityam ākunnu
draṣṭāvām enne śarīram enn-ōrkkumbōḷ
kaṣṭam! ñān dṛśyam ākunnu

The body is an object of perception, and all perceptions are impermanent. What a pity when the seer mistakes himself to be the seen, the mere physical body.

65
onnillēl onnum illallo – ellām
onninōṭ-ottu varttikkum
onninōṭ-ottu ninnīṭunna pūjyaṅgaḷkk-
onnin-onn-ēṟunnu mūlyam

Zeros have value only when preceded by a one. Value increases in proportion to the zeros that come after the one.

66
entum tapass-ākki māṫṫām – ōrō
cintayum indhanam ākkām
agni-sphuṭam ceyta hṛttil nirantaram
satya-anubhūti sphurikkum

Let each action become an act of austerity to attain realization. Let each thought kindle the purifying fire within. A heart thus purified constantly experiences the blissful Truth.

www.ingramcontent.com/pod-product-compliance
Lightning Source LLC
Chambersburg PA
CBHW051412090426
42737CB00014B/2625
* 9 7 8 1 6 8 0 3 7 8 5 8 0 *